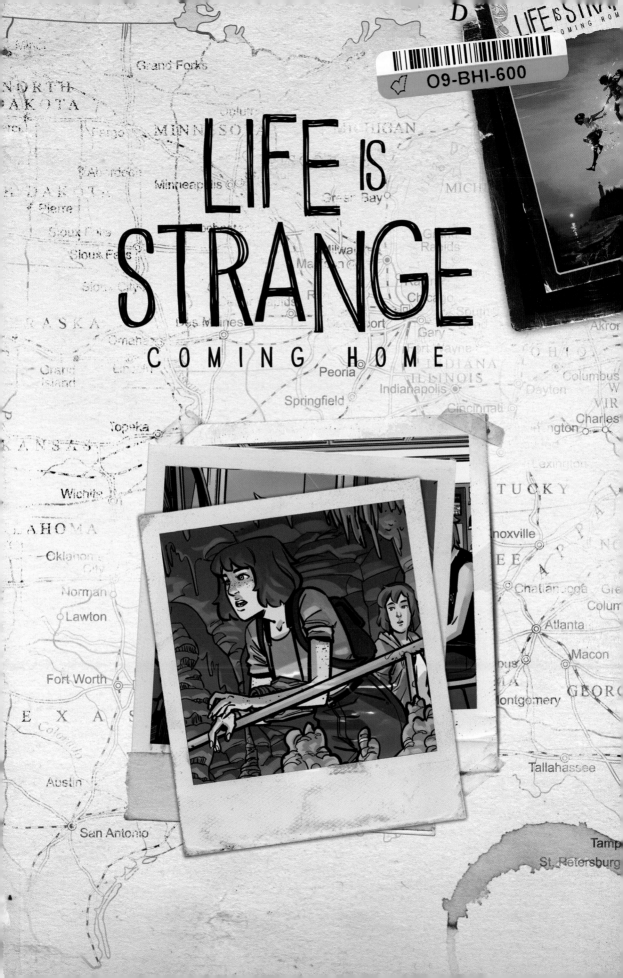

LIFE IS STRANGE
COMING HOME

O9-BHI-600

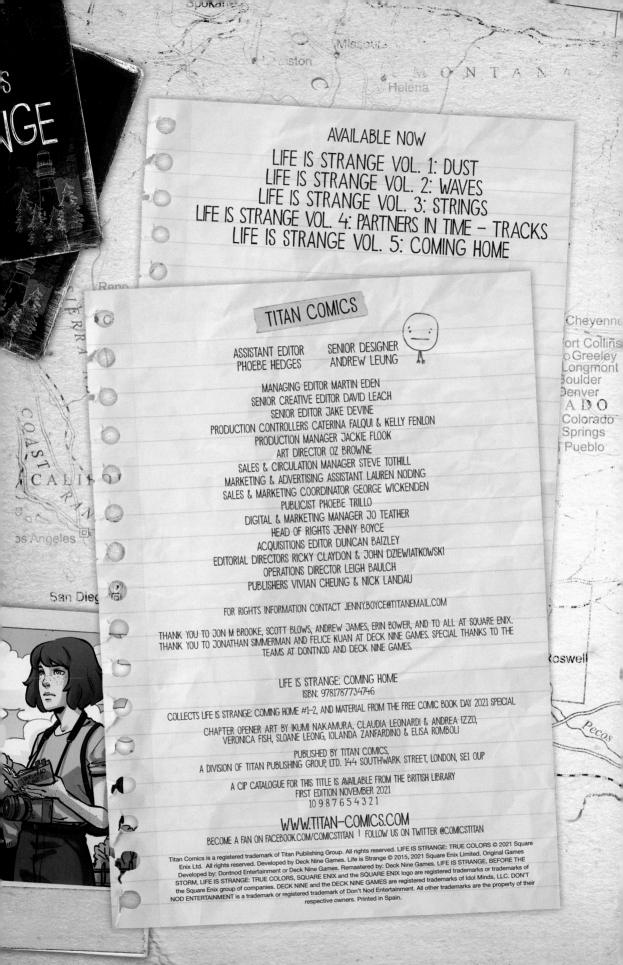

AVAILABLE NOW
LIFE IS STRANGE VOL. 1: DUST
LIFE IS STRANGE VOL. 2: WAVES
LIFE IS STRANGE VOL. 3: STRINGS
LIFE IS STRANGE VOL. 4: PARTNERS IN TIME — TRACKS
LIFE IS STRANGE VOL. 5: COMING HOME

TITAN COMICS

ASSISTANT EDITOR
PHOEBE HEDGES

SENIOR DESIGNER
ANDREW LEUNG

MANAGING EDITOR MARTIN EDEN
SENIOR CREATIVE EDITOR DAVID LEACH
SENIOR EDITOR JAKE DEVINE
PRODUCTION CONTROLLERS CATERINA FALQUI & KELLY FENLON
PRODUCTION MANAGER JACKIE FLOOK
ART DIRECTOR OZ BROWNE
SALES & CIRCULATION MANAGER STEVE TOTHILL
MARKETING & ADVERTISING ASSISTANT LAUREN NODING
SALES & MARKETING COORDINATOR GEORGE WICKENDEN
PUBLICIST PHOEBE TRILLO
DIGITAL & MARKETING MANAGER JO TEATHER
HEAD OF RIGHTS JENNY BOYCE
ACQUISITIONS EDITOR DUNCAN BAIZLEY
EDITORIAL DIRECTORS RICKY CLAYDON & JOHN DZIEWIATKOWSKI
OPERATIONS DIRECTOR LEIGH BAULCH
PUBLISHERS VIVIAN CHEUNG & NICK LANDAU

FOR RIGHTS INFORMATION CONTACT JENNY.BOYCE@TITANEMAIL.COM

THANK YOU TO JON M BROOKE, SCOTT BLOWS, ANDREW JAMES, ERIN BOWER, AND TO ALL AT SQUARE ENIX.
THANK YOU TO JONATHAN SIMMERMAN AND FELICE KUAN AT DECK NINE GAMES. SPECIAL THANKS TO THE
TEAMS AT DONTNOD AND DECK NINE GAMES.

LIFE IS STRANGE: COMING HOME
ISBN: 9781787734746

COLLECTS LIFE IS STRANGE: COMING HOME #1-2, AND MATERIAL FROM THE FREE COMIC BOOK DAY 2021 SPECIAL

CHAPTER OPENER ART BY IKUMI NAKAMURA, CLAUDIA LEONARDI & ANDREA IZZO,
VERONICA FISH, SLOANE LEONG, IOLANDA ZANFARDINO & ELISA ROMBOLI

PUBLISHED BY TITAN COMICS,
A DIVISION OF TITAN PUBLISHING GROUP, LTD. 144 SOUTHWARK STREET, LONDON, SE1 OUP

A CIP CATALOGUE FOR THIS TITLE IS AVAILABLE FROM THE BRITISH LIBRARY
FIRST EDITION NOVEMBER 2021
10 9 8 7 6 5 4 3 2 1

WWW.TITAN-COMICS.COM
BECOME A FAN ON FACEBOOK.COM/COMICSTITAN | FOLLOW US ON TWITTER @COMICSTITAN

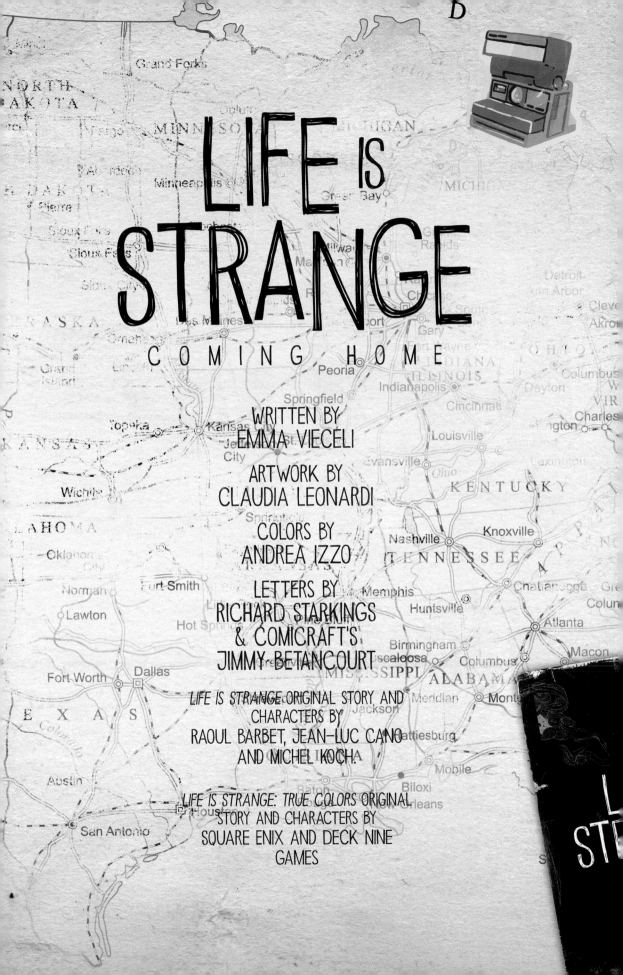

LIFE IS STRANGE
COMING HOME

WRITTEN BY
EMMA VIECELI

ARTWORK BY
CLAUDIA LEONARDI

COLORS BY
ANDREA IZZO

LETTERS BY
RICHARD STARKINGS
& COMICRAFT'S
JIMMY BETANCOURT

LIFE IS STRANGE ORIGINAL STORY AND
CHARACTERS BY
RAOUL BARBET, JEAN-LUC CANO
AND MICHEL KOCH

LIFE IS STRANGE: TRUE COLORS ORIGINAL
STORY AND CHARACTERS BY
SQUARE ENIX AND DECK NINE
GAMES

PREVIOUSLY...

Mysteriously gifted with the power to rewind time, photography student Max Caulfield never anticipated that her strange temporal abilities would put her at the center of the dark secrets of Arcadia Bay. In a bid to save her oldest friend, Chloe Price, from being murdered and to find justice for the death of Rachel Amber - Chloe's closest confidante - Max's powers caused a hurricane which threatened to destroy Arcadia Bay. Max chose to sacrifice the town rather than lose Chloe once again. Afterwards, Max and Chloe moved to Seattle - but a year later, Max's abilities threatened to tear her apart. To stabilize her powers and her reality, Max jumped to another timeline - where Rachel was still alive. Though two years have passed, Max never forgot where she came from, and now with the help of Tristan - a boy with the power to "phase" out of reality - she's ready to push her powers to their limit if it means finally coming home...

Still, life waits for no-one. When Rachel landed a role in a touring production of Hamlet, she, Max, and Chloe headed out on a cross-country roadtrip towards the site of her first performance. Their route also aligned with that of their friends' band - The High Seas. In Max's original timeline, her Chloe and Tristan embarked on their own mirrored journey.

Two years after Max was forced to leave her original timeline - and her Chloe - Max thought she was ready to return home. But combining her powers with Tristan's wasn't enough to get her home. While Tristan was stranded in the original timeline, Max was firmly stuck in her new reality.

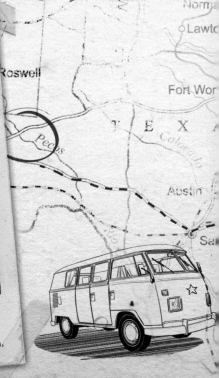

Roswell

Fort Wor

TEXA

Pecos

Austin

Norma

Lawto

Sa

Since her first failed jump home, Max and Chloe - across the timelines - began to notice strange phenomena. The veil between realities was thinning, and, though Tristan struggled to regain his strength, Max grew more confident with each passing day.

HOLE TO THE UNIVERSE

D

MINNESOTA

After another successful gig, the High Seas headed out onto the next leg of their tour. But Max, Chloe, and Rachel watched in horror as the stormy weather felled a tree trunk into the road, directly into the path of the High Seas' tour van, which overturned to avoid a collision.

Without waiting to see how bad the damage was, Max rushed forward to use her powers and undo the crash. But as time began to rewind, Tristan appeared in the wreckage! He shouted for Max to stop, but it was too late. Worse, when Chloe caught up with Max, she was furious at Max's recklessness.

Tristan was forced back into Max's original timeline, but lost control of his powers. He yelled for the High Seas to realize that their own crash was imminent, but his cries fell on deaf ears. Yet, despite his helplessness, the van stopped just in time...

CAST OF CHARACTERS

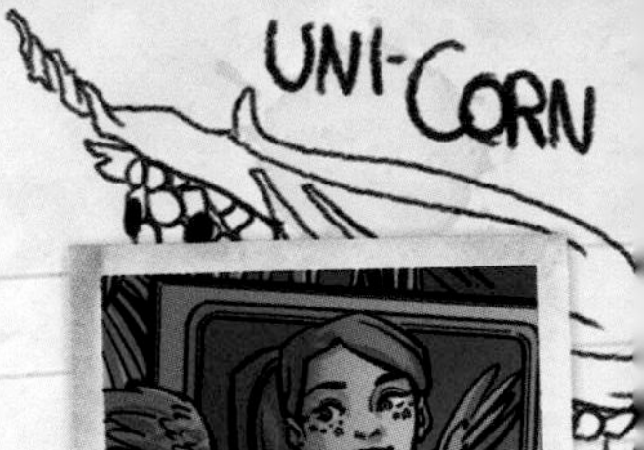
UNI-CORN

CHLOE AND RACHEL'S UNIVERSE

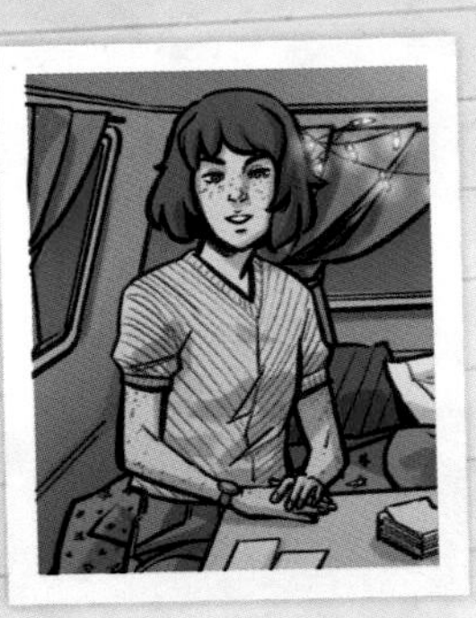

MAX

Time traveler. Photographer. Refugee from her original universe, now trying to get back to the Chloe she loves.

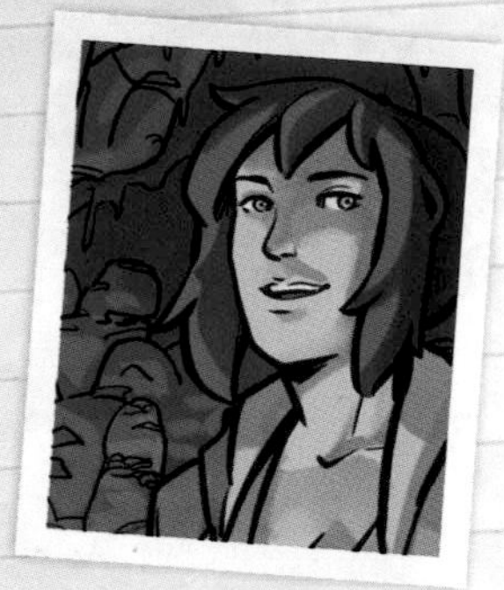

CHLOE

A different Chloe than the one Max fell in love with. Still a punky rebel mechanic with an artistic streak, now dating Rachel. Fiercely loyal to Max, even though she's not the friend Chloe once knew.

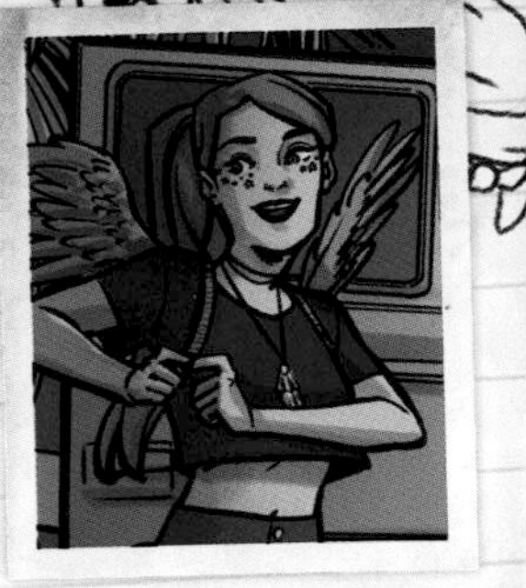

RACHEL

Intuencer, actor, just heading out on her first theatrical tour of Hamlet. Dating Chloe. Murdered in Max's original timeline, but alive and kicking in this one.

MAX AND CHLOE'S UNIVERSE

TRISTAN

Timeline castaway with the ability to phase out of reality. Tristan first crossed the timelines alone, but now may have found a way to cross the realities at will - with a little help...

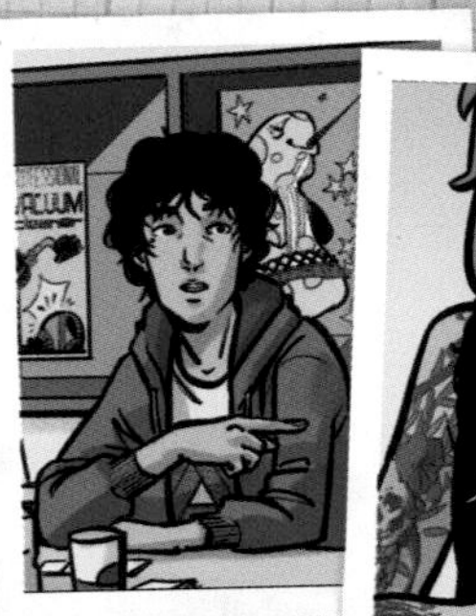

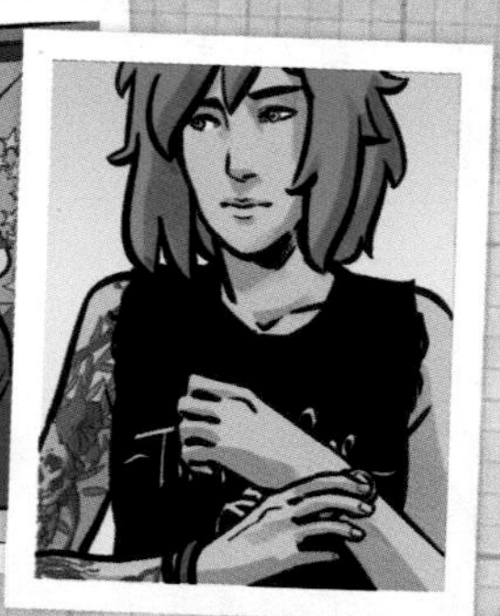

CHLOE

The Chloe Max had to leave behind. Now that both are aware that the other is still alive, Chloe is actively looking for a way to bring Max home.

VICTORIA

A survivor of Arcadia Bay, now Ophelia in her timeline's Hamlet cast. No longer Queen Bee, Victoria is taking the first step in making amends.

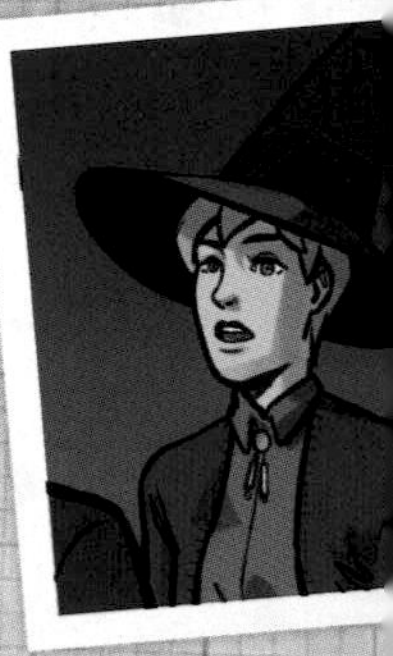

SUPPORTING CAST (IN BOTH UNIVERSES)

BAND ON TOUR

The High Seas

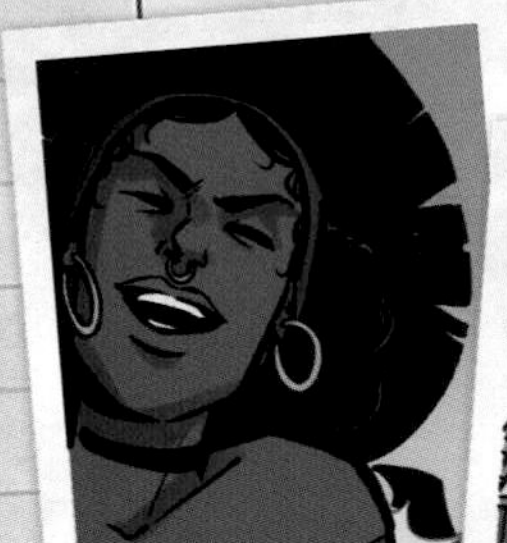

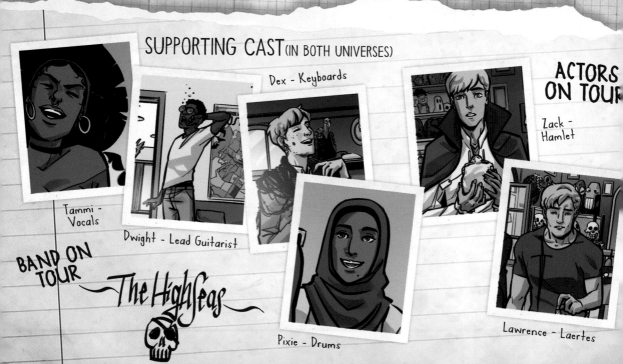

Tammi - Vocals

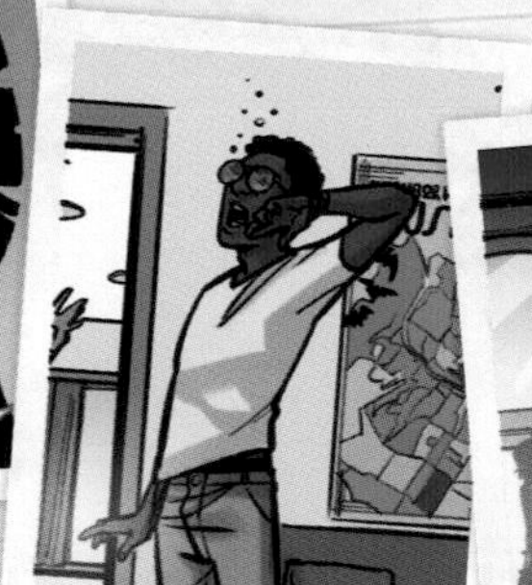

Dwight - Lead Guitarist

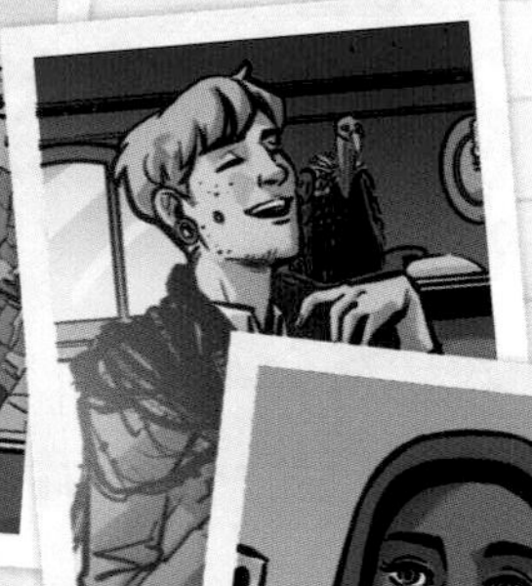

Dex - Keyboards

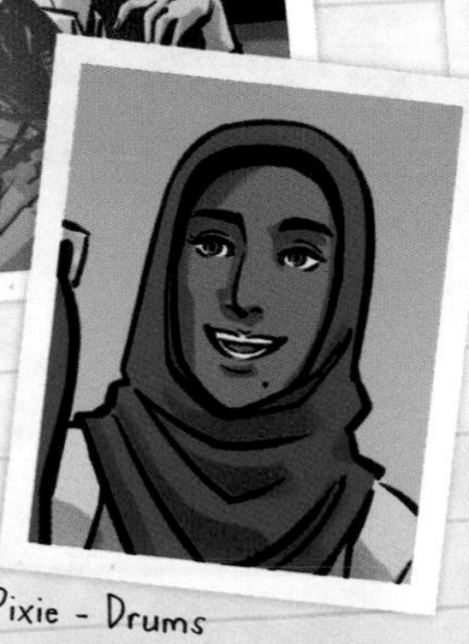

Pixie - Drums

ACTORS ON TOUR

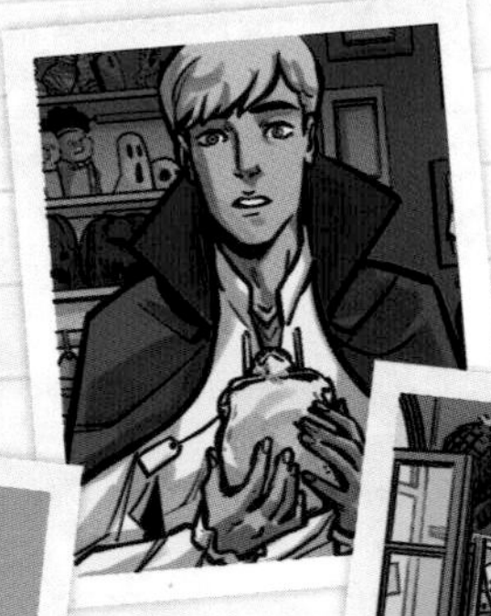

Zack - Hamlet

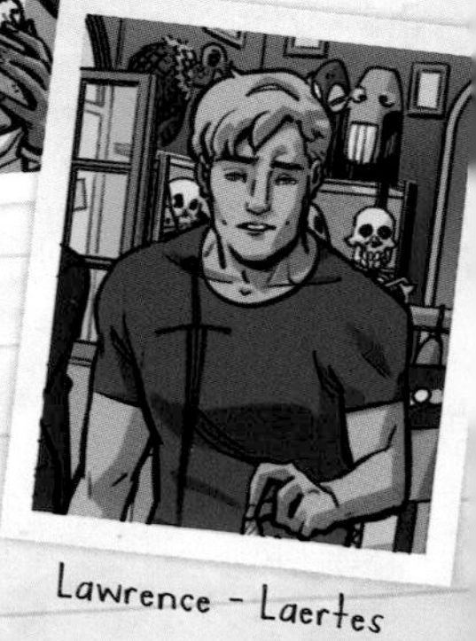

Lawrence - Laertes

CHAPTER 1

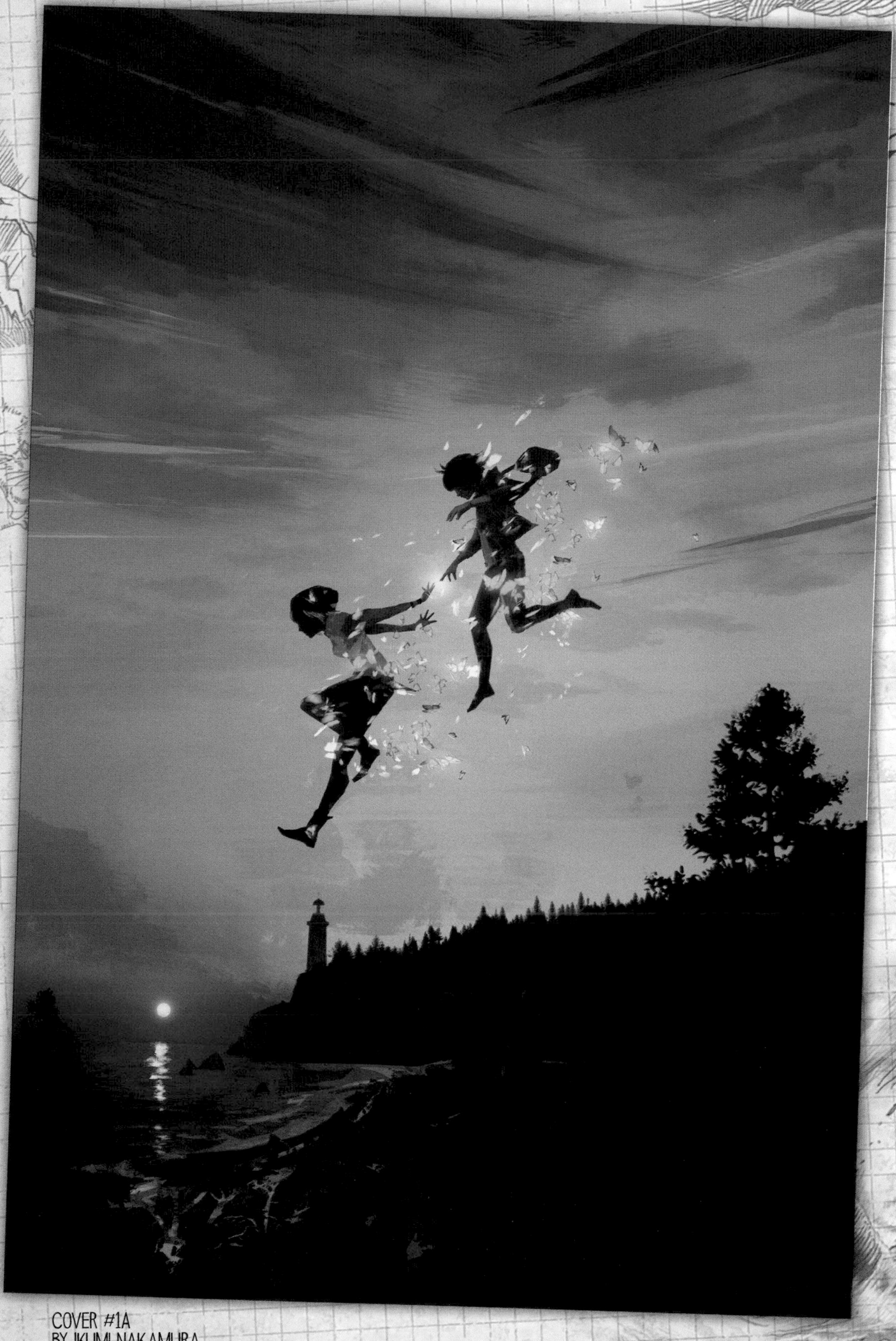

COVER #1A
BY IKUMI NAKAMURA

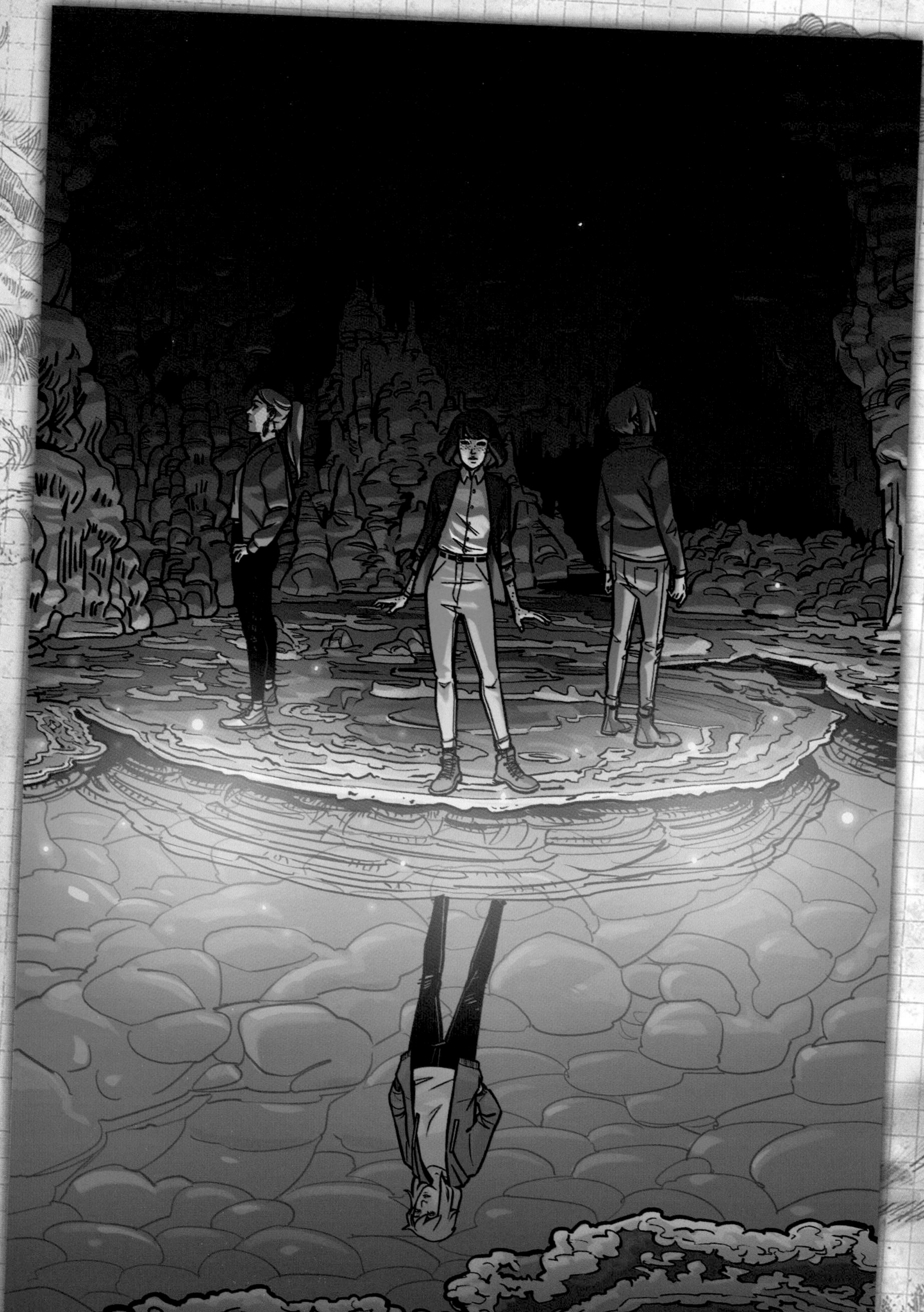

COVER #1B
BY CLAUDIA LEONARDI & ANDREA IZZO

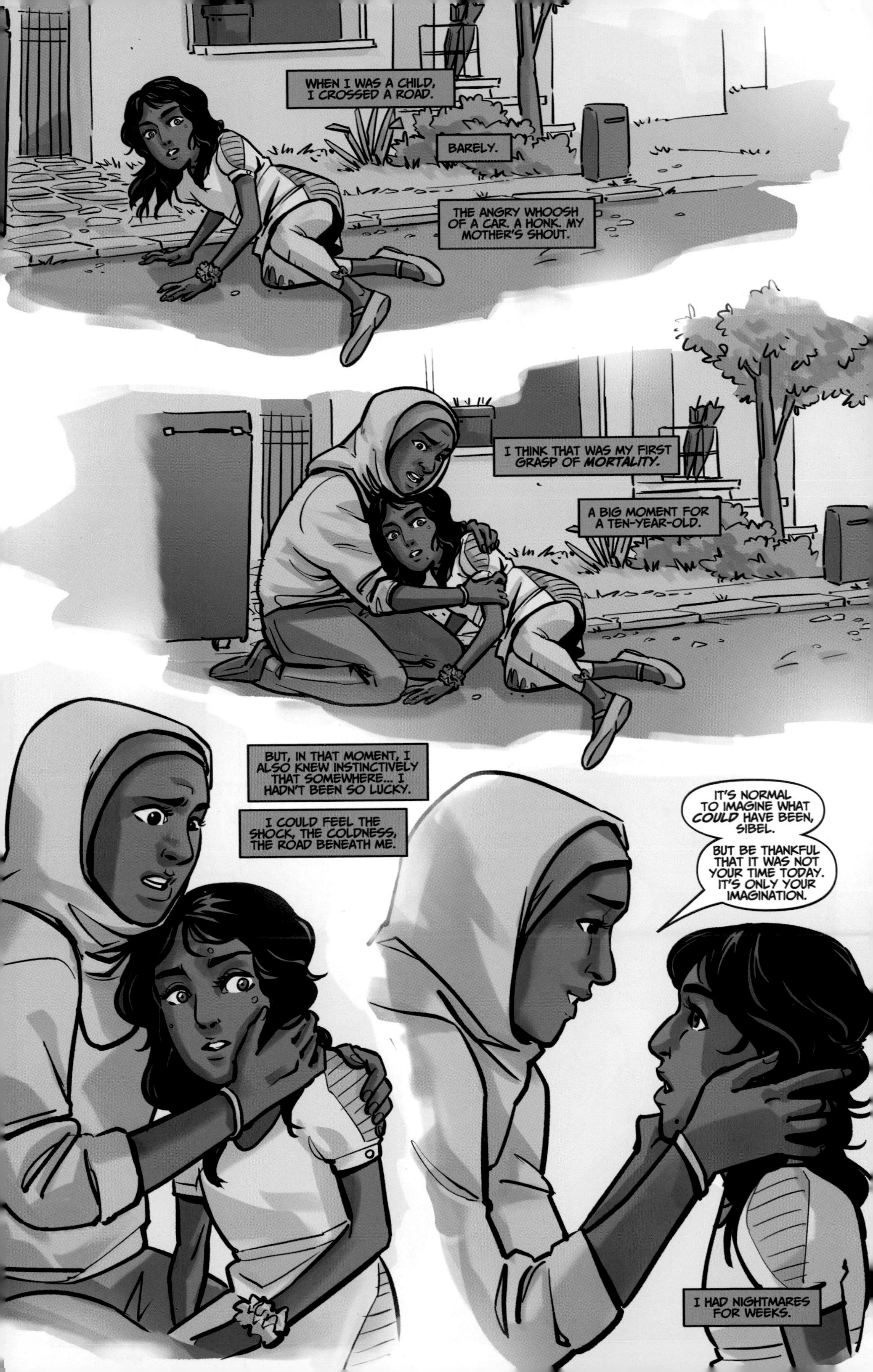
WHEN I WAS A CHILD, I CROSSED A ROAD.
BARELY.
THE ANGRY WHOOSH OF A CAR. A HONK. MY MOTHER'S SHOUT.
I THINK THAT WAS MY FIRST GRASP OF MORTALITY.
A BIG MOMENT FOR A TEN-YEAR-OLD.
BUT, IN THAT MOMENT, I ALSO KNEW INSTINCTIVELY THAT SOMEWHERE... I HADN'T BEEN SO LUCKY.
I COULD FEEL THE SHOCK, THE COLDNESS, THE ROAD BENEATH ME.
IT'S NORMAL TO IMAGINE WHAT COULD HAVE BEEN, SIBEL.
BUT BE THANKFUL THAT IT WAS NOT YOUR TIME TODAY. IT'S ONLY YOUR IMAGINATION.
I HAD NIGHTMARES FOR WEEKS.

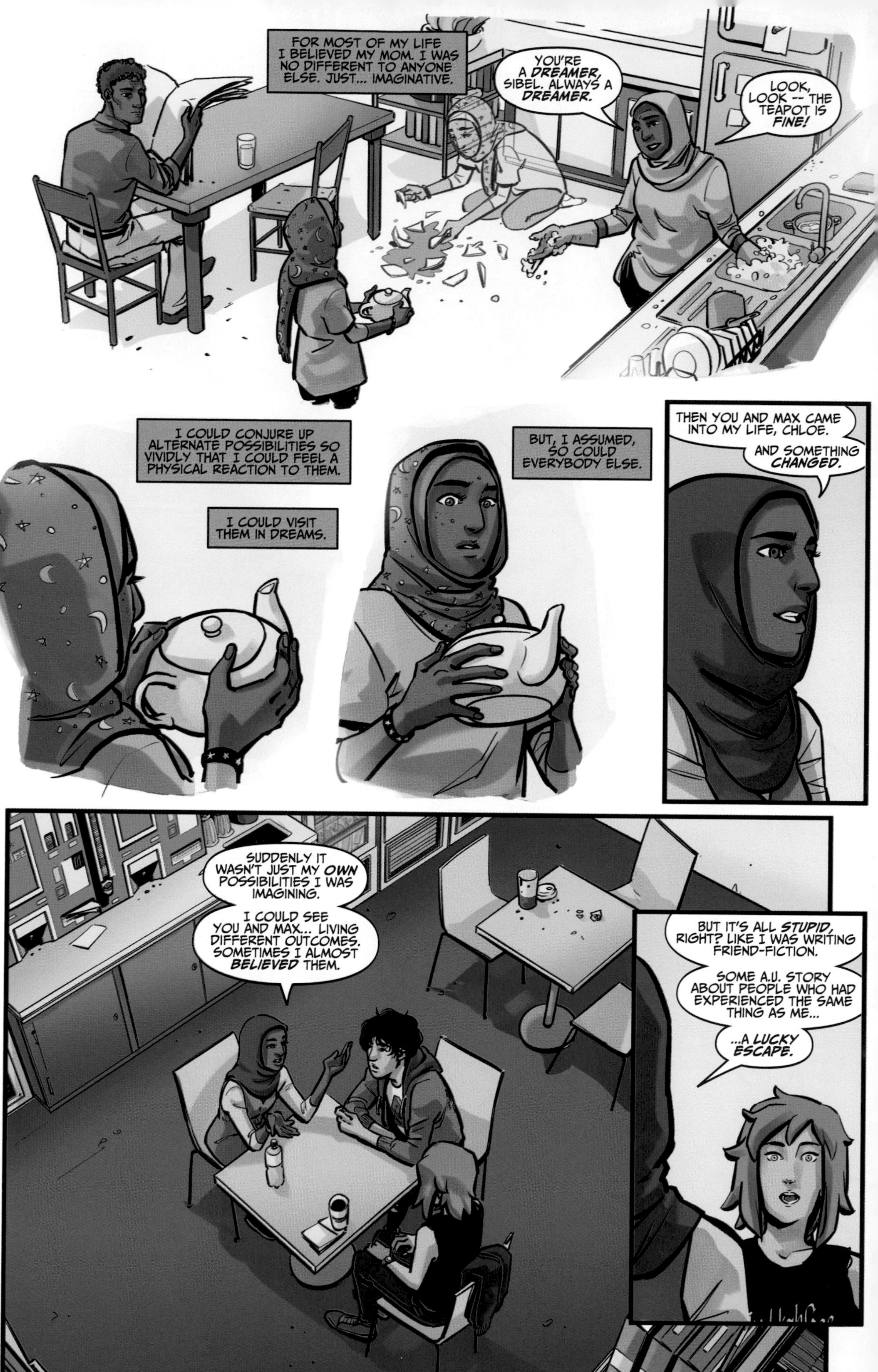
FOR MOST OF MY LIFE I BELIEVED MY MOM. I WAS NO DIFFERENT TO ANYONE ELSE. JUST... IMAGINATIVE.
YOU'RE A DREAMER, SIBEL. ALWAYS A DREAMER.
LOOK, LOOK -- THE TEAPOT IS FINE!
I COULD CONJURE UP ALTERNATE POSSIBILITIES SO VIVIDLY THAT I COULD FEEL A PHYSICAL REACTION TO THEM.
I COULD VISIT THEM IN DREAMS.
BUT, I ASSUMED, SO COULD EVERYBODY ELSE.
THEN YOU AND MAX CAME INTO MY LIFE, CHLOE.
AND SOMETHING CHANGED.
SUDDENLY IT WASN'T JUST MY OWN POSSIBILITIES I WAS IMAGINING.
I COULD SEE YOU AND MAX... LIVING DIFFERENT OUTCOMES. SOMETIMES I ALMOST BELIEVED THEM.
BUT IT'S ALL STUPID, RIGHT? LIKE I WAS WRITING FRIEND-FICTION.
SOME A.U. STORY ABOUT PEOPLE WHO HAD EXPERIENCED THE SAME THING AS ME...
...A LUCKY ESCAPE.

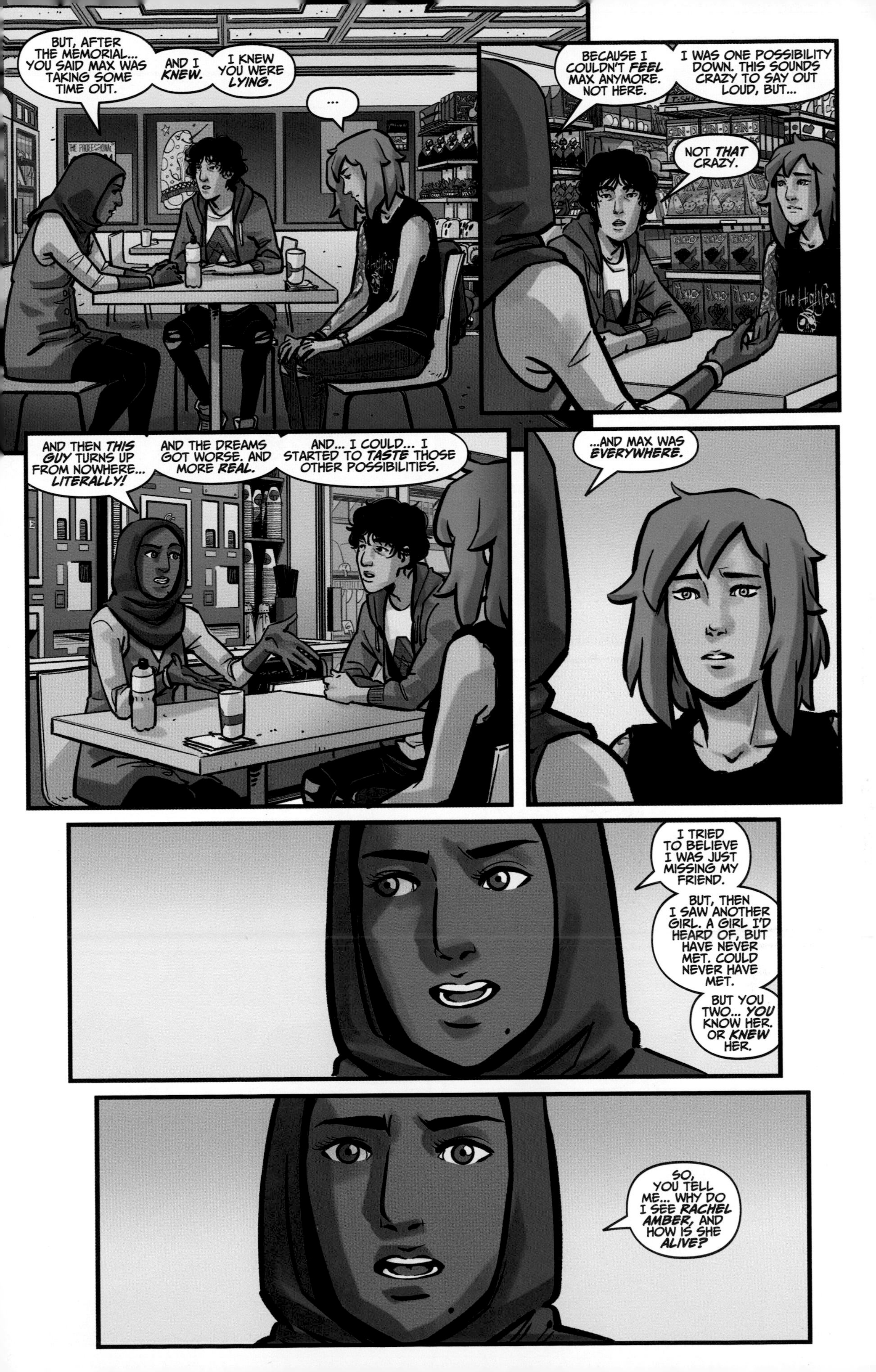
BUT, AFTER THE MEMORIAL... YOU SAID MAX WAS TAKING SOME TIME OUT.
AND I KNEW.
I KNEW YOU WERE LYING.
...
BECAUSE I COULDN'T FEEL MAX ANYMORE. NOT HERE.
I WAS ONE POSSIBILITY DOWN. THIS SOUNDS CRAZY TO SAY OUT LOUD, BUT...
NOT THAT CRAZY.
AND THEN THIS GUY TURNS UP FROM NOWHERE... LITERALLY!
AND THE DREAMS GOT WORSE. AND MORE REAL.
AND... I COULD... I STARTED TO TASTE THOSE OTHER POSSIBILITIES.
...AND MAX WAS EVERYWHERE.
I TRIED TO BELIEVE I WAS JUST MISSING MY FRIEND.
BUT, THEN I SAW ANOTHER GIRL. A GIRL I'D HEARD OF, BUT HAVE NEVER MET. COULD NEVER HAVE MET.
BUT YOU TWO... YOU KNOW HER. OR KNEW HER.
SO, YOU TELL ME... WHY DO I SEE RACHEL AMBER, AND HOW IS SHE ALIVE?

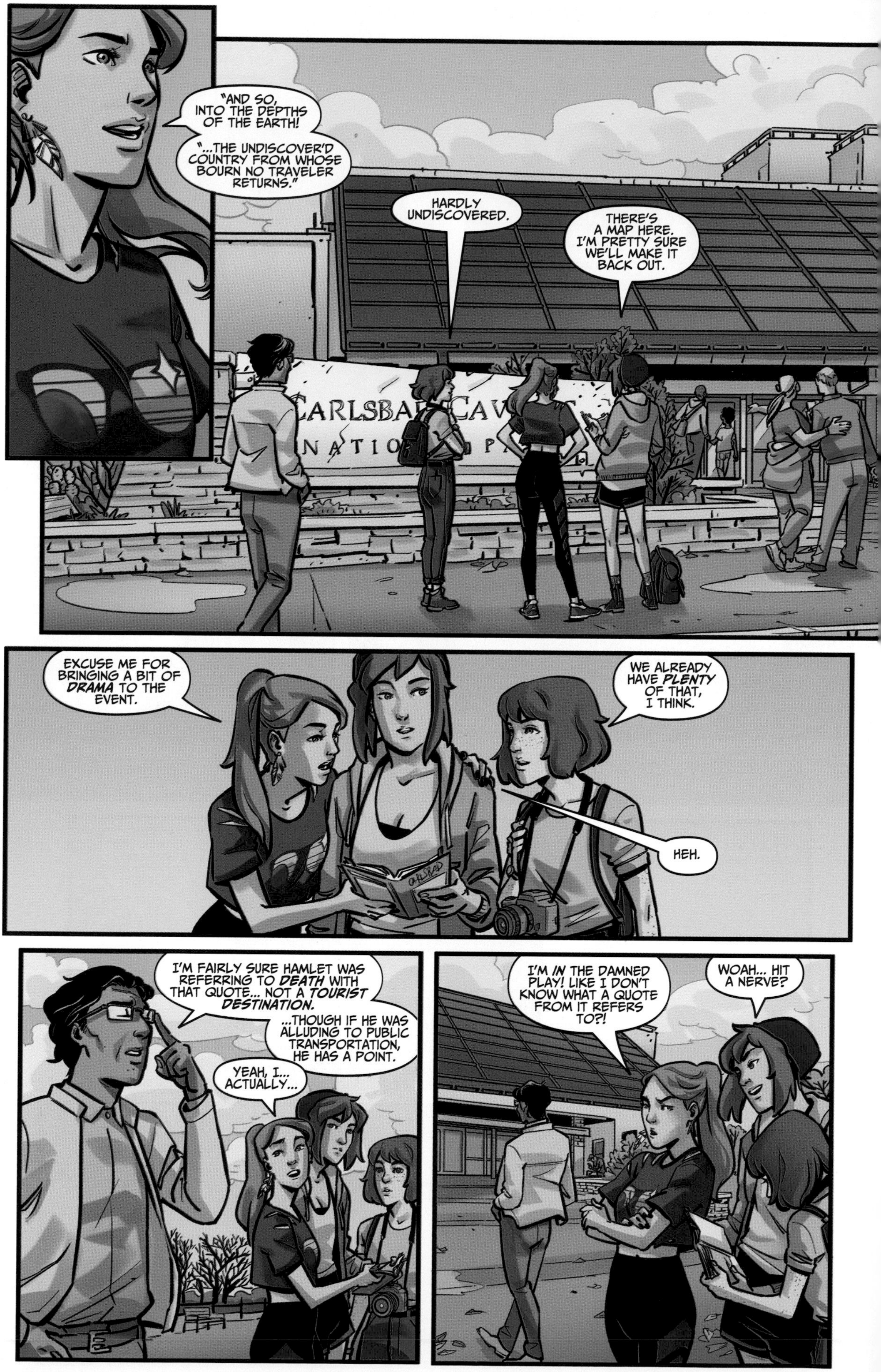
"AND SO, INTO THE DEPTHS OF THE EARTH!
"...THE UNDISCOVER'D COUNTRY FROM WHOSE BOURN NO TRAVELER RETURNS."
HARDLY UNDISCOVERED.
THERE'S A MAP HERE. I'M PRETTY SURE WE'LL MAKE IT BACK OUT.
CARLSBAD CAV
NATIO P
EXCUSE ME FOR BRINGING A BIT OF DRAMA TO THE EVENT.
WE ALREADY HAVE PLENTY OF THAT, I THINK.
HEH.
CARLSBAD
I'M FAIRLY SURE HAMLET WAS REFERRING TO DEATH WITH THAT QUOTE... NOT A TOURIST DESTINATION.
...THOUGH IF HE WAS ALLUDING TO PUBLIC TRANSPORTATION, HE HAS A POINT.
YEAH, I... ACTUALLY...
I'M IN THE DAMNED PLAY! LIKE I DON'T KNOW WHAT A QUOTE FROM IT REFERS TO?!
WOAH... HIT A NERVE?

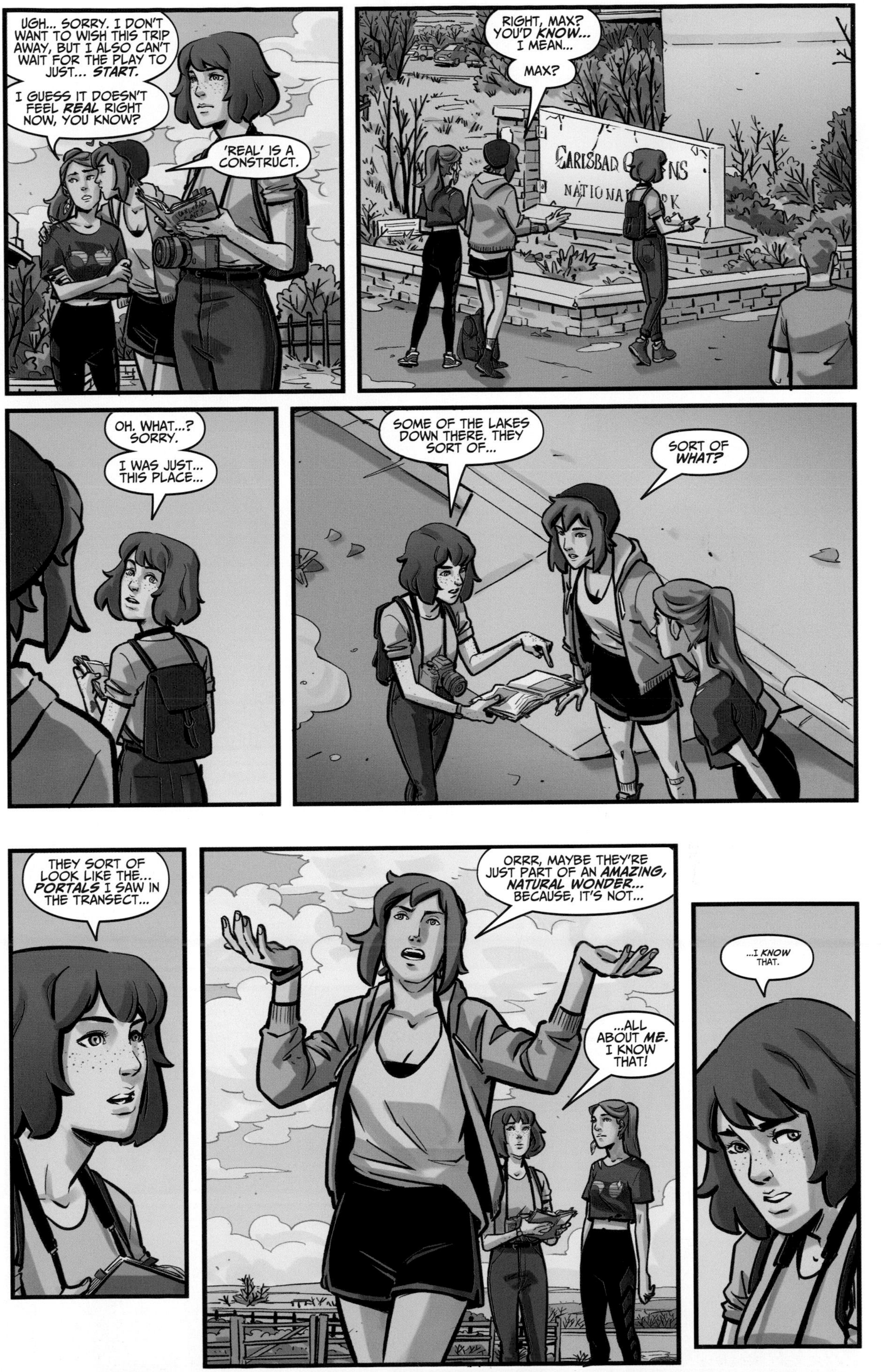
UGH... SORRY. I DON'T WANT TO WISH THIS TRIP AWAY, BUT I ALSO CAN'T WAIT FOR THE PLAY TO JUST... START.
I GUESS IT DOESN'T FEEL REAL RIGHT NOW, YOU KNOW?
'REAL' IS A CONSTRUCT.
RIGHT, MAX? YOU'D KNOW... I MEAN...
MAX?
CARLSBAD C... NS NATIONA... RK
OH. WHAT...? SORRY.
I WAS JUST... THIS PLACE...
SOME OF THE LAKES DOWN THERE. THEY SORT OF...
SORT OF WHAT?
THEY SORT OF LOOK LIKE THE... PORTALS I SAW IN THE TRANSECT...
ORRR, MAYBE THEY'RE JUST PART OF AN AMAZING, NATURAL WONDER... BECAUSE, IT'S NOT...
...ALL ABOUT ME. I KNOW THAT!
...I KNOW THAT.

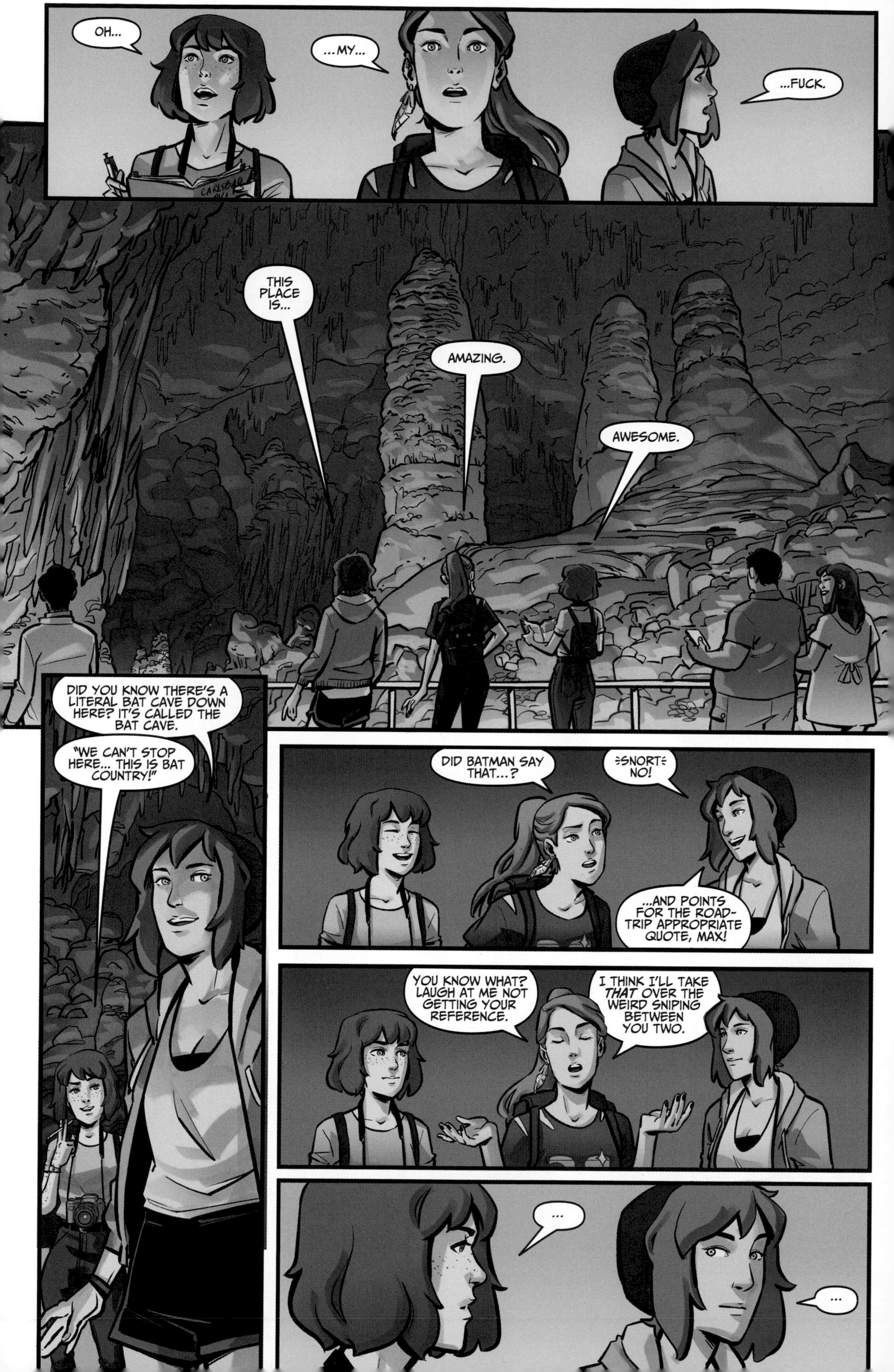
OH...
...MY...
...FUCK.
THIS PLACE IS...
AMAZING.
AWESOME.
DID YOU KNOW THERE'S A LITERAL BAT CAVE DOWN HERE? IT'S CALLED THE BAT CAVE.
"WE CAN'T STOP HERE... THIS IS BAT COUNTRY!"
DID BATMAN SAY THAT...?
SNORT NO!
...AND POINTS FOR THE ROAD-TRIP APPROPRIATE QUOTE, MAX!
YOU KNOW WHAT? LAUGH AT ME NOT GETTING YOUR REFERENCE.
I THINK I'LL TAKE *THAT* OVER THE WEIRD SNIPING BETWEEN YOU TWO.
...
...

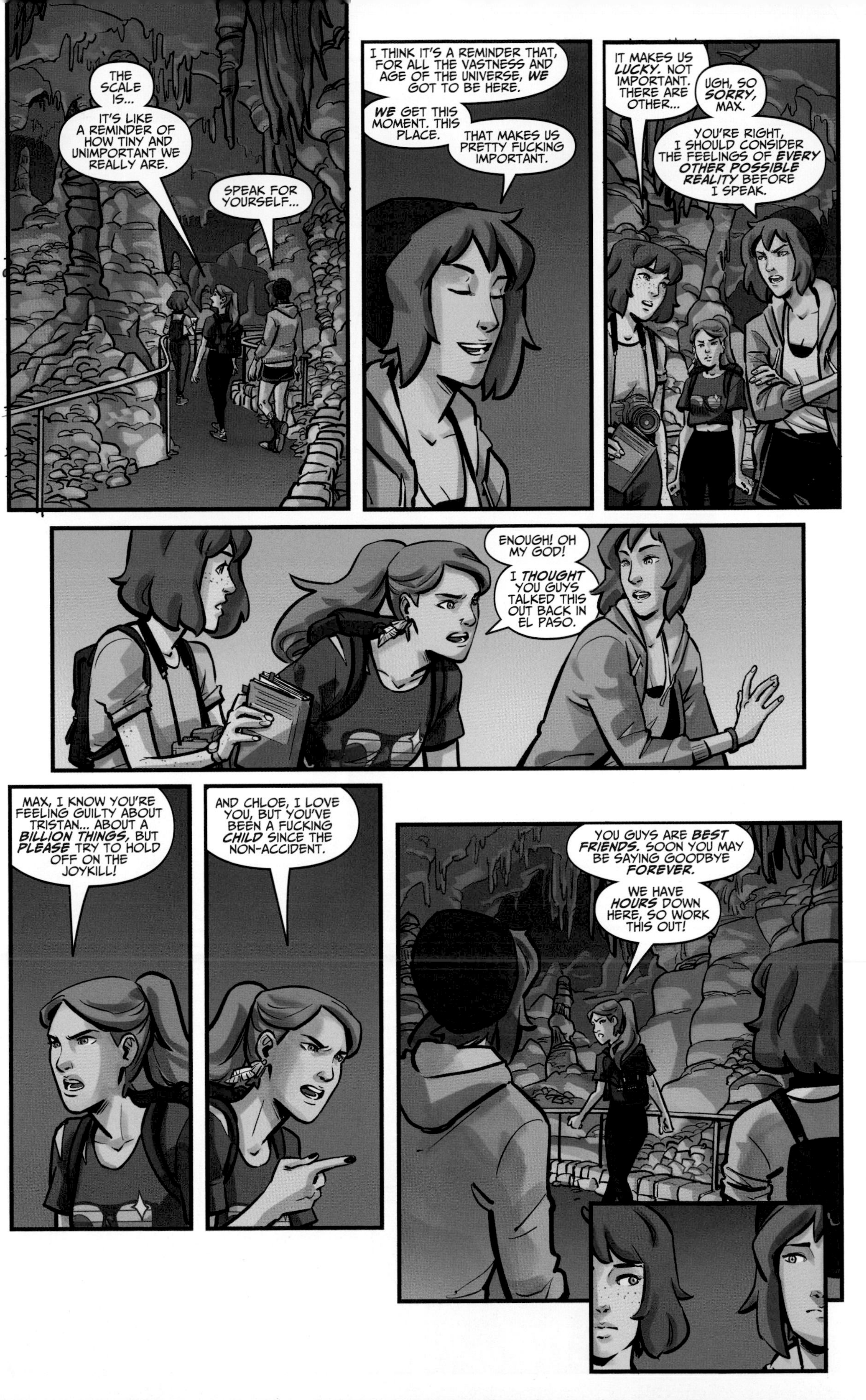
THE SCALE IS...
IT'S LIKE A REMINDER OF HOW TINY AND UNIMPORTANT WE REALLY ARE.
SPEAK FOR YOURSELF...
I THINK IT'S A REMINDER THAT, FOR ALL THE VASTNESS AND AGE OF THE UNIVERSE, WE GOT TO BE HERE.
WE GET THIS MOMENT. THIS PLACE.
THAT MAKES US PRETTY FUCKING IMPORTANT.
IT MAKES US LUCKY. NOT IMPORTANT. THERE ARE OTHER...
UGH, SO SORRY, MAX.
YOU'RE RIGHT, I SHOULD CONSIDER THE FEELINGS OF EVERY OTHER POSSIBLE REALITY BEFORE I SPEAK.
ENOUGH! OH MY GOD!
I THOUGHT YOU GUYS TALKED THIS OUT BACK IN EL PASO.
MAX, I KNOW YOU'RE FEELING GUILTY ABOUT TRISTAN... ABOUT A BILLION THINGS, BUT PLEASE TRY TO HOLD OFF ON THE JOYKILL!
AND CHLOE, I LOVE YOU, BUT YOU'VE BEEN A FUCKING CHILD SINCE THE NON-ACCIDENT.
YOU GUYS ARE BEST FRIENDS. SOON YOU MAY BE SAYING GOODBYE FOREVER.
WE HAVE HOURS DOWN HERE, SO WORK THIS OUT!

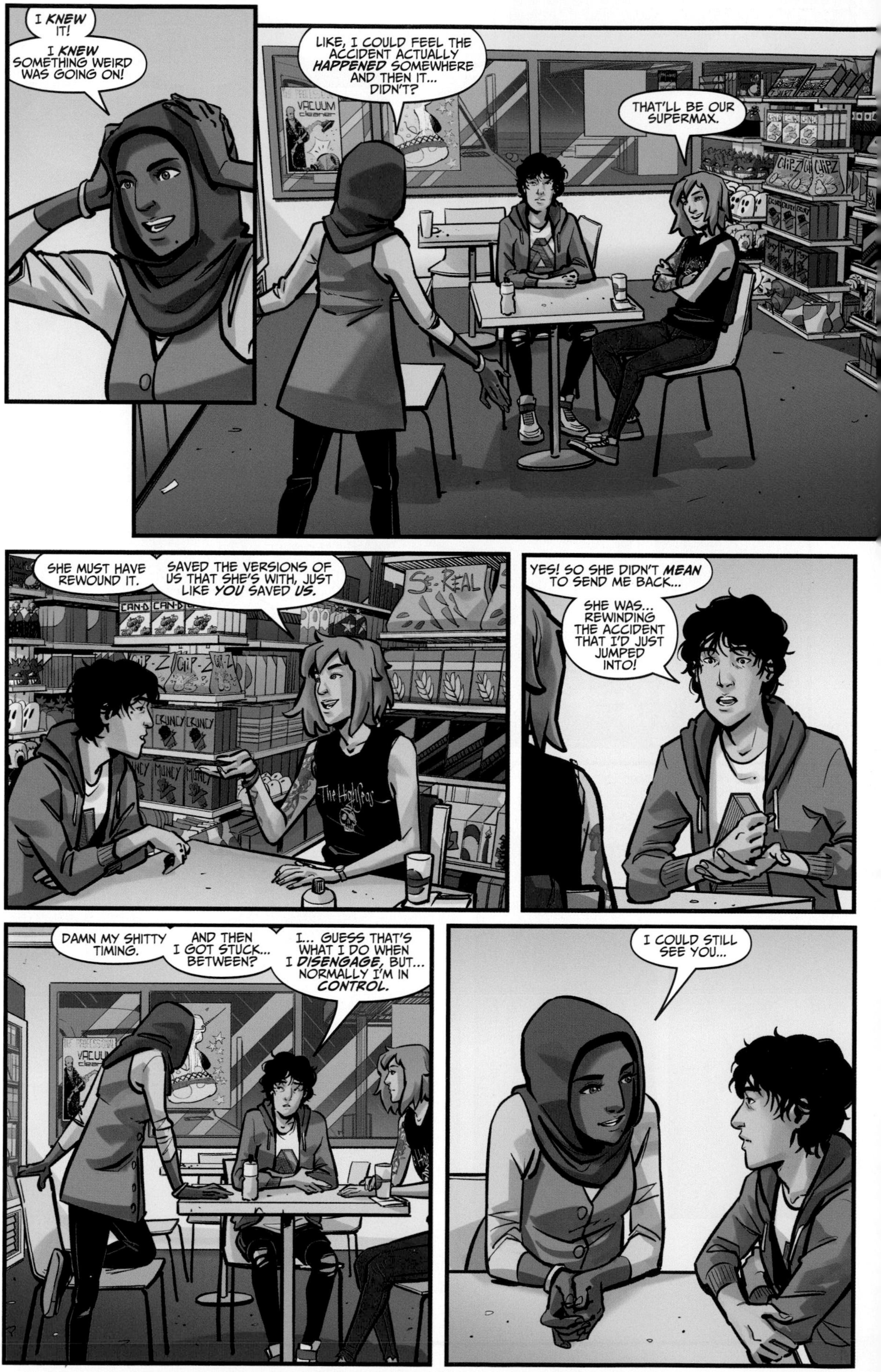
I KNEW IT!
I KNEW SOMETHING WEIRD WAS GOING ON!
LIKE, I COULD FEEL THE ACCIDENT ACTUALLY HAPPENED SOMEWHERE AND THEN IT... DIDN'T?
THAT'LL BE OUR SUPERMAX.
VACUUM cleaner
CHIPZ
SHE MUST HAVE REWOUND IT.
SAVED THE VERSIONS OF US THAT SHE'S WITH, JUST LIKE YOU SAVED US.
SE-REAL
CAN-D
CRUNCY
MUNCY
The HighSeas
YES! SO SHE DIDN'T MEAN TO SEND ME BACK...
SHE WAS... REWINDING THE ACCIDENT THAT I'D JUST JUMPED INTO!
DAMN MY SHITTY TIMING.
AND THEN I GOT STUCK... BETWEEN?
I... GUESS THAT'S WHAT I DO WHEN I DISENGAGE, BUT... NORMALLY I'M IN CONTROL.
VACUUM
I COULD STILL SEE YOU...

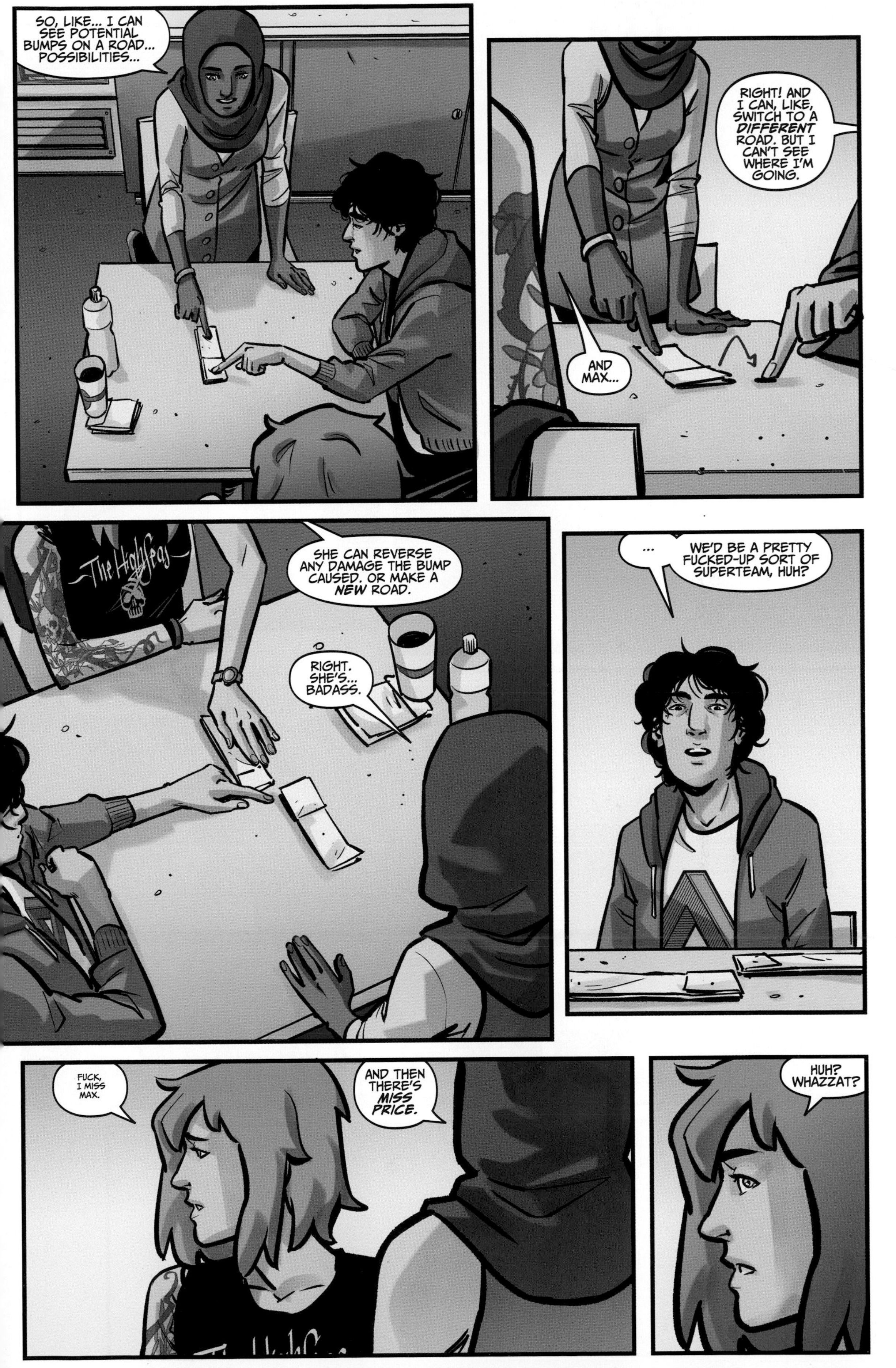
SO, LIKE... I CAN SEE POTENTIAL BUMPS ON A ROAD... POSSIBILITIES...
RIGHT! AND I CAN, LIKE, SWITCH TO A DIFFERENT ROAD. BUT I CAN'T SEE WHERE I'M GOING.
AND MAX...
SHE CAN REVERSE ANY DAMAGE THE BUMP CAUSED. OR MAKE A NEW ROAD.
RIGHT. SHE'S... BADASS.
...
WE'D BE A PRETTY FUCKED-UP SORT OF SUPERTEAM, HUH?
FUCK, I MISS MAX.
AND THEN THERE'S MISS PRICE.
HUH? WHAZZAT?

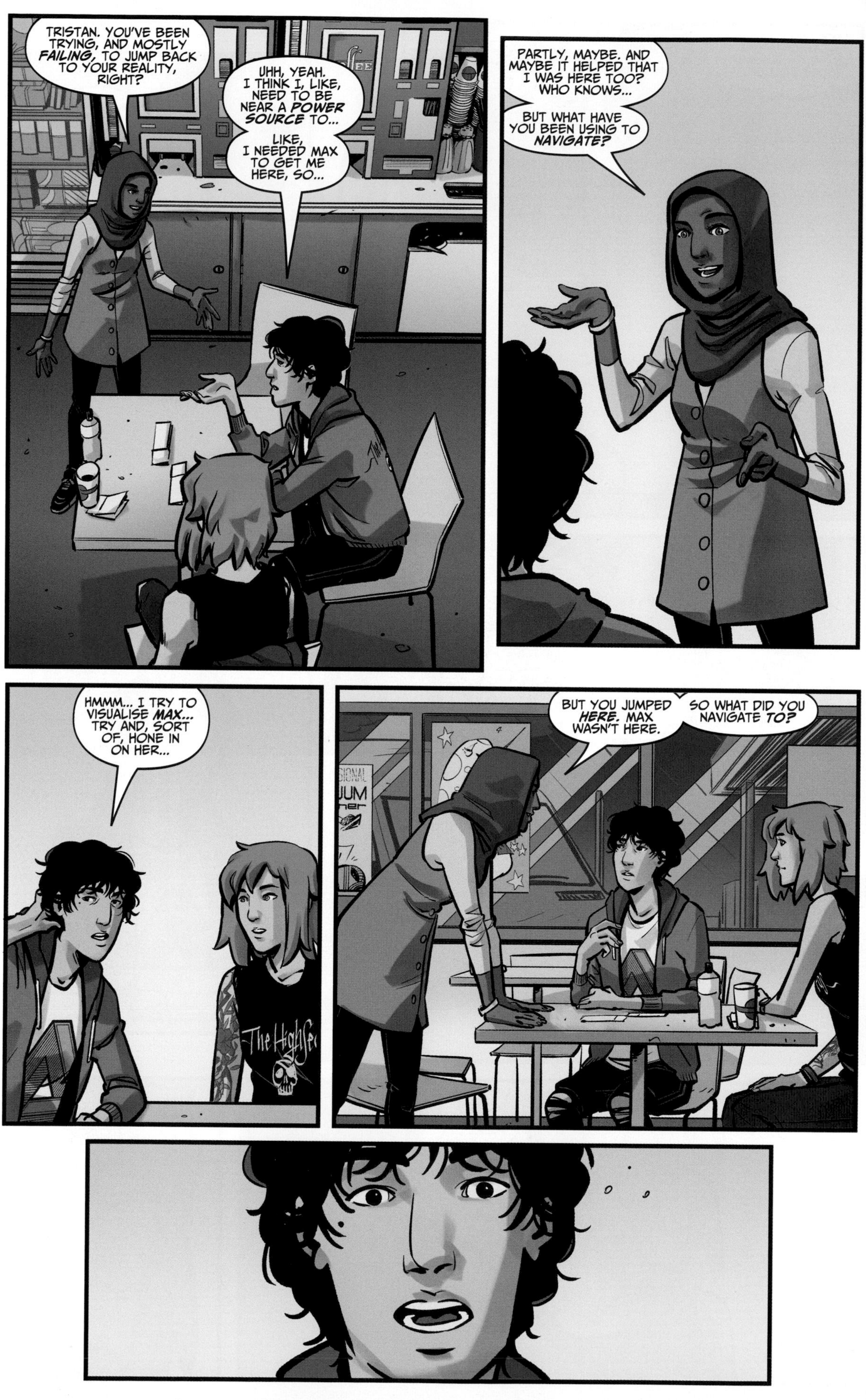
TRISTAN. YOU'VE BEEN TRYING, AND MOSTLY FAILING, TO JUMP BACK TO YOUR REALITY, RIGHT?
UHH, YEAH. I THINK I, LIKE, NEED TO BE NEAR A POWER SOURCE TO...
LIKE, I NEEDED MAX TO GET ME HERE, SO...
PARTLY, MAYBE. AND MAYBE IT HELPED THAT I WAS HERE TOO? WHO KNOWS...
BUT WHAT HAVE YOU BEEN USING TO NAVIGATE?
HMMM... I TRY TO VISUALISE MAX... TRY AND, SORT OF, HONE IN ON HER...
BUT YOU JUMPED HERE. MAX WASN'T HERE.
SO WHAT DID YOU NAVIGATE TO?

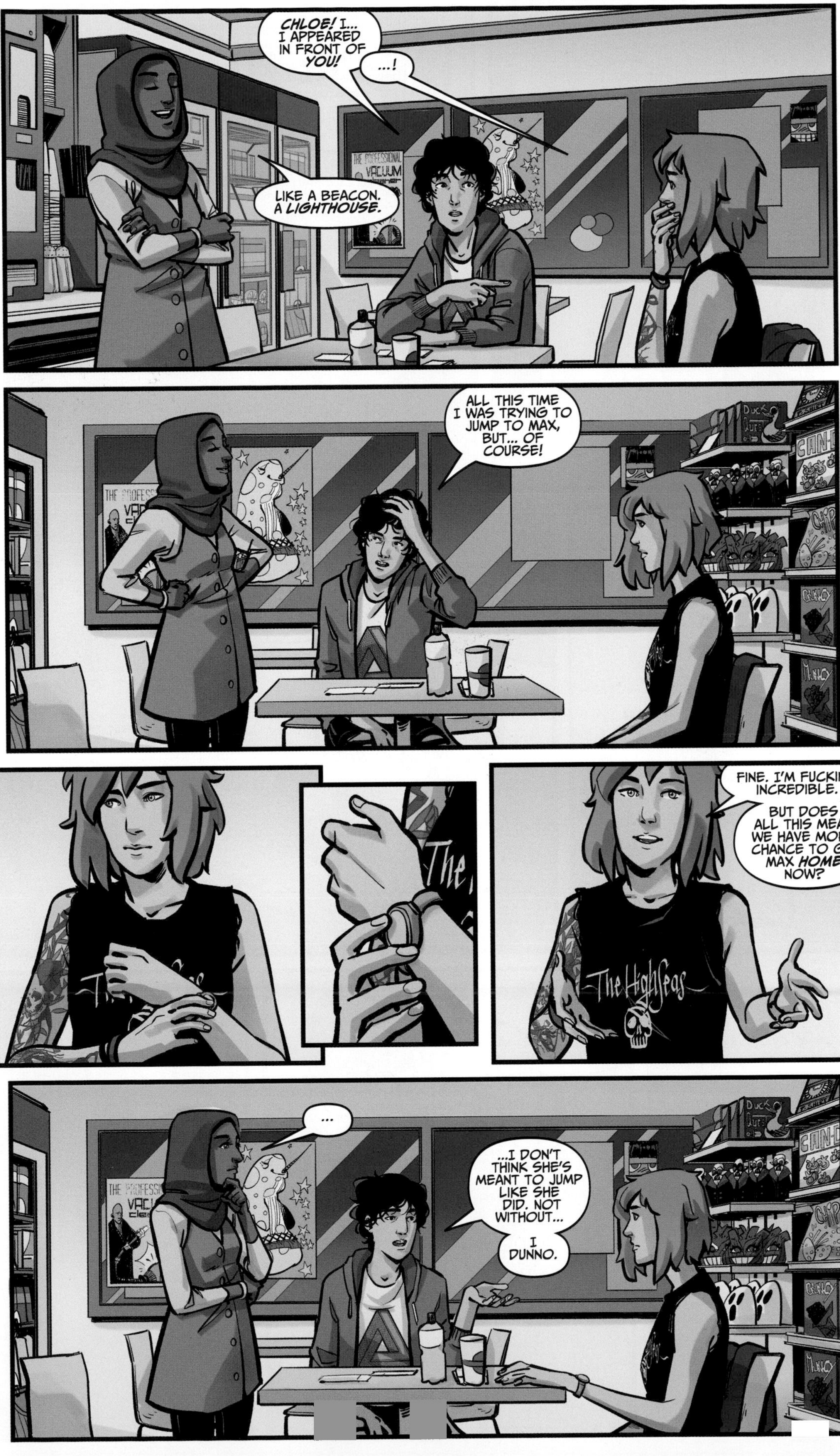
CHLOE! I... I APPEARED IN FRONT OF YOU!
...!
LIKE A BEACON. A LIGHTHOUSE.
THE PROFESSIONAL VACUUM
ALL THIS TIME I WAS TRYING TO JUMP TO MAX, BUT... OF COURSE!
FINE. I'M FUCKING INCREDIBLE.
BUT DOES ALL THIS MEAN WE HAVE MORE CHANCE TO GET MAX HOME NOW?
The HighSeas
...
...I DON'T THINK SHE'S MEANT TO JUMP LIKE SHE DID. NOT WITHOUT...
I DUNNO.

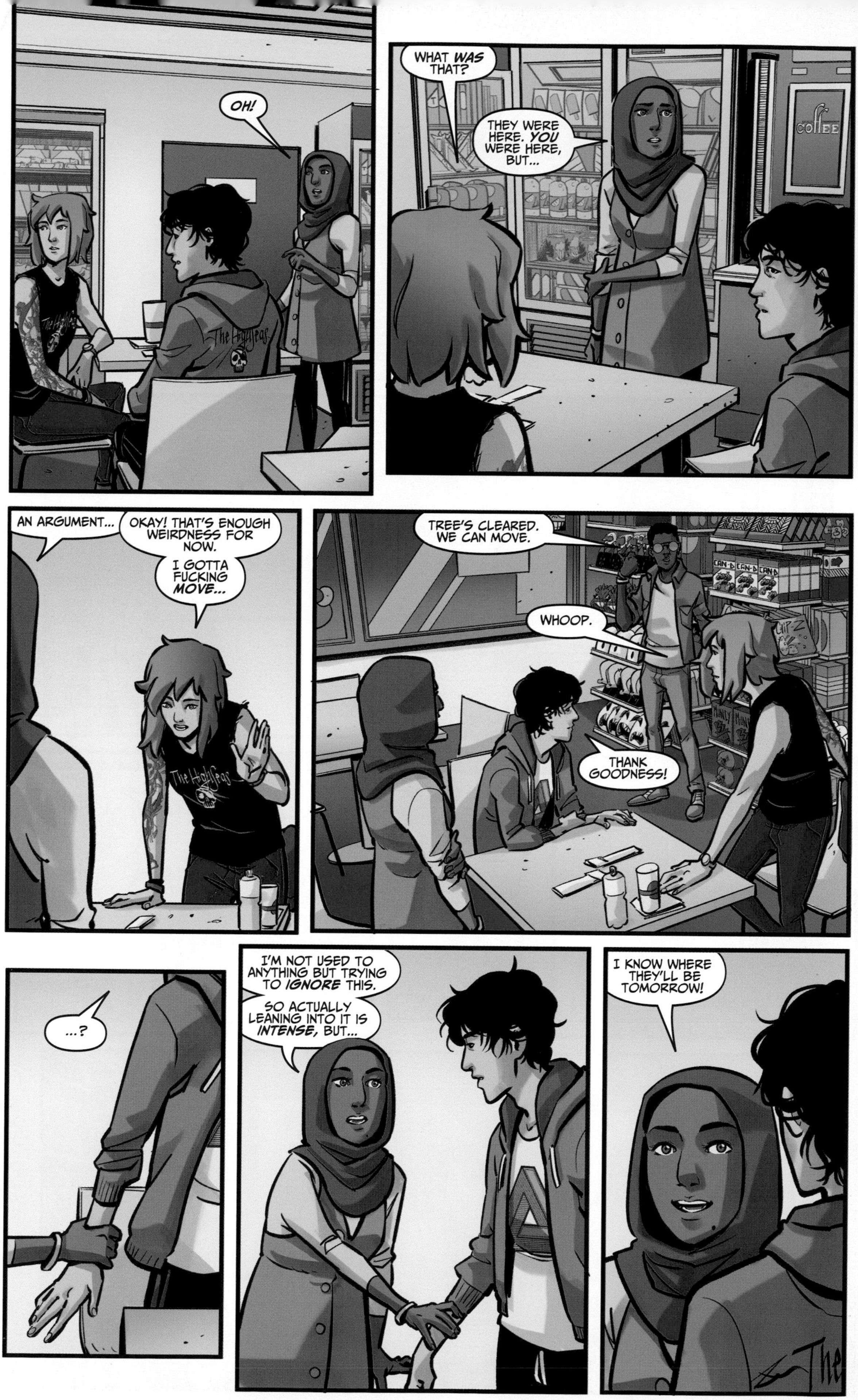
OH!
WHAT WAS THAT?
THEY WERE HERE. YOU WERE HERE, BUT...
AN ARGUMENT...
OKAY! THAT'S ENOUGH WEIRDNESS FOR NOW.
I GOTTA FUCKING MOVE...
TREE'S CLEARED. WE CAN MOVE.
WHOOP.
THANK GOODNESS!
...?
I'M NOT USED TO ANYTHING BUT TRYING TO IGNORE THIS.
SO ACTUALLY LEANING INTO IT IS INTENSE, BUT...
I KNOW WHERE THEY'LL BE TOMORROW!

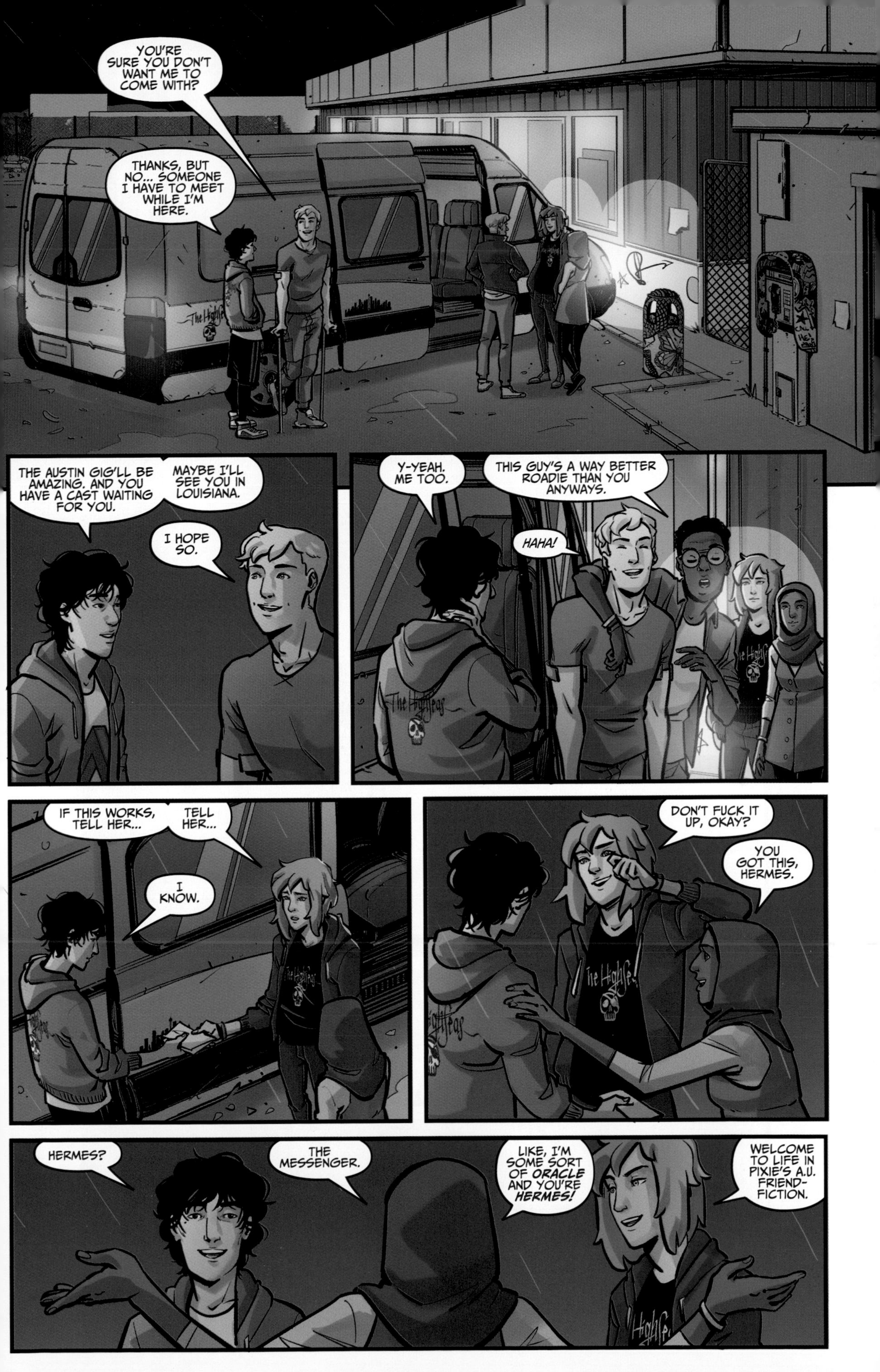
YOU'RE SURE YOU DON'T WANT ME TO COME WITH?
THANKS, BUT NO... SOMEONE I HAVE TO MEET WHILE I'M HERE.
THE AUSTIN GIG'LL BE AMAZING. AND YOU HAVE A CAST WAITING FOR YOU.
MAYBE I'LL SEE YOU IN LOUISIANA.
I HOPE SO.
Y-YEAH. ME TOO.
THIS GUY'S A WAY BETTER ROADIE THAN YOU ANYWAYS.
HAHA!
IF THIS WORKS, TELL HER...
TELL HER...
I KNOW.
DON'T FUCK IT UP, OKAY?
YOU GOT THIS, HERMES.
HERMES?
THE MESSENGER.
LIKE, I'M SOME SORT OF ORACLE AND YOU'RE HERMES!
WELCOME TO LIFE IN PIXIE'S A.U. FRIEND-FICTION.

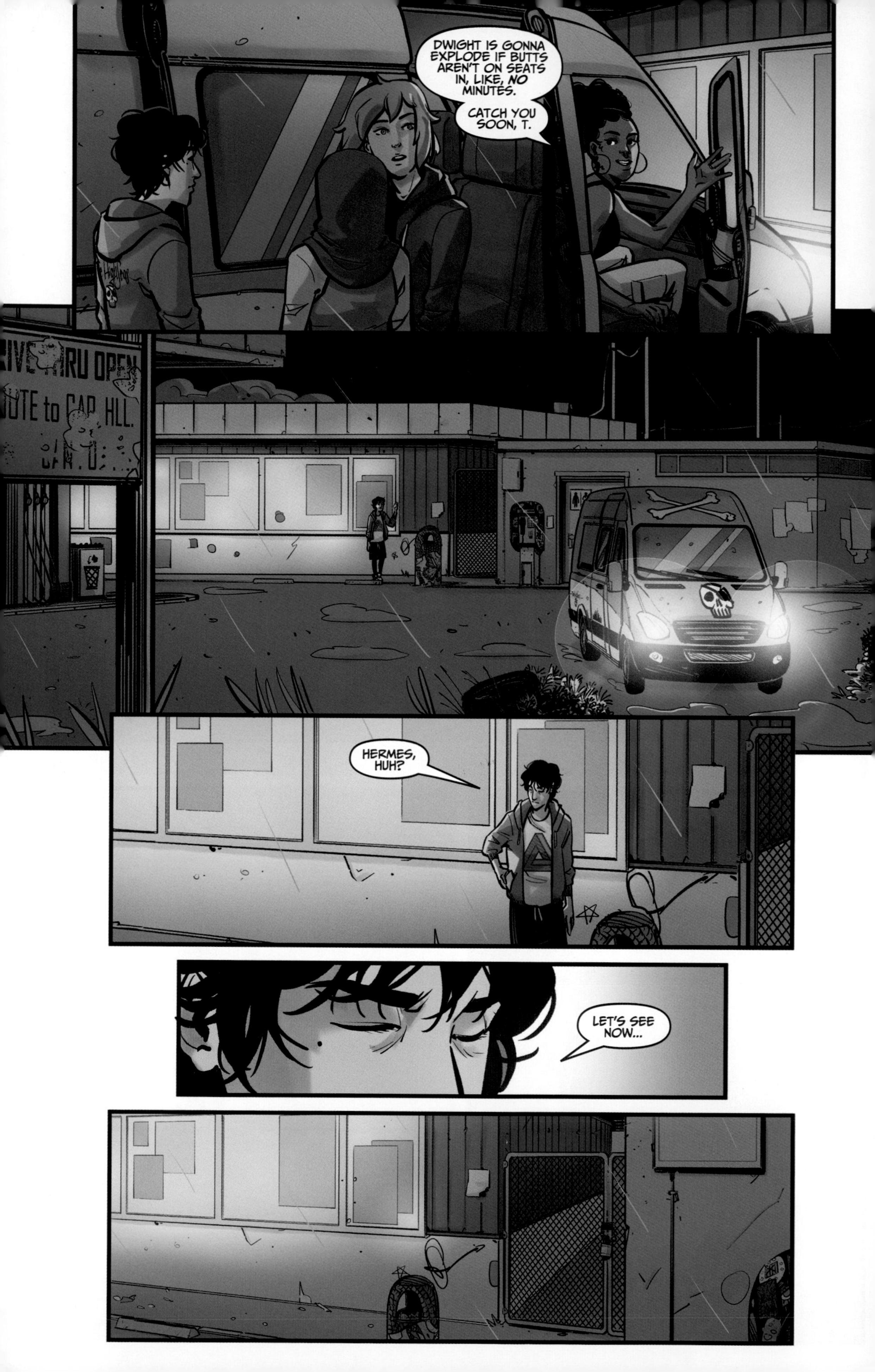
DWIGHT IS GONNA EXPLODE IF BUTTS AREN'T ON SEATS IN, LIKE, *NO* MINUTES.
CATCH YOU SOON, T.
HERMES, HUH?
LET'S SEE NOW...

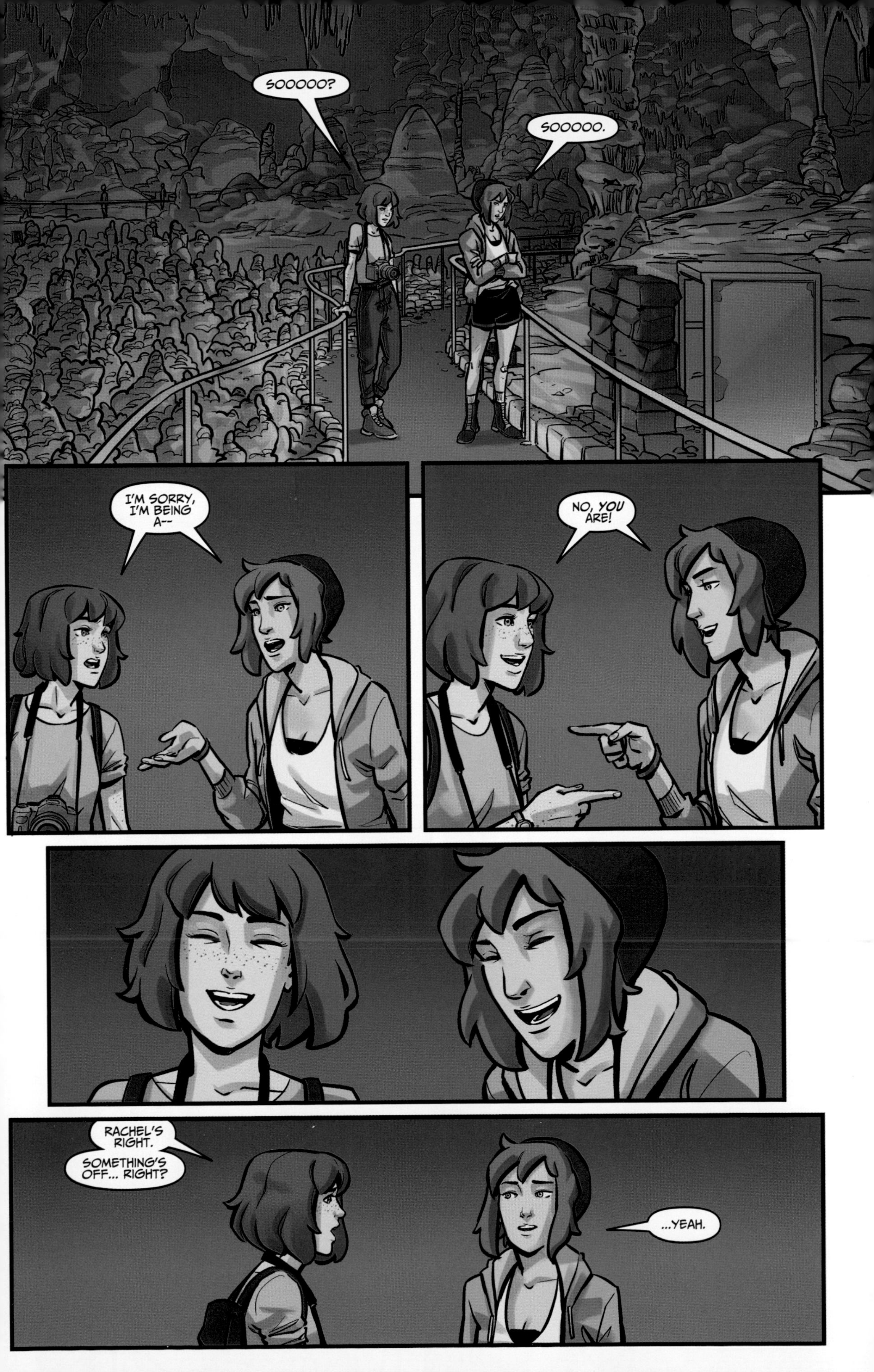
SOOOOO?
SOOOOO.
I'M SORRY, I'M BEING A--
NO, YOU ARE!
RACHEL'S RIGHT.
SOMETHING'S OFF... RIGHT?
...YEAH.

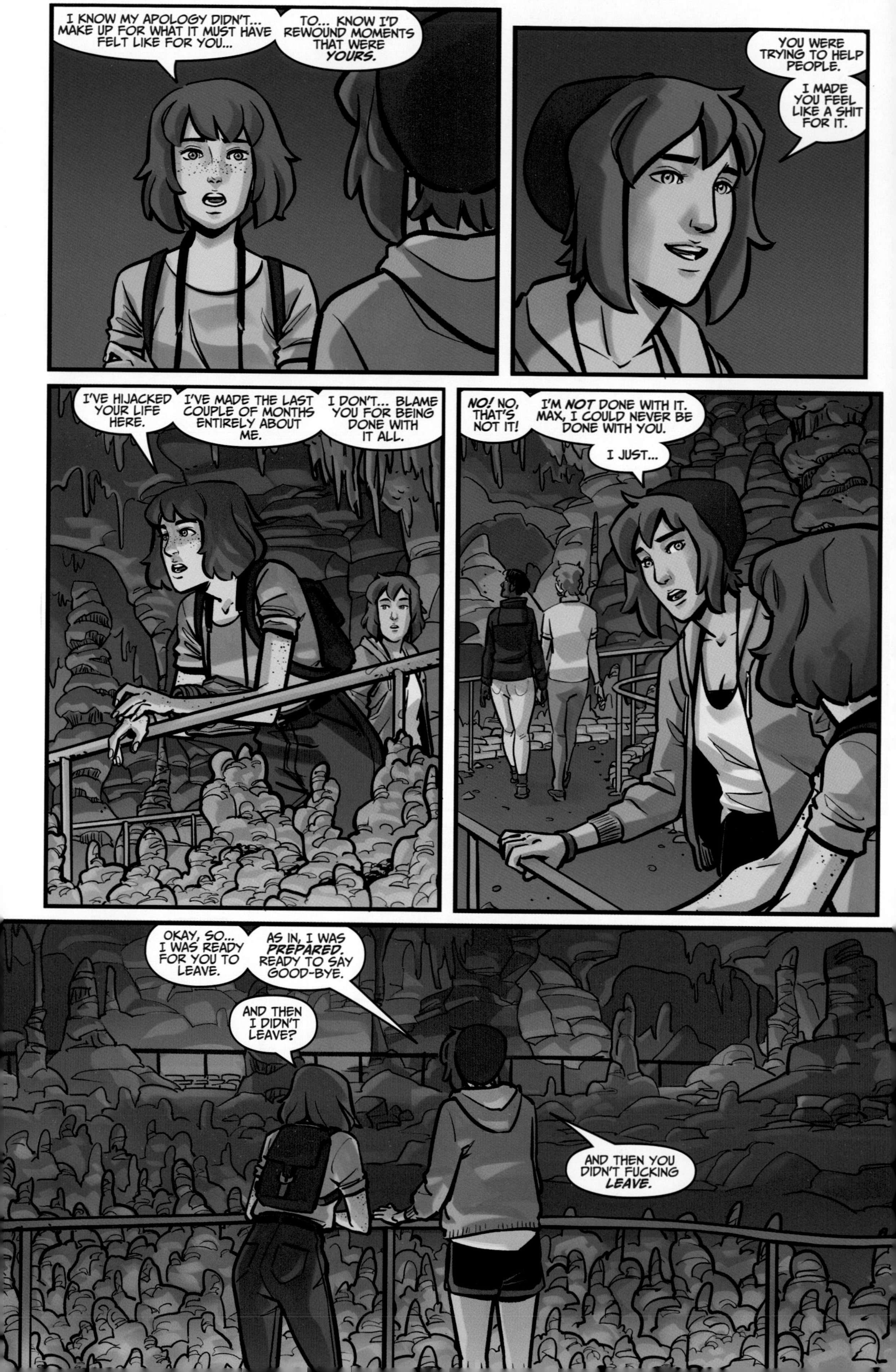
I KNOW MY APOLOGY DIDN'T... MAKE UP FOR WHAT IT MUST HAVE FELT LIKE FOR YOU...
TO... KNOW I'D REWOUND MOMENTS THAT WERE *YOURS.*
YOU WERE TRYING TO HELP PEOPLE.
I MADE YOU FEEL LIKE A SHIT FOR IT.
I'VE HIJACKED YOUR LIFE HERE.
I'VE MADE THE LAST COUPLE OF MONTHS ENTIRELY ABOUT ME.
I DON'T... BLAME YOU FOR BEING DONE WITH IT ALL.
NO! NO, THAT'S NOT IT!
I'M *NOT* DONE WITH IT. MAX, I COULD NEVER BE DONE WITH YOU.
I JUST...
OKAY, SO... I WAS READY FOR YOU TO LEAVE.
AS IN, I WAS *PREPARED.* READY TO SAY GOOD-BYE.
AND THEN I DIDN'T LEAVE?
AND THEN YOU DIDN'T FUCKING *LEAVE.*

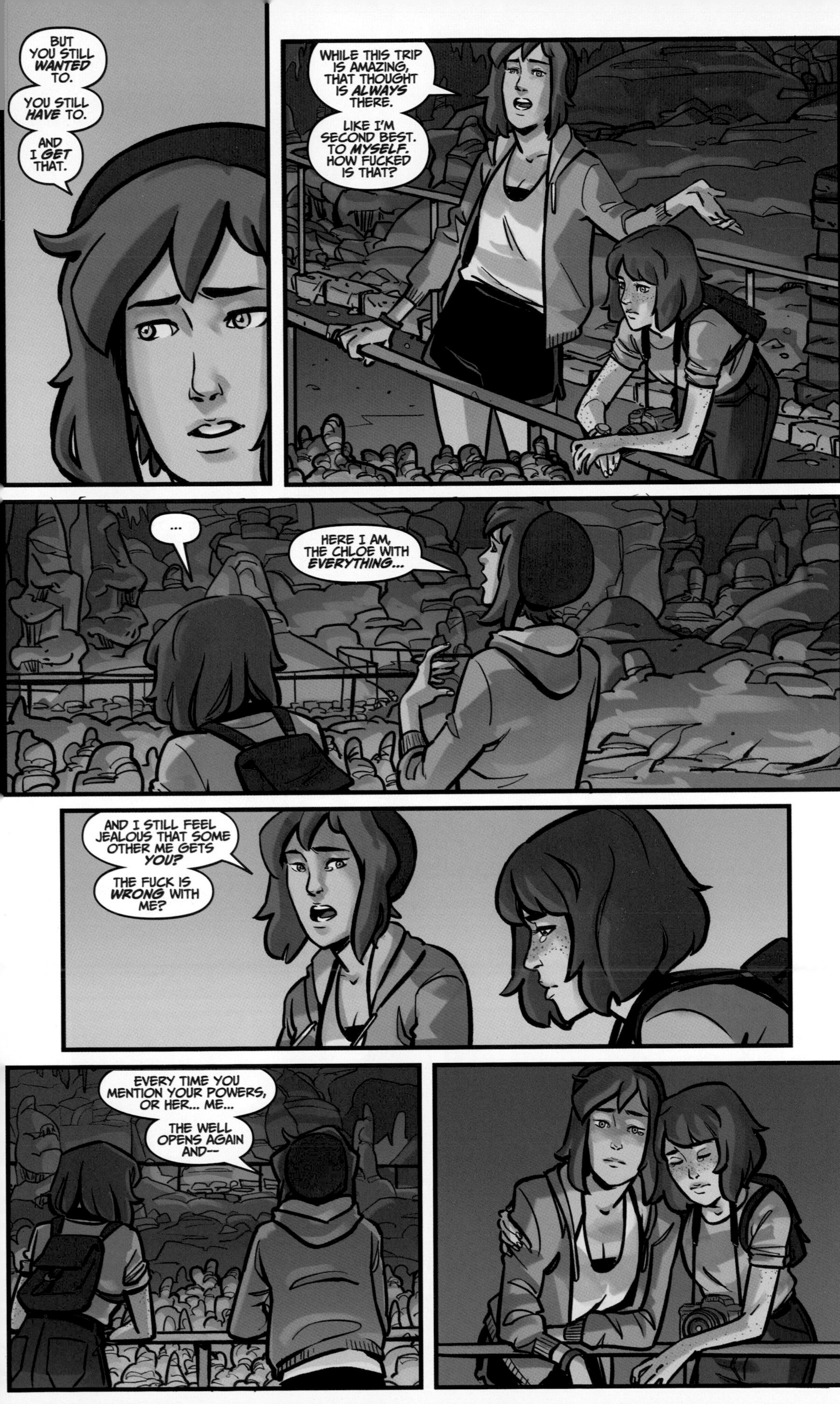
BUT YOU STILL *WANTED* TO.
YOU STILL *HAVE* TO.
AND I *GET* THAT.
WHILE THIS TRIP IS AMAZING, THAT THOUGHT IS *ALWAYS* THERE.
LIKE I'M SECOND BEST. TO *MYSELF*. HOW FUCKED IS THAT?
...
HERE I AM, THE CHLOE WITH *EVERYTHING*...
AND I STILL FEEL JEALOUS THAT SOME OTHER ME GETS *YOU?*
THE FUCK IS *WRONG* WITH ME?
EVERY TIME YOU MENTION YOUR POWERS, OR HER... ME...
THE WELL OPENS AGAIN AND--

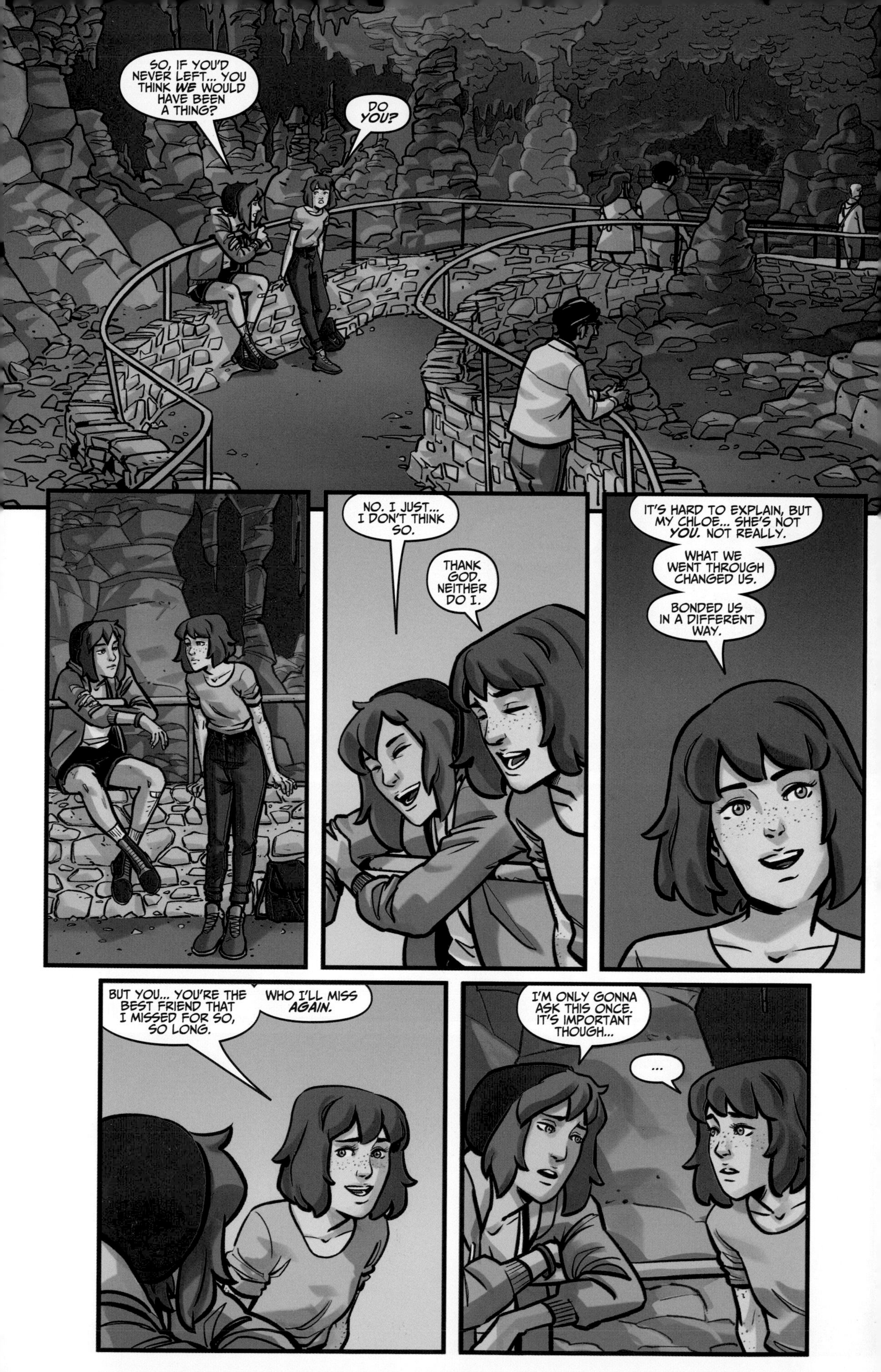
SO, IF YOU'D NEVER LEFT... YOU THINK **WE** WOULD HAVE BEEN A THING?
DO *YOU?*
NO. I JUST... I DON'T THINK SO.
THANK GOD. NEITHER DO I.
IT'S HARD TO EXPLAIN, BUT MY CHLOE... SHE'S NOT *YOU.* NOT REALLY.
WHAT WE WENT THROUGH CHANGED US.
BONDED US IN A DIFFERENT WAY.
BUT YOU... YOU'RE THE BEST FRIEND THAT I MISSED FOR SO, SO LONG.
WHO I'LL MISS *AGAIN.*
I'M ONLY GONNA ASK THIS ONCE. IT'S IMPORTANT THOUGH...
...

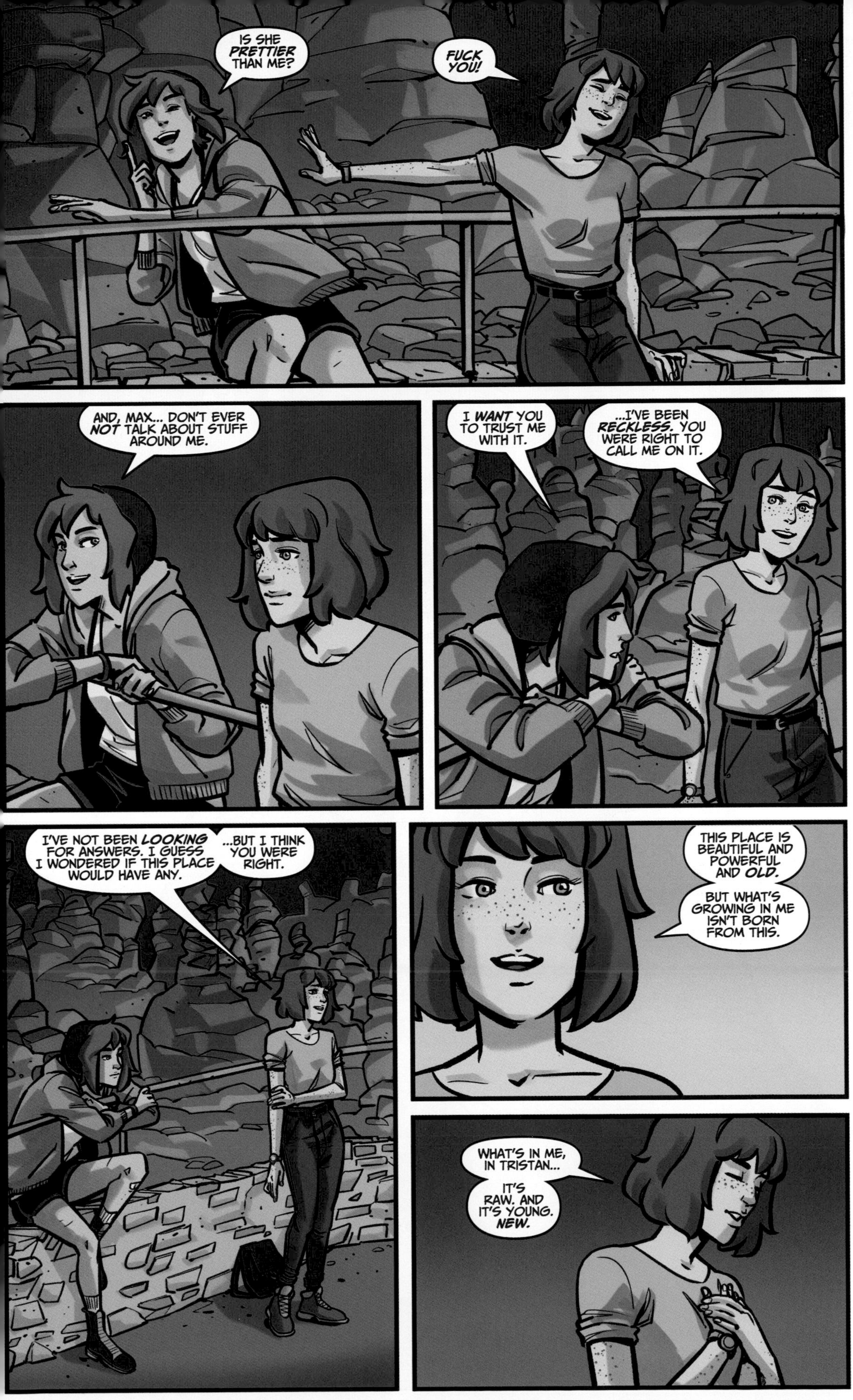
IS SHE PRETTIER THAN ME?
FUCK YOU!
AND, MAX... DON'T EVER NOT TALK ABOUT STUFF AROUND ME.
I WANT YOU TO TRUST ME WITH IT.
...I'VE BEEN RECKLESS. YOU WERE RIGHT TO CALL ME ON IT.
I'VE NOT BEEN LOOKING FOR ANSWERS. I GUESS I WONDERED IF THIS PLACE WOULD HAVE ANY.
...BUT I THINK YOU WERE RIGHT.
THIS PLACE IS BEAUTIFUL AND POWERFUL AND OLD.
BUT WHAT'S GROWING IN ME ISN'T BORN FROM THIS.
WHAT'S IN ME, IN TRISTAN...
IT'S RAW. AND IT'S YOUNG. NEW.

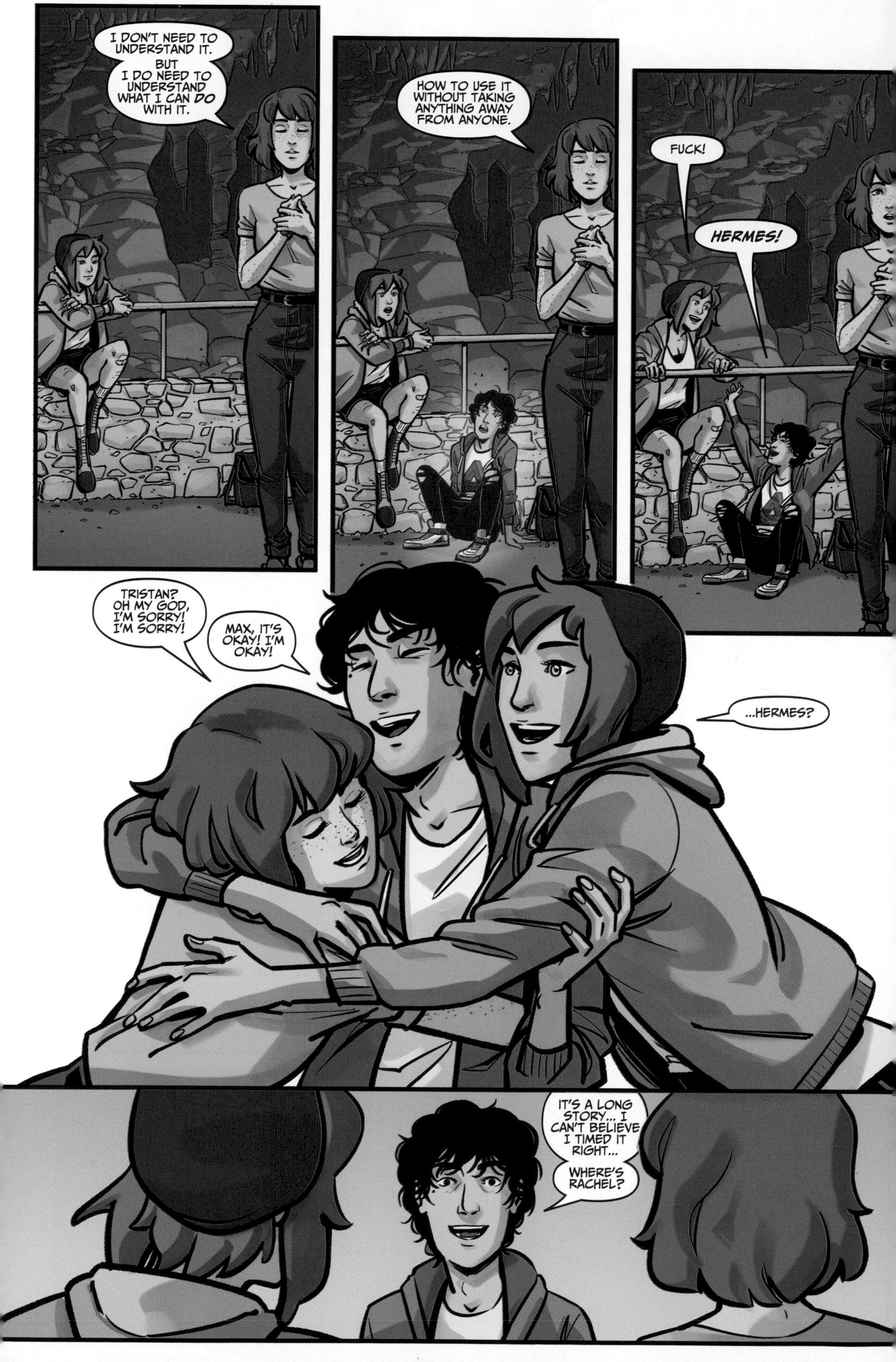
I DON'T NEED TO UNDERSTAND IT.
BUT I DO NEED TO UNDERSTAND WHAT I CAN *DO* WITH IT.
HOW TO USE IT WITHOUT TAKING ANYTHING AWAY FROM ANYONE.
FUCK!
HERMES!
TRISTAN? OH MY GOD, I'M SORRY! I'M SORRY!
MAX, IT'S OKAY! I'M OKAY!
...HERMES?
IT'S A LONG STORY... I CAN'T BELIEVE I TIMED IT RIGHT...
WHERE'S RACHEL?

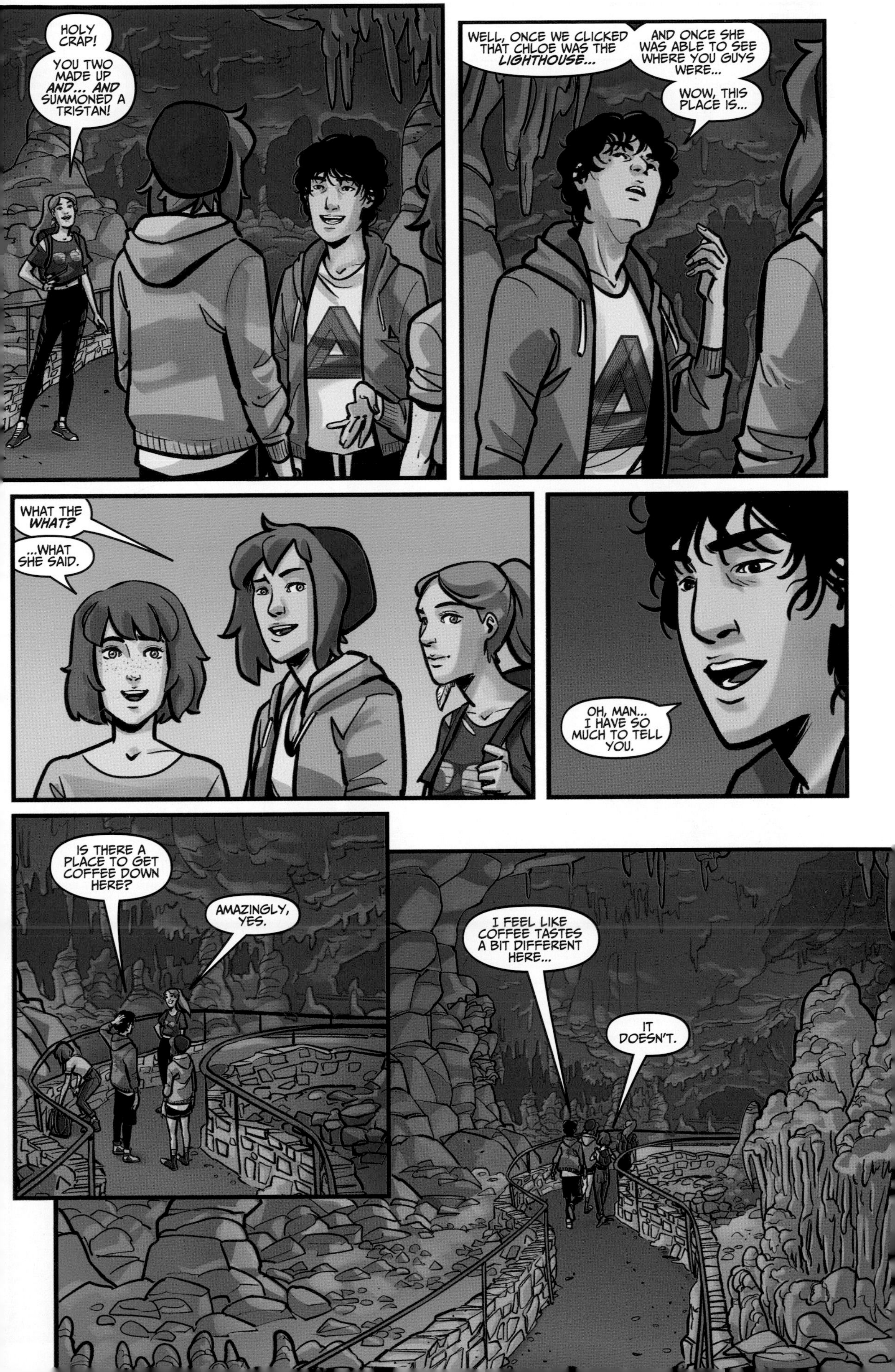
HOLY CRAP!
YOU TWO MADE UP AND... AND SUMMONED A TRISTAN!
WELL, ONCE WE CLICKED THAT CHLOE WAS THE LIGHTHOUSE...
AND ONCE SHE WAS ABLE TO SEE WHERE YOU GUYS WERE...
WOW, THIS PLACE IS...
WHAT THE WHAT?
...WHAT SHE SAID.
OH, MAN... I HAVE SO MUCH TO TELL YOU.
IS THERE A PLACE TO GET COFFEE DOWN HERE?
AMAZINGLY, YES.
I FEEL LIKE COFFEE TASTES A BIT DIFFERENT HERE...
IT DOESN'T.

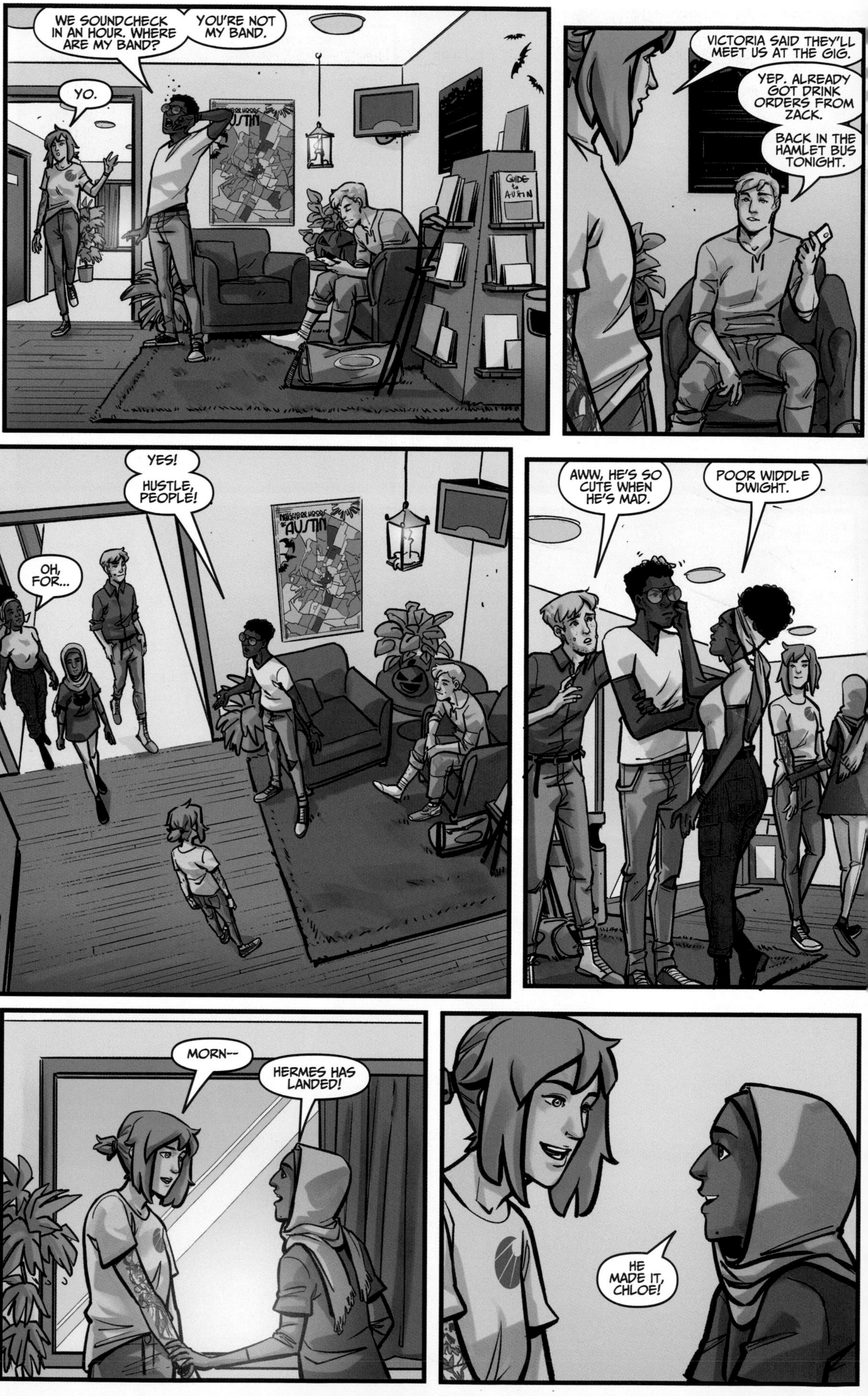
WE SOUNDCHECK IN AN HOUR. WHERE ARE MY BAND?
YOU'RE NOT MY BAND.
YO.
VICTORIA SAID THEY'LL MEET US AT THE GIG.
YEP. ALREADY GOT DRINK ORDERS FROM ZACK.
BACK IN THE HAMLET BUS TONIGHT.
GUIDE to AUSTIN
YES!
HUSTLE, PEOPLE!
OH, FOR...
AWW, HE'S SO CUTE WHEN HE'S MAD.
POOR WIDDLE DWIGHT.
MORN--
HERMES HAS LANDED!
HE MADE IT, CHLOE!

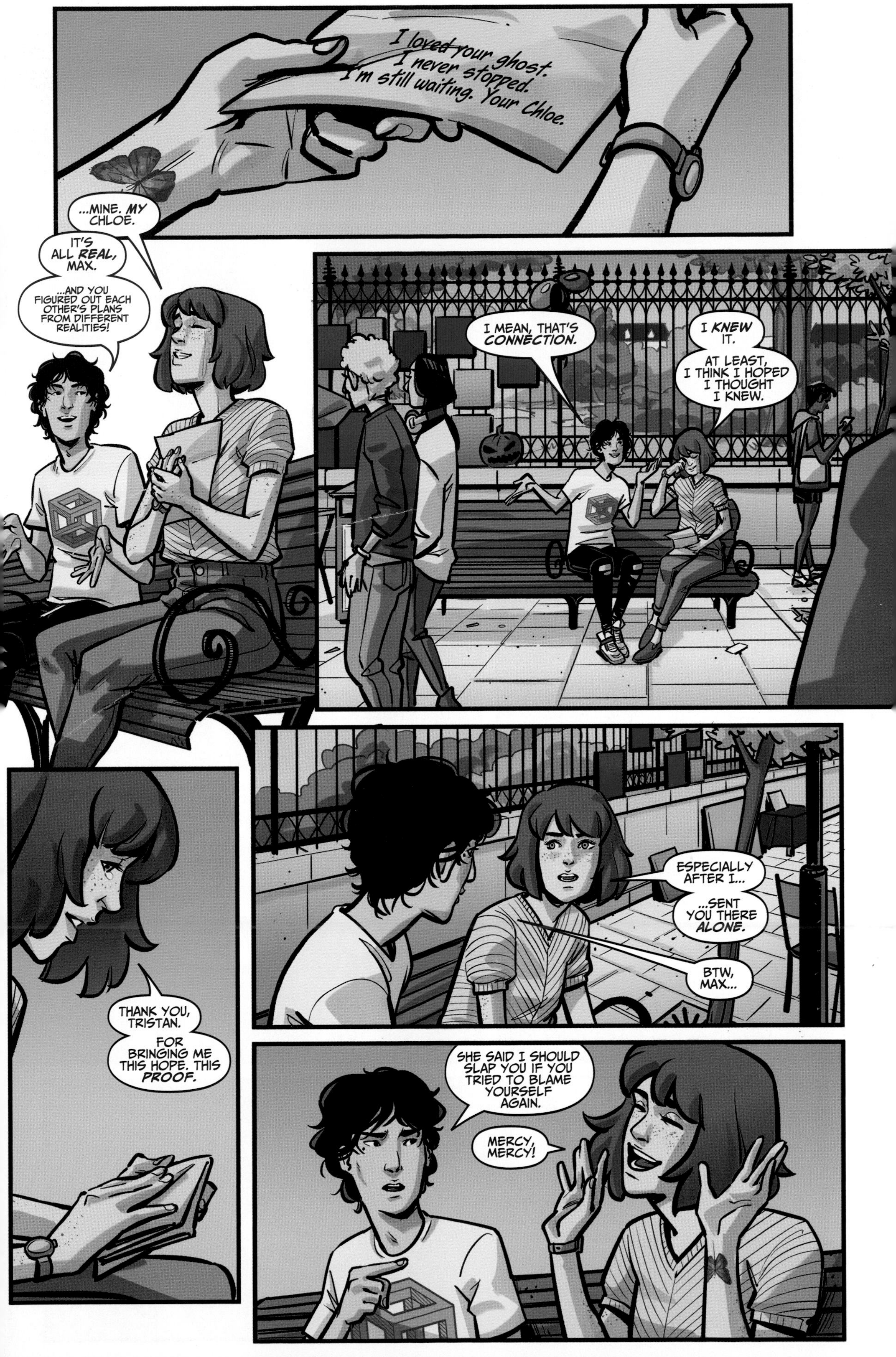
I loved your ghost.
I never stopped.
I'm still waiting. Your Chloe.
...MINE. MY CHLOE.
IT'S ALL REAL, MAX.
...AND YOU FIGURED OUT EACH OTHER'S PLANS FROM DIFFERENT REALITIES!
I MEAN, THAT'S CONNECTION.
I KNEW IT.
AT LEAST, I THINK I HOPED I THOUGHT I KNEW.
THANK YOU, TRISTAN.
FOR BRINGING ME THIS HOPE. THIS PROOF.
ESPECIALLY AFTER I...
...SENT YOU THERE ALONE.
BTW, MAX...
SHE SAID I SHOULD SLAP YOU IF YOU TRIED TO BLAME YOURSELF AGAIN.
MERCY, MERCY!

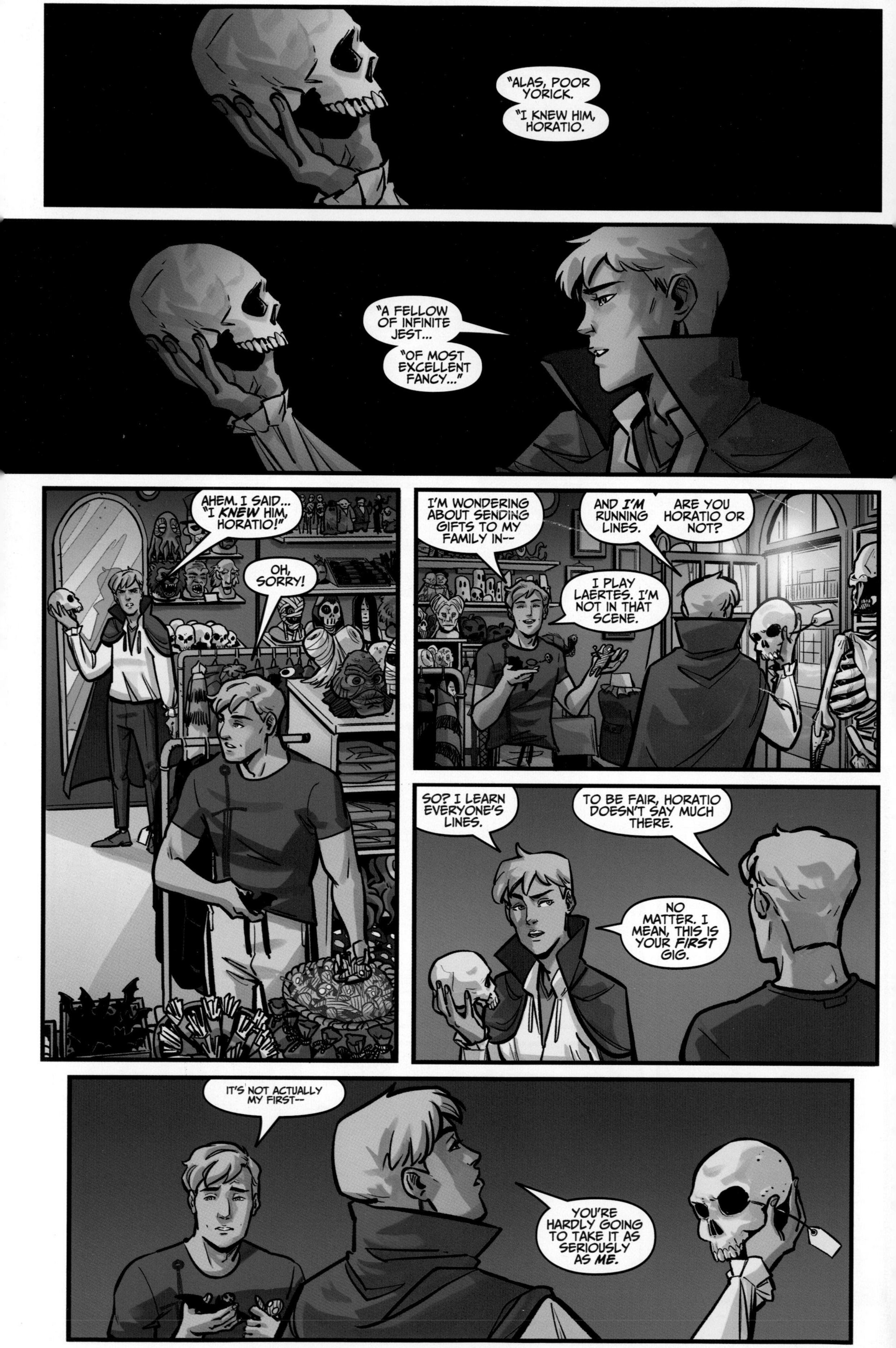
"ALAS, POOR YORICK.
"I KNEW HIM, HORATIO.
"A FELLOW OF INFINITE JEST...
"OF MOST EXCELLENT FANCY..."
AHEM. I SAID... "I *KNEW* HIM, HORATIO!"
OH, SORRY!
I'M WONDERING ABOUT SENDING GIFTS TO MY FAMILY IN--
AND *I'M* RUNNING LINES.
ARE YOU HORATIO OR NOT?
I PLAY LAERTES. I'M NOT IN THAT SCENE.
SO? I LEARN EVERYONE'S LINES.
TO BE FAIR, HORATIO DOESN'T SAY MUCH THERE.
NO MATTER. I MEAN, THIS IS YOUR *FIRST* GIG.
IT'S NOT ACTUALLY MY FIRST--
YOU'RE HARDLY GOING TO TAKE IT AS SERIOUSLY AS *ME*.

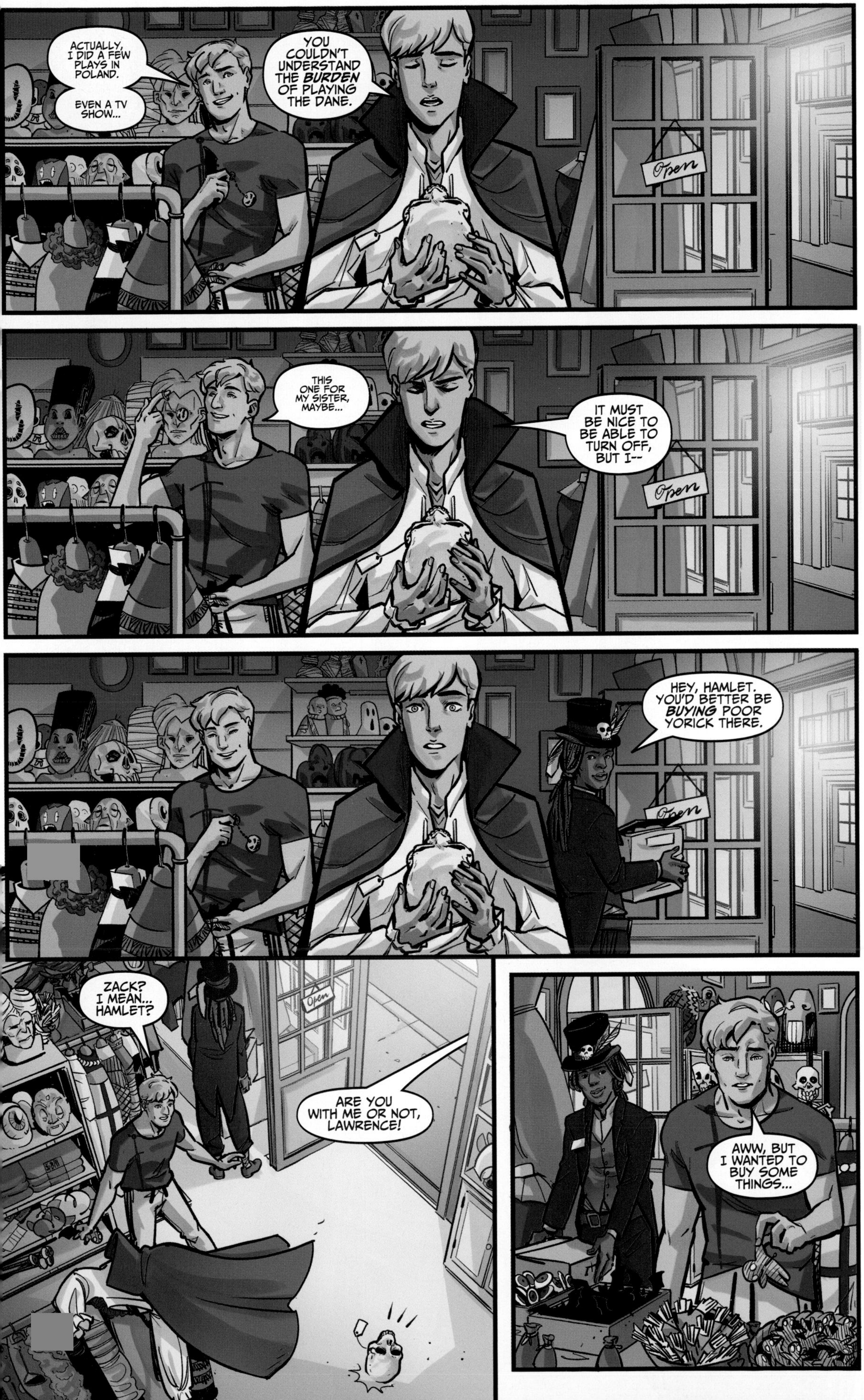
ACTUALLY, I DID A FEW PLAYS IN POLAND.
EVEN A TV SHOW...
YOU COULDN'T UNDERSTAND THE BURDEN OF PLAYING THE DANE.
Open
THIS ONE FOR MY SISTER, MAYBE...
IT MUST BE NICE TO BE ABLE TO TURN OFF, BUT I--
HEY, HAMLET. YOU'D BETTER BE BUYING POOR YORICK THERE.
ZACK? I MEAN... HAMLET?
ARE YOU WITH ME OR NOT, LAWRENCE!
AWW, BUT I WANTED TO BUY SOME THINGS...

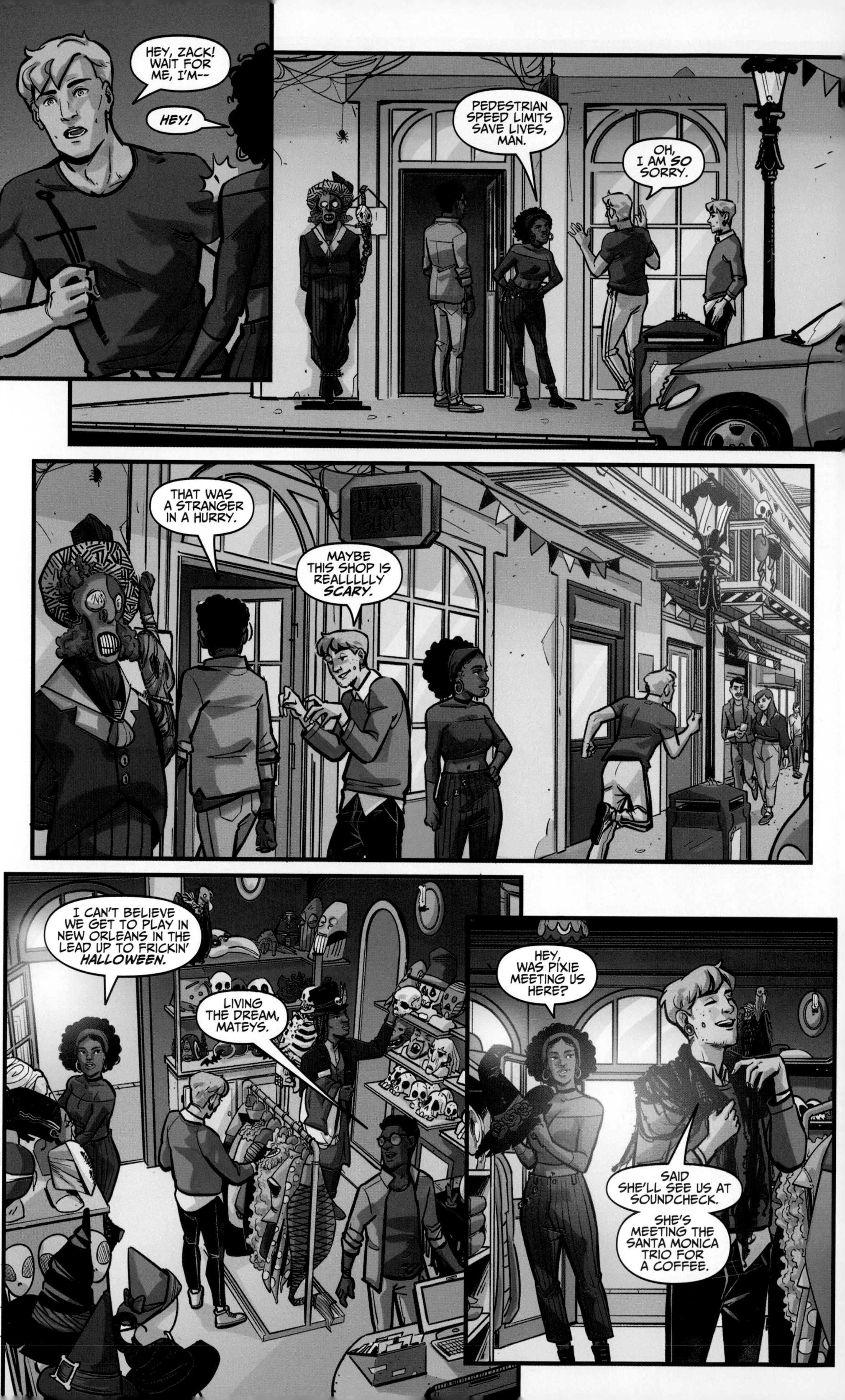
HEY, ZACK! WAIT FOR ME, I'M--
HEY!
PEDESTRIAN SPEED LIMITS SAVE LIVES, MAN.
OH, I AM SO SORRY.
THAT WAS A STRANGER IN A HURRY.
HORROR SHOP
MAYBE THIS SHOP IS REALLLLLY SCARY.
I CAN'T BELIEVE WE GET TO PLAY IN NEW ORLEANS IN THE LEAD UP TO FRICKIN' HALLOWEEN.
LIVING THE DREAM, MATEYS.
HEY, WAS PIXIE MEETING US HERE?
SAID SHE'LL SEE US AT SOUNDCHECK.
SHE'S MEETING THE SANTA MONICA TRIO FOR A COFFEE.

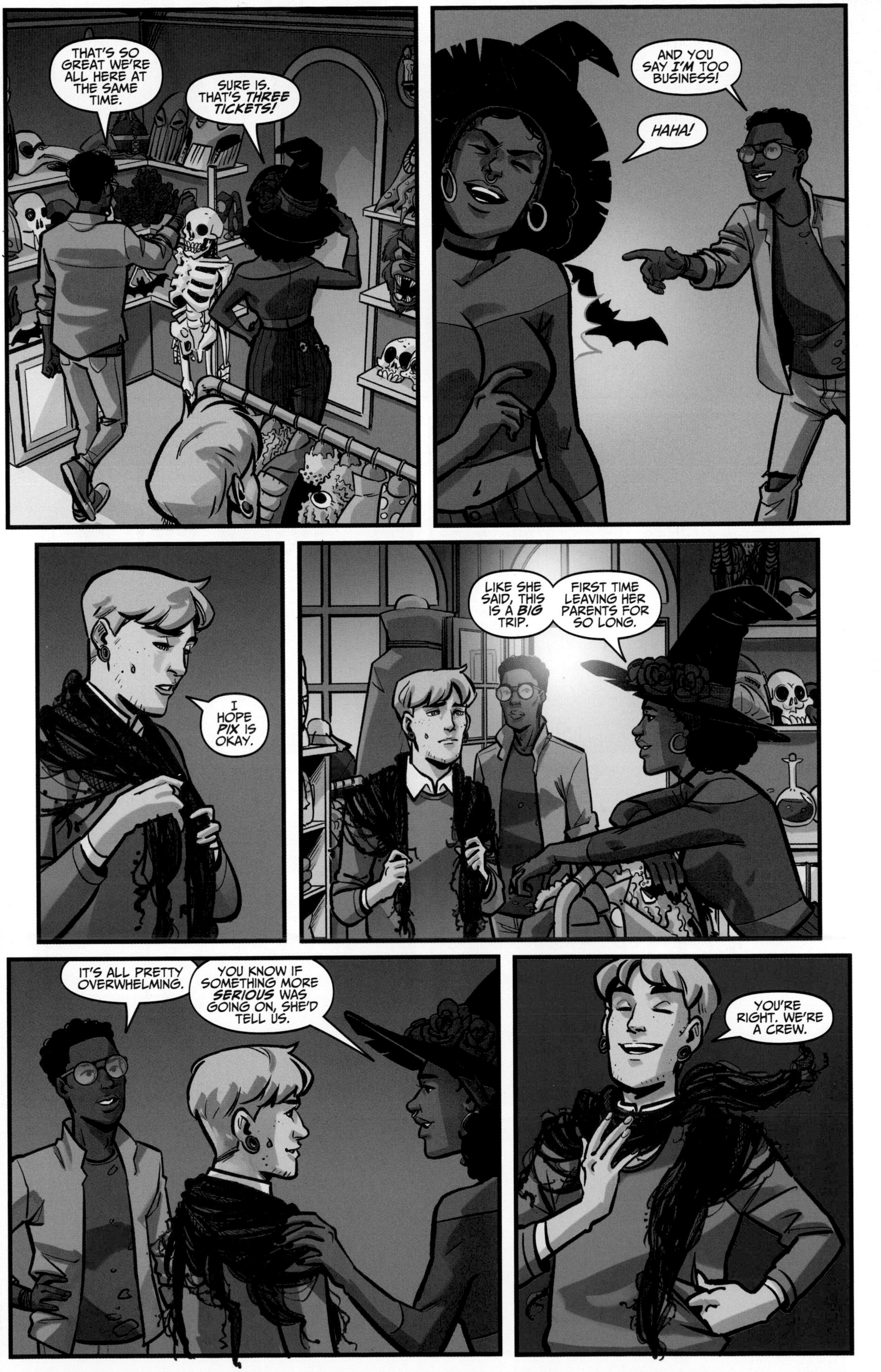
THAT'S SO GREAT WE'RE ALL HERE AT THE SAME TIME.
SURE IS. THAT'S THREE TICKETS!
AND YOU SAY I'M TOO BUSINESS!
HAHA!
I HOPE PIX IS OKAY.
LIKE SHE SAID, THIS IS A BIG TRIP.
FIRST TIME LEAVING HER PARENTS FOR SO LONG.
IT'S ALL PRETTY OVERWHELMING.
YOU KNOW IF SOMETHING MORE SERIOUS WAS GOING ON, SHE'D TELL US.
YOU'RE RIGHT. WE'RE A CREW.

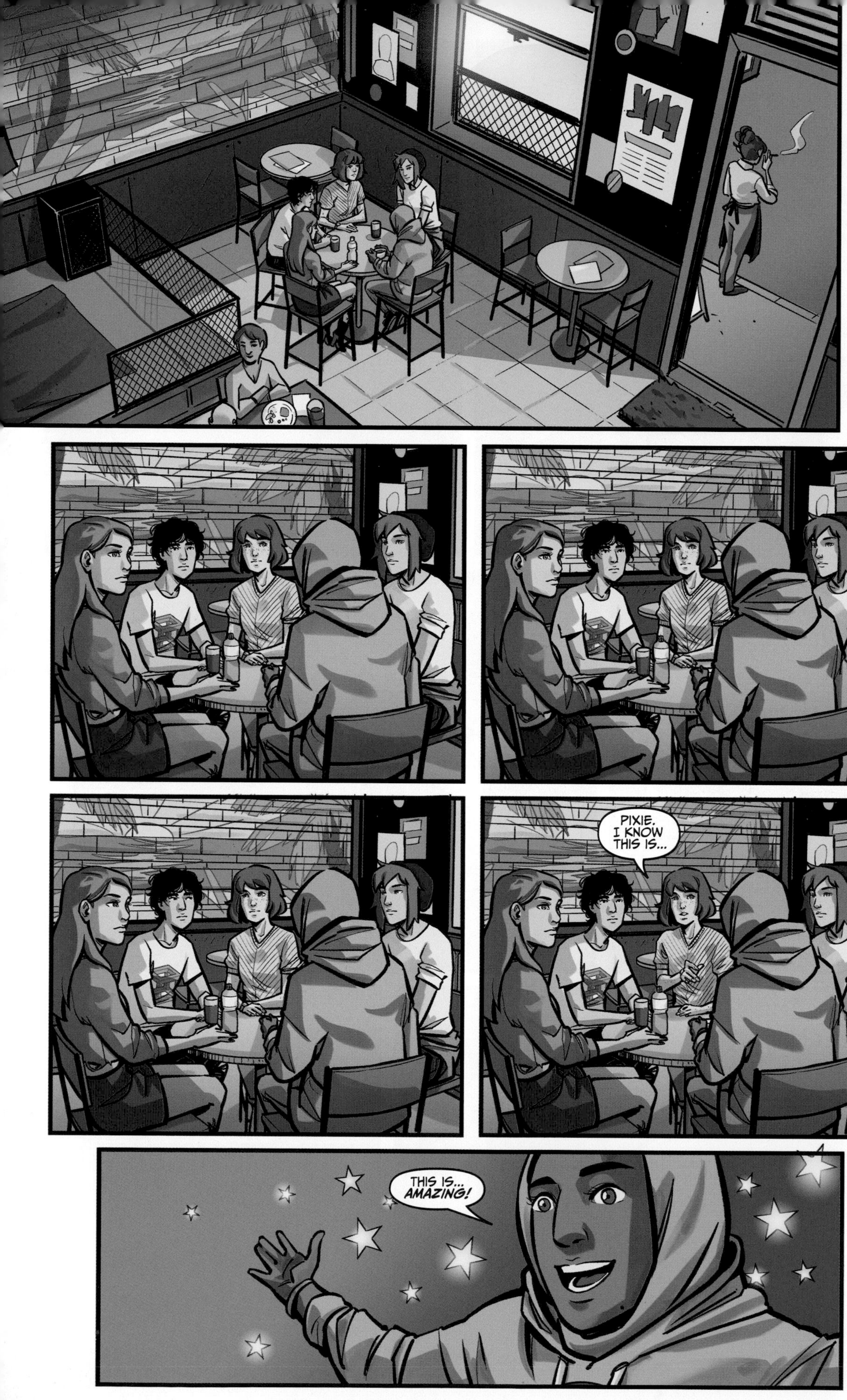
PIXIE. I KNOW THIS IS...
THIS IS... AMAZING!

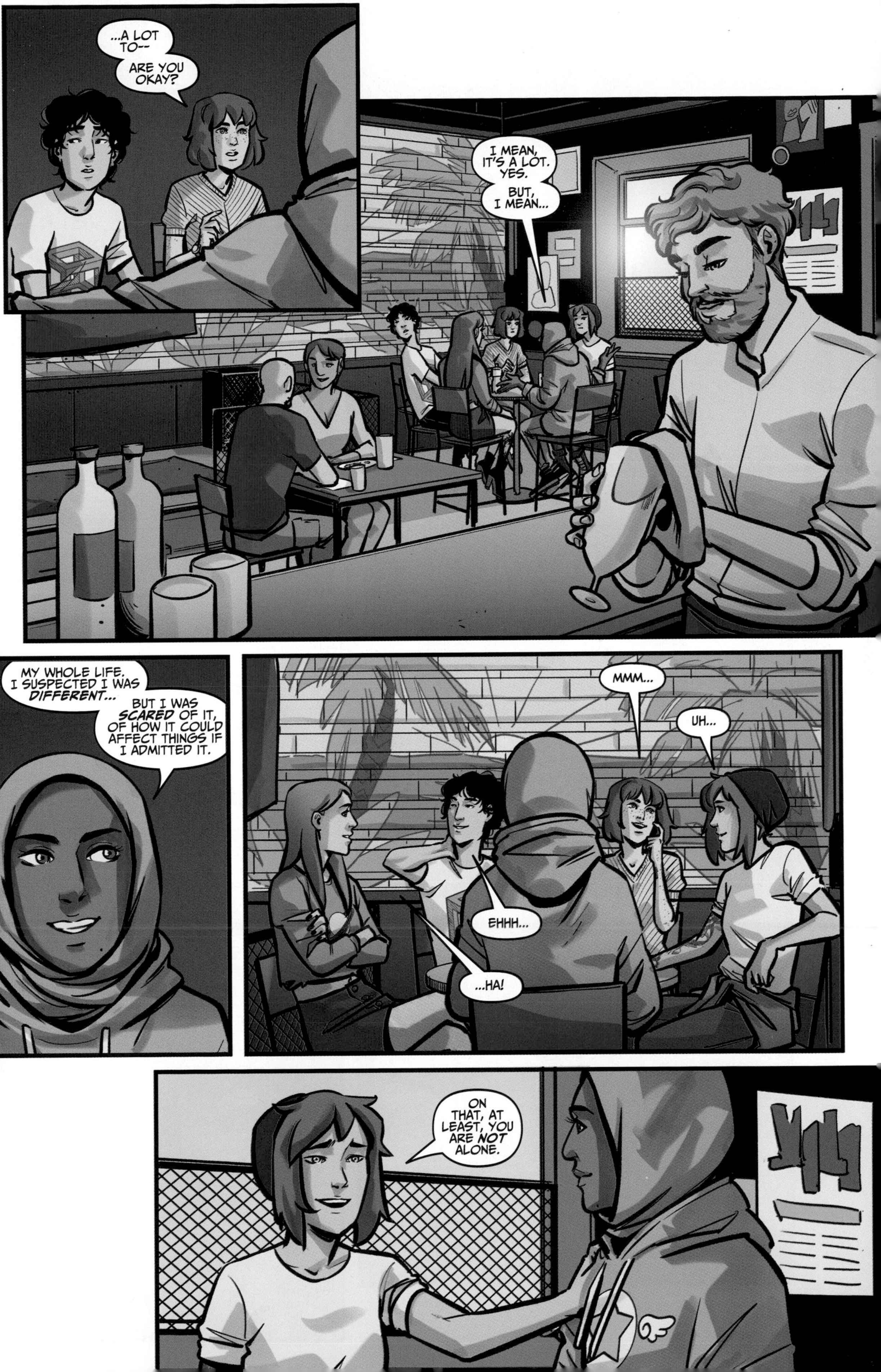

...A LOT TO--
ARE YOU OKAY?
I MEAN, IT'S A LOT. YES.
BUT, I MEAN...
MY WHOLE LIFE. I SUSPECTED I WAS DIFFERENT...
BUT I WAS SCARED OF IT, OF HOW IT COULD AFFECT THINGS IF I ADMITTED IT.
MMM...
UH...
EHHH...
...HA!
ON THAT, AT LEAST, YOU ARE NOT ALONE.

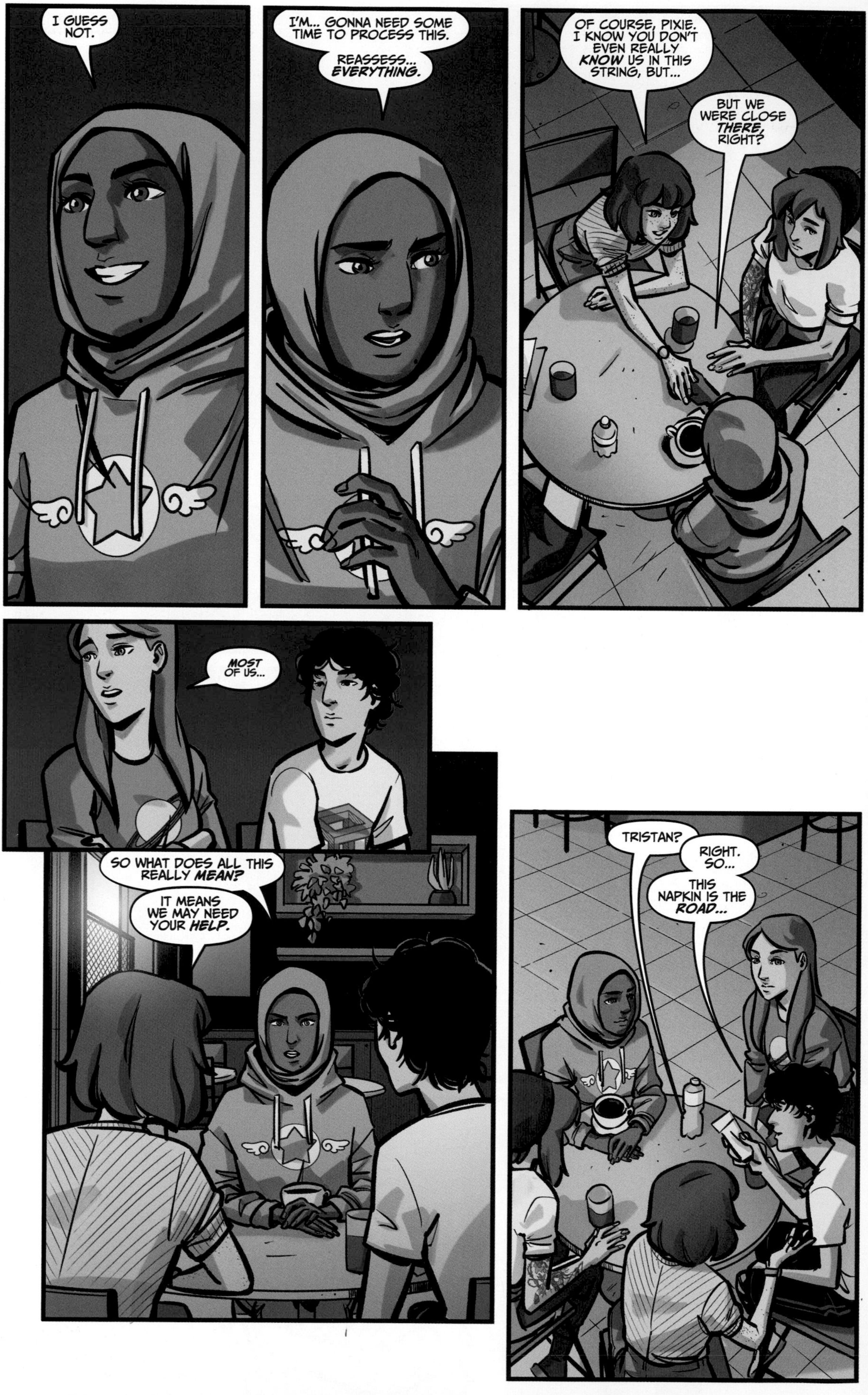

I GUESS NOT.
I'M... GONNA NEED SOME TIME TO PROCESS THIS.
REASSESS... *EVERYTHING.*
OF COURSE, PIXIE. I KNOW YOU DON'T EVEN REALLY *KNOW* US IN THIS STRING, BUT...
BUT WE WERE CLOSE *THERE,* RIGHT?
MOST OF US...
SO WHAT DOES ALL THIS REALLY *MEAN?*
IT MEANS WE MAY NEED YOUR *HELP.*
TRISTAN?
RIGHT. SO...
THIS NAPKIN IS THE *ROAD...*

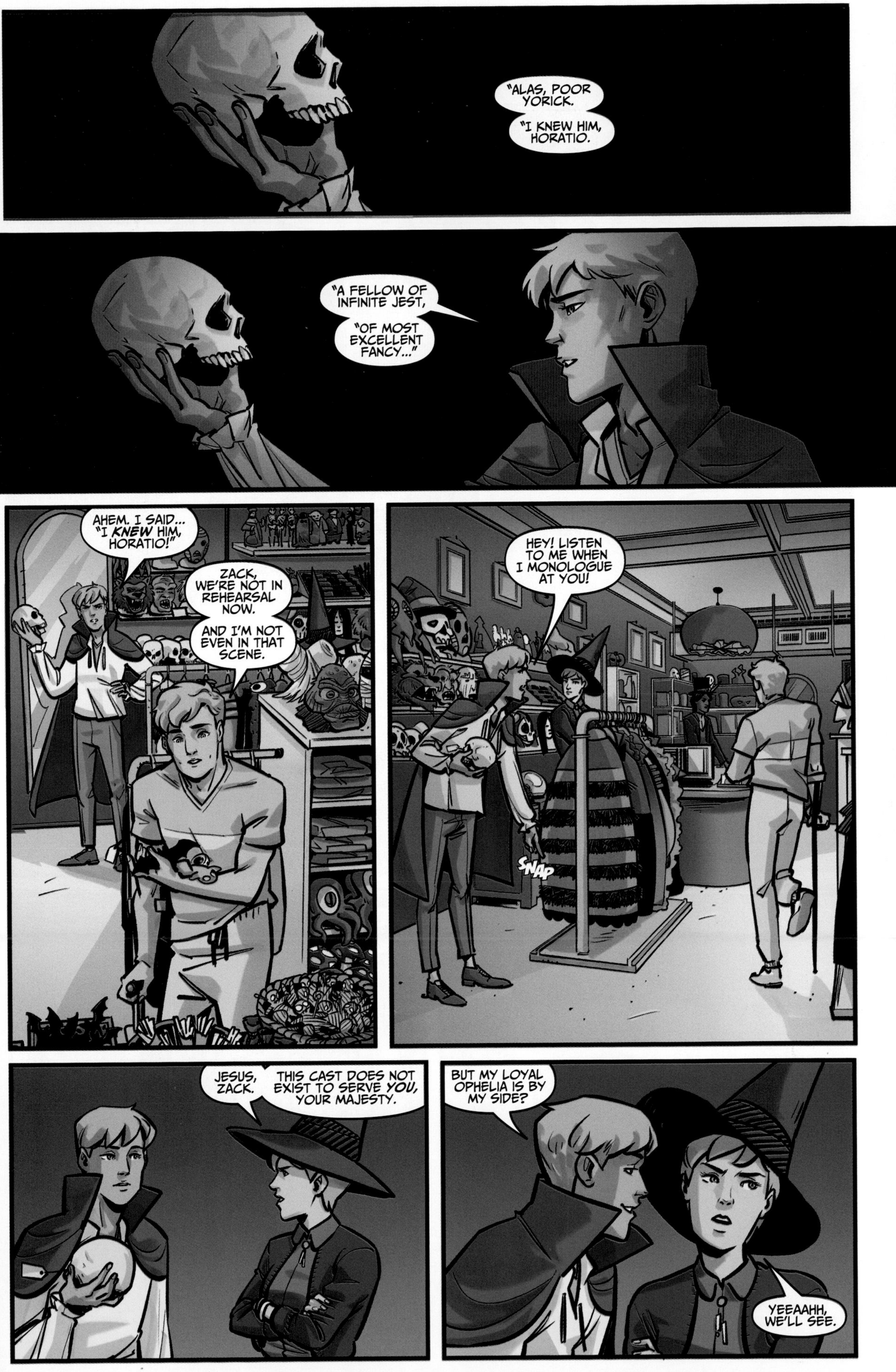
"ALAS, POOR YORICK.
"I KNEW HIM, HORATIO.
"A FELLOW OF INFINITE JEST,
"OF MOST EXCELLENT FANCY..."
AHEM. I SAID... "I KNEW HIM, HORATIO!"
ZACK, WE'RE NOT IN REHEARSAL NOW.
AND I'M NOT EVEN IN THAT SCENE.
HEY! LISTEN TO ME WHEN I MONOLOGUE AT YOU!
SNAP
JESUS, ZACK.
THIS CAST DOES NOT EXIST TO SERVE YOU, YOUR MAJESTY.
BUT MY LOYAL OPHELIA IS BY MY SIDE?
YEEAAHH, WE'LL SEE.

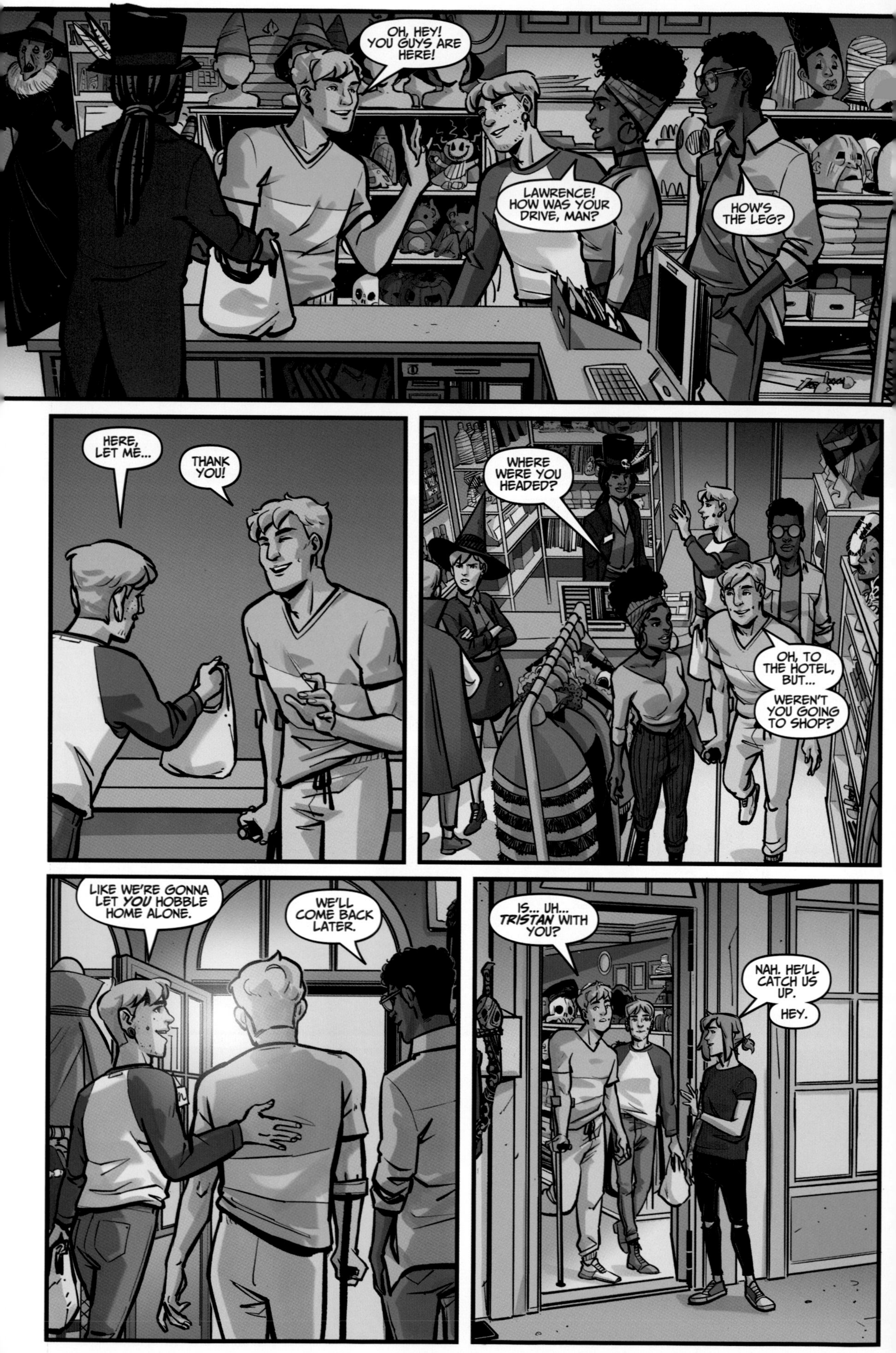
OH, HEY! YOU GUYS ARE HERE!
LAWRENCE! HOW WAS YOUR DRIVE, MAN?
HOW'S THE LEG?
HERE, LET ME...
THANK YOU!
WHERE WERE YOU HEADED?
OH, TO THE HOTEL, BUT...
WEREN'T YOU GOING TO SHOP?
LIKE WE'RE GONNA LET *YOU* HOBBLE HOME ALONE.
WE'LL COME BACK LATER.
IS... UH... *TRISTAN* WITH YOU?
NAH. HE'LL CATCH US UP.
HEY.

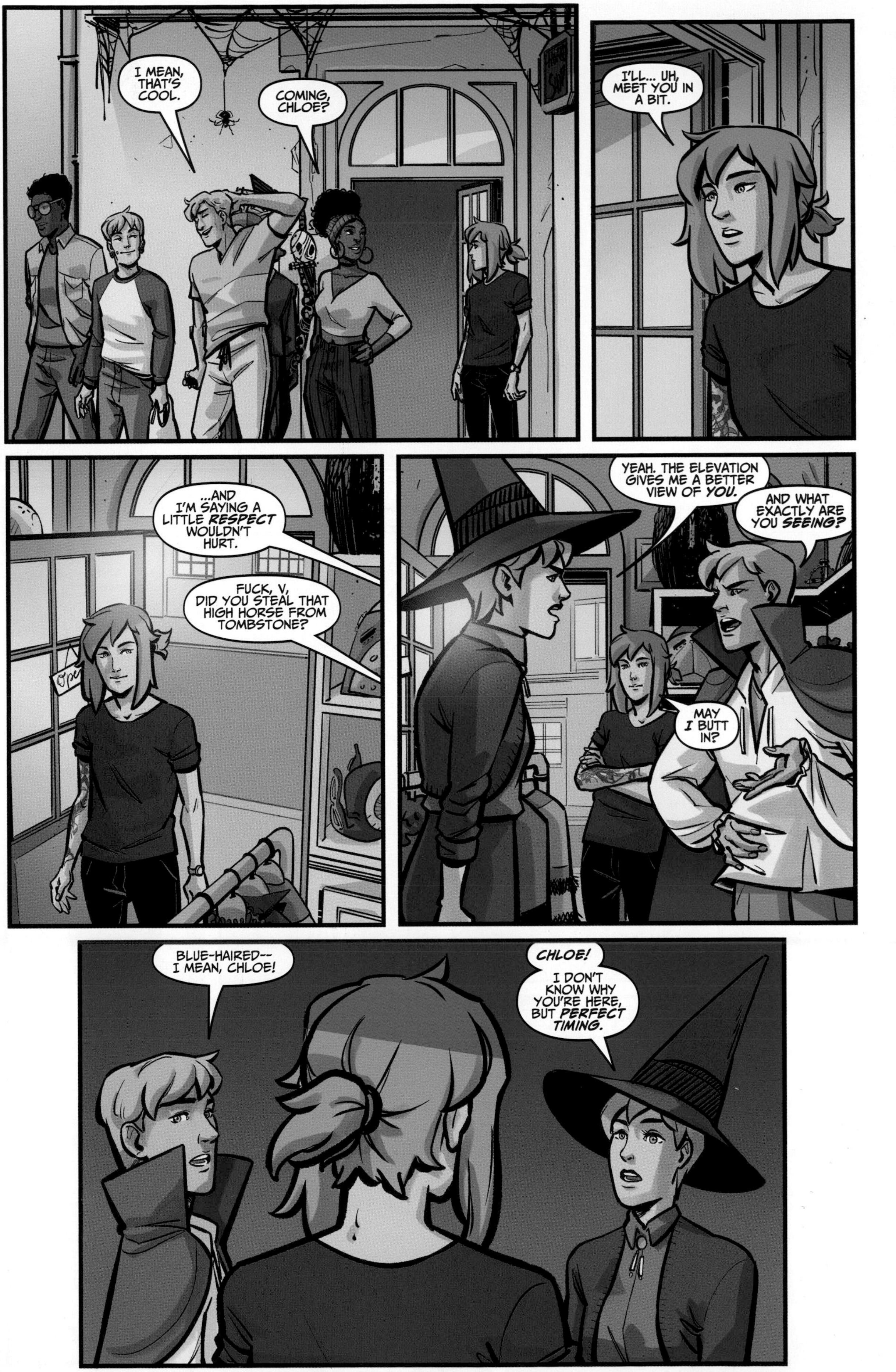
I MEAN, THAT'S COOL.
COMING, CHLOE?
I'LL... UH, MEET YOU IN A BIT.
...AND I'M SAYING A LITTLE RESPECT WOULDN'T HURT.
FUCK, V, DID YOU STEAL THAT HIGH HORSE FROM TOMBSTONE?
YEAH. THE ELEVATION GIVES ME A BETTER VIEW OF YOU.
AND WHAT EXACTLY ARE YOU SEEING?
MAY I BUTT IN?
BLUE-HAIRED-- I MEAN, CHLOE!
CHLOE!
I DON'T KNOW WHY YOU'RE HERE, BUT PERFECT TIMING.

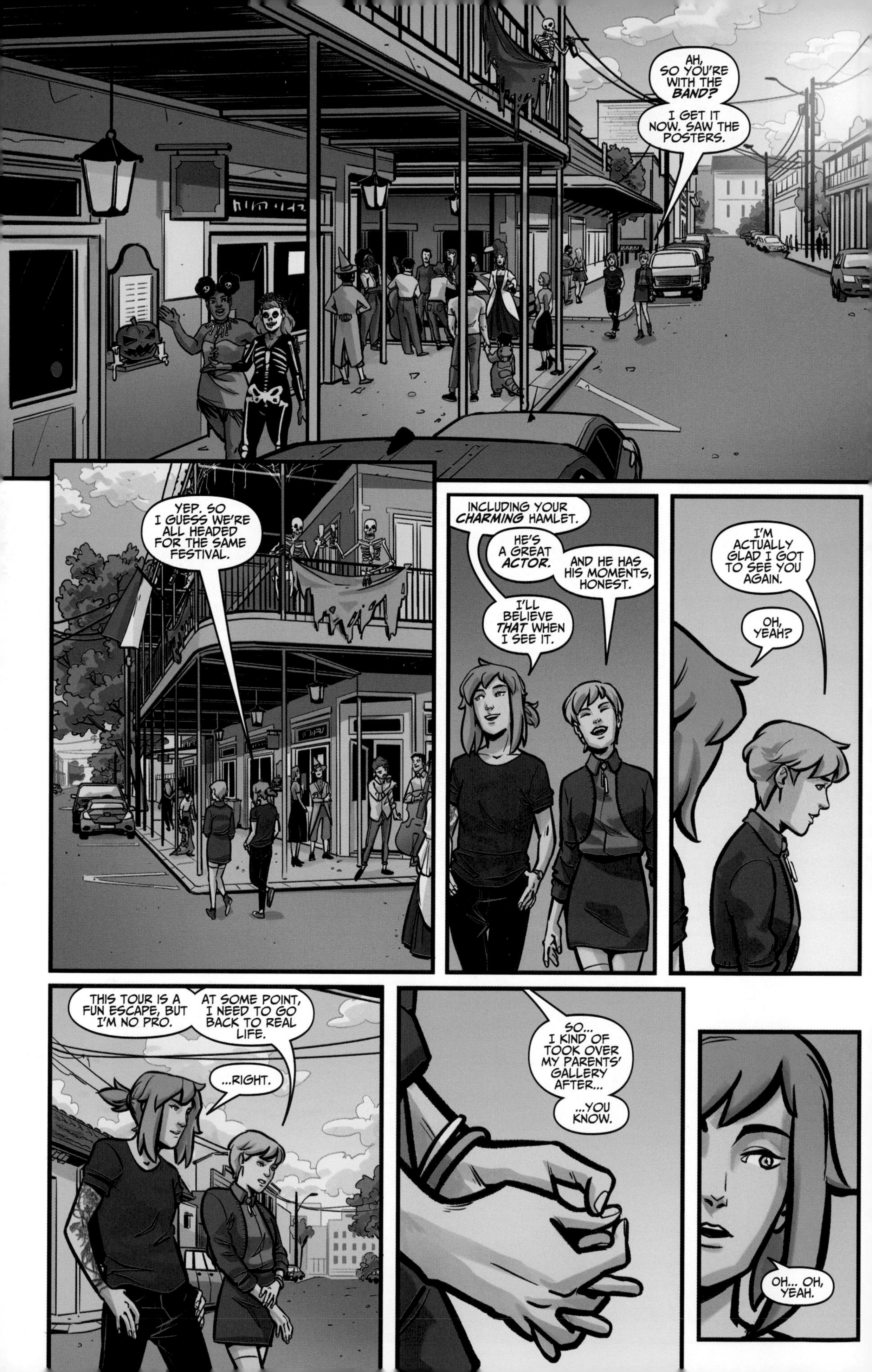
AH, SO YOU'RE WITH THE BAND?
I GET IT NOW. SAW THE POSTERS.
YEP. SO I GUESS WE'RE ALL HEADED FOR THE SAME FESTIVAL.
INCLUDING YOUR CHARMING HAMLET.
HE'S A GREAT ACTOR.
AND HE HAS HIS MOMENTS, HONEST.
I'LL BELIEVE THAT WHEN I SEE IT.
I'M ACTUALLY GLAD I GOT TO SEE YOU AGAIN.
OH, YEAH?
THIS TOUR IS A FUN ESCAPE, BUT I'M NO PRO.
AT SOME POINT, I NEED TO GO BACK TO REAL LIFE.
...RIGHT.
SO... I KIND OF TOOK OVER MY PARENTS' GALLERY AFTER...
...YOU KNOW.
OH... OH, YEAH.

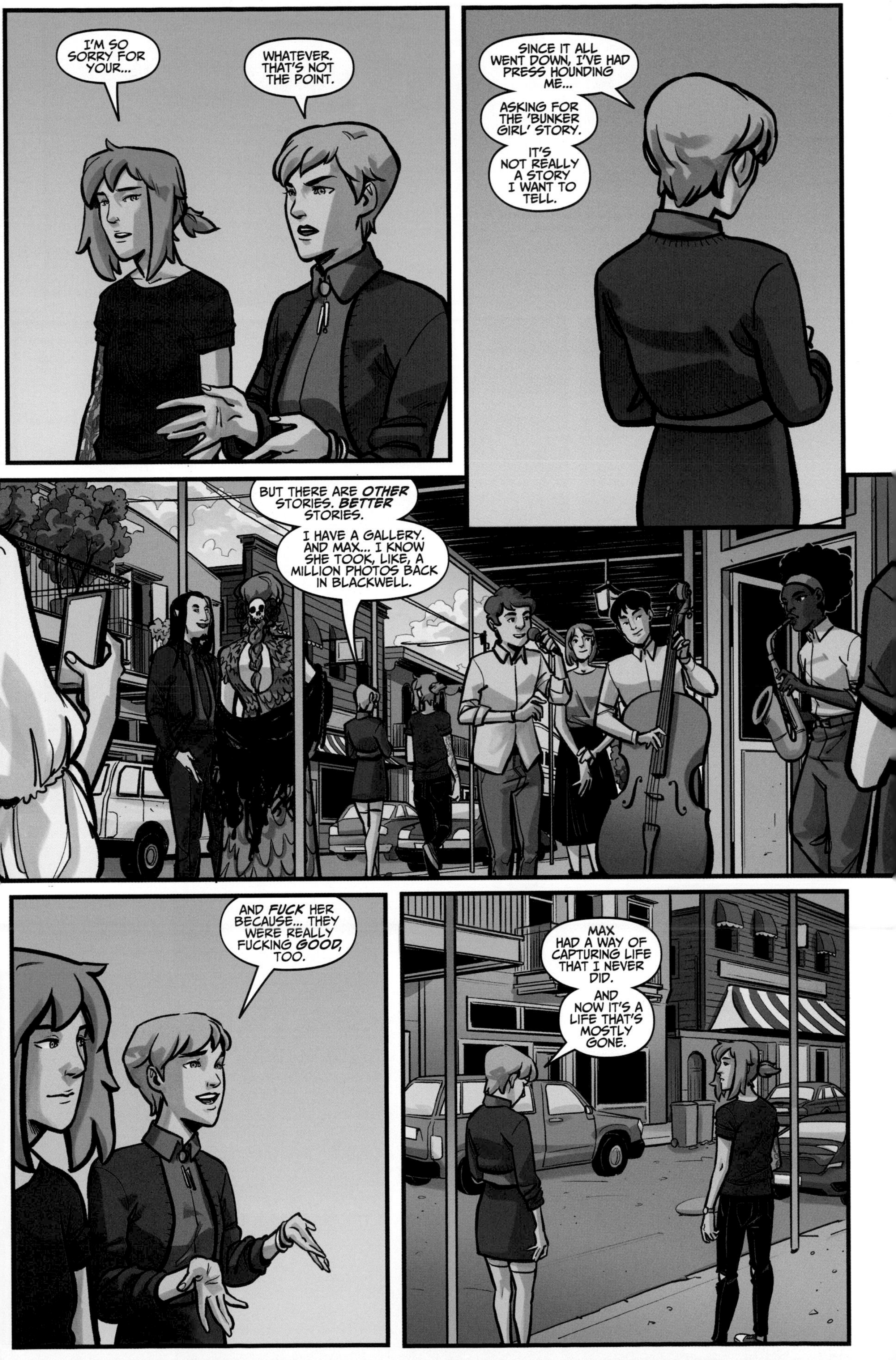
I'M SO SORRY FOR YOUR...
WHATEVER. THAT'S NOT THE POINT.
SINCE IT ALL WENT DOWN, I'VE HAD PRESS HOUNDING ME...
ASKING FOR THE 'BUNKER GIRL' STORY.
IT'S NOT REALLY A STORY I WANT TO TELL.
BUT THERE ARE *OTHER* STORIES. *BETTER* STORIES.
I HAVE A GALLERY. AND MAX... I KNOW SHE TOOK, LIKE, A MILLION PHOTOS BACK IN BLACKWELL.
AND *FUCK* HER BECAUSE... THEY WERE REALLY FUCKING *GOOD*, TOO.
MAX HAD A WAY OF CAPTURING LIFE THAT I NEVER DID.
AND NOW IT'S A LIFE THAT'S MOSTLY GONE.

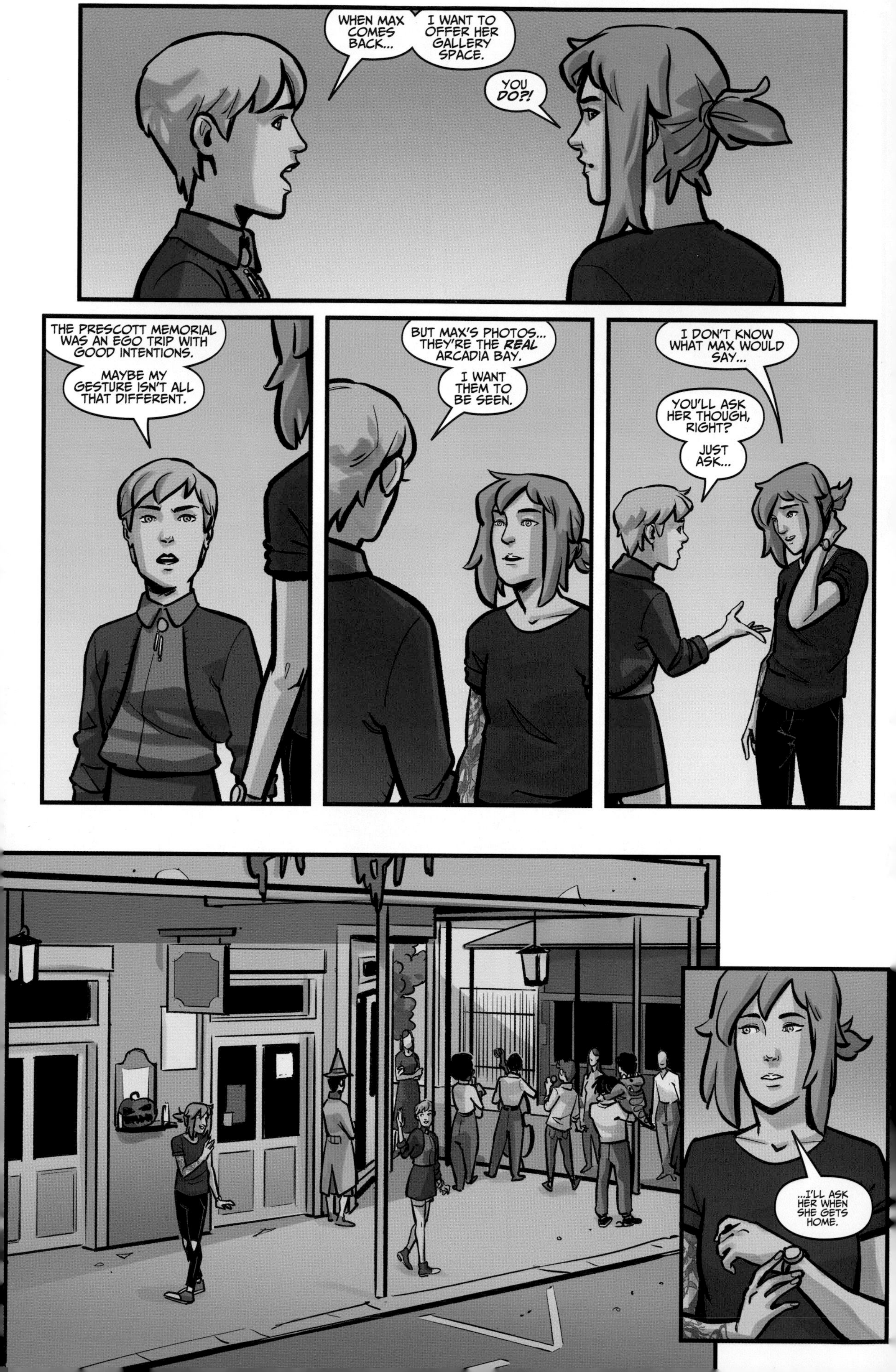
WHEN MAX COMES BACK...
I WANT TO OFFER HER GALLERY SPACE.
YOU DO?!
THE PRESCOTT MEMORIAL WAS AN EGO TRIP WITH GOOD INTENTIONS.
MAYBE MY GESTURE ISN'T ALL THAT DIFFERENT.
BUT MAX'S PHOTOS... THEY'RE THE REAL ARCADIA BAY.
I WANT THEM TO BE SEEN.
I DON'T KNOW WHAT MAX WOULD SAY...
YOU'LL ASK HER THOUGH, RIGHT?
JUST ASK...
...I'LL ASK HER WHEN SHE GETS HOME.

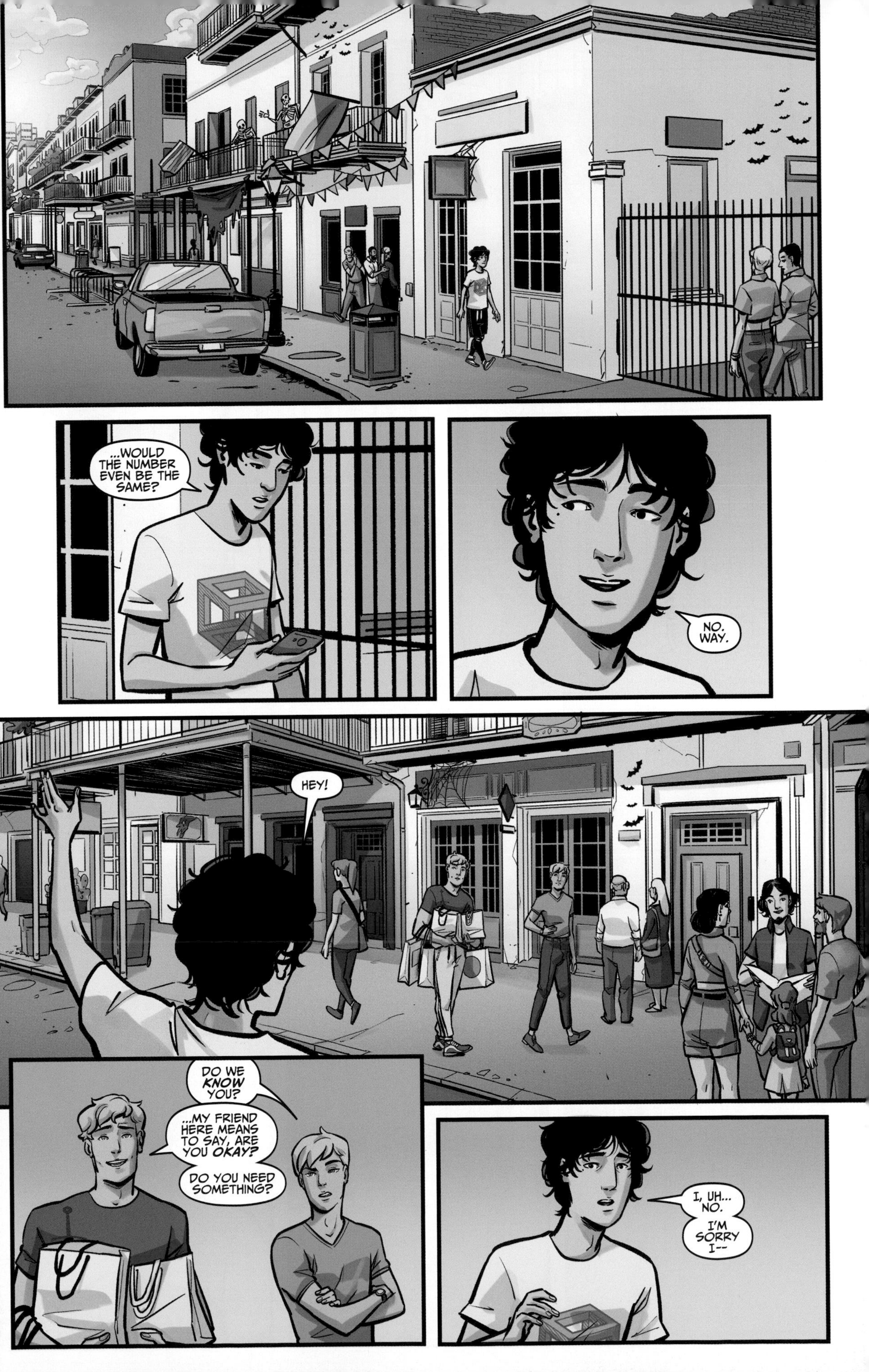
...WOULD THE NUMBER EVEN BE THE SAME?
NO. WAY.
HEY!
DO WE *KNOW* YOU?
...MY FRIEND HERE MEANS TO SAY, ARE YOU *OKAY?*
DO YOU NEED SOMETHING?
I, UH... NO.
I'M SORRY I--

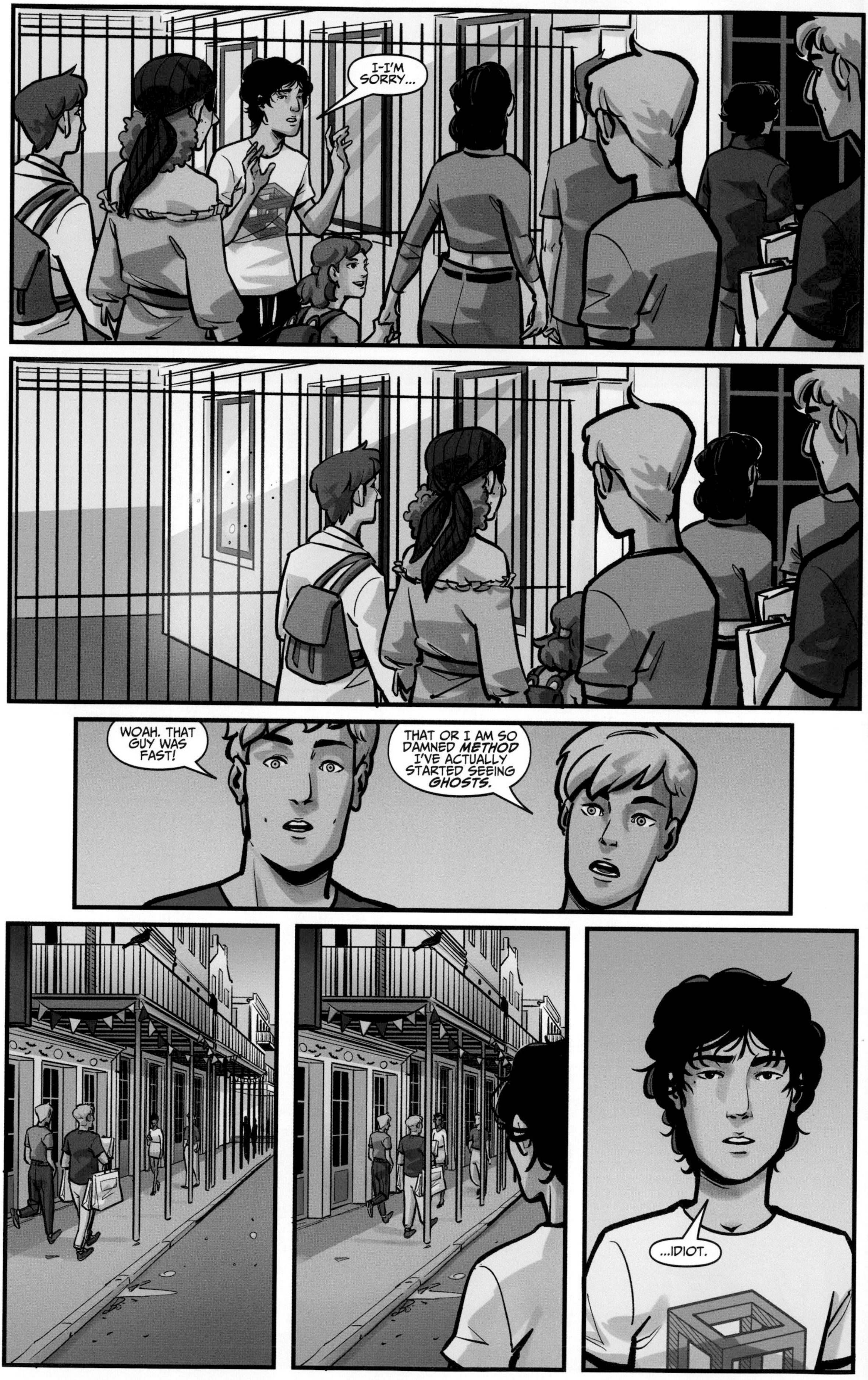
I-I'M SORRY...
WOAH. THAT GUY WAS FAST!
THAT OR I AM SO DAMNED METHOD I'VE ACTUALLY STARTED SEEING GHOSTS.
...IDIOT.

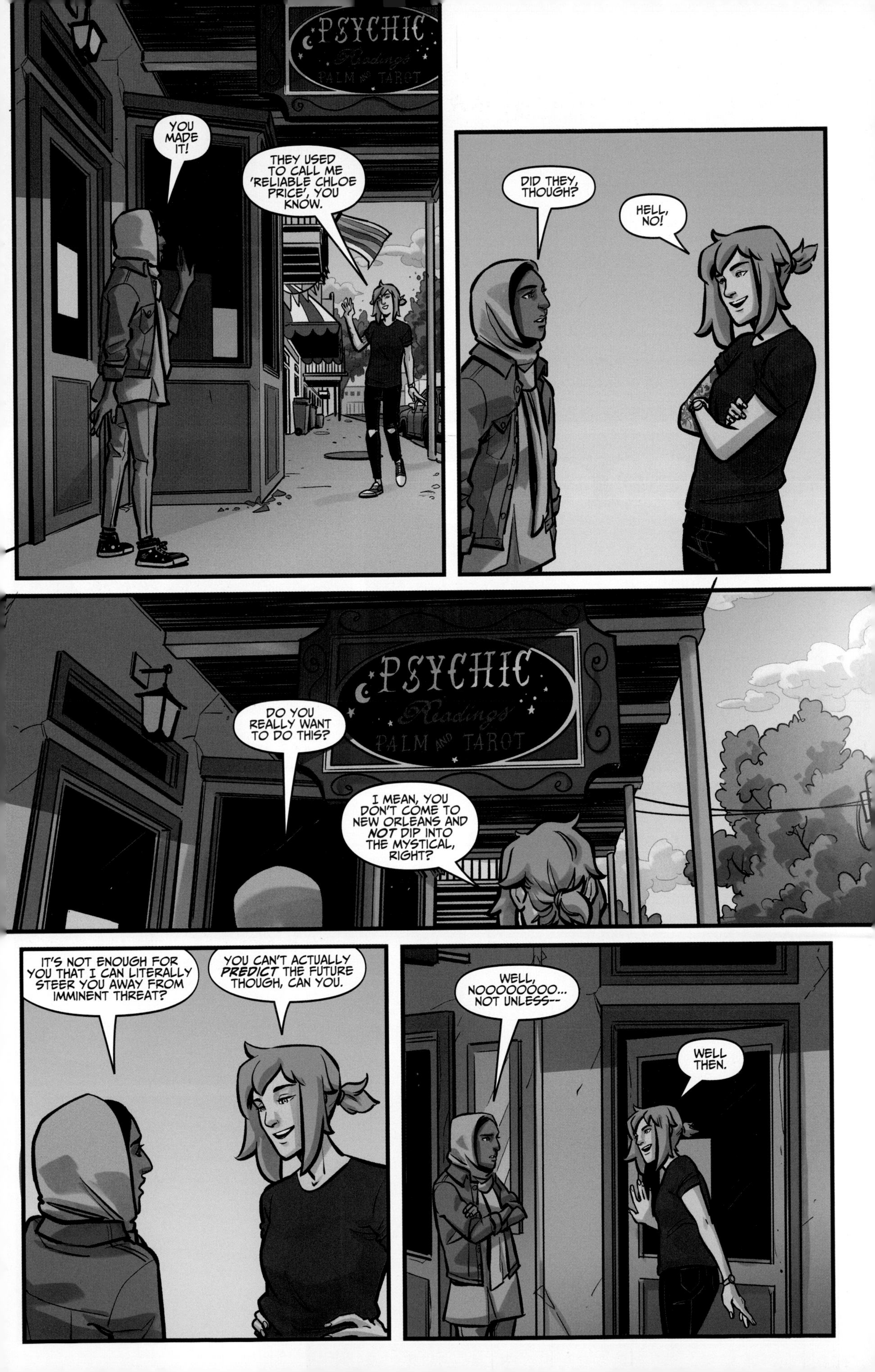
PSYCHIC
Readings
PALM AND TAROT
YOU MADE IT!
THEY USED TO CALL ME 'RELIABLE CHLOE PRICE', YOU KNOW.
DID THEY, THOUGH?
HELL, NO!
PSYCHIC
Readings
PALM AND TAROT
DO YOU REALLY WANT TO DO THIS?
I MEAN, YOU DON'T COME TO NEW ORLEANS AND NOT DIP INTO THE MYSTICAL, RIGHT?
IT'S NOT ENOUGH FOR YOU THAT I CAN LITERALLY STEER YOU AWAY FROM IMMINENT THREAT?
YOU CAN'T ACTUALLY PREDICT THE FUTURE THOUGH, CAN YOU.
WELL, NOOOOOOOO... NOT UNLESS--
WELL THEN.

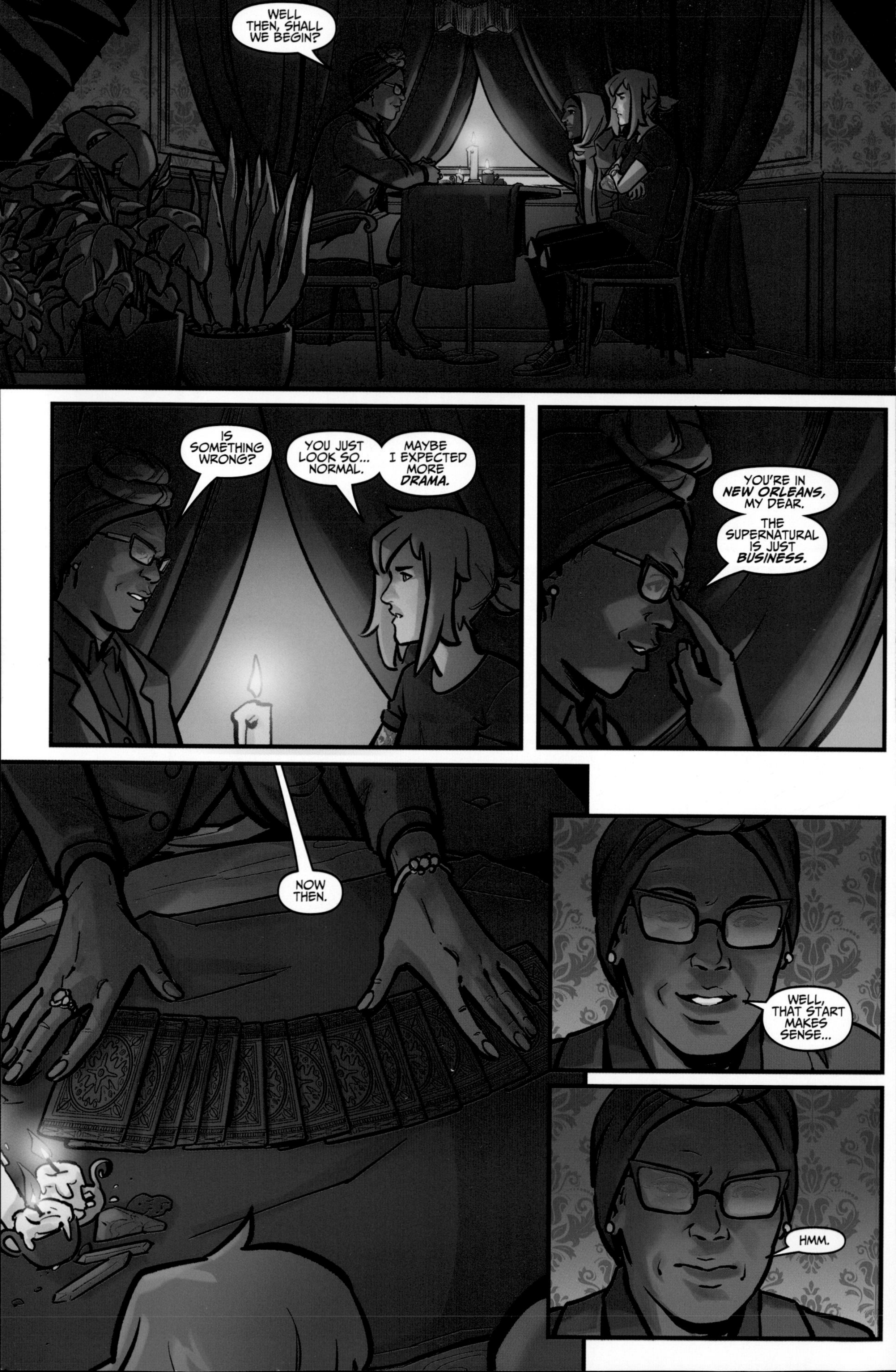
WELL THEN, SHALL WE BEGIN?
IS SOMETHING WRONG?
YOU JUST LOOK SO... NORMAL.
MAYBE I EXPECTED MORE *DRAMA.*
YOU'RE IN *NEW ORLEANS,* MY DEAR.
THE SUPERNATURAL IS JUST *BUSINESS.*
NOW THEN.
WELL, THAT START MAKES SENSE...
HMM.

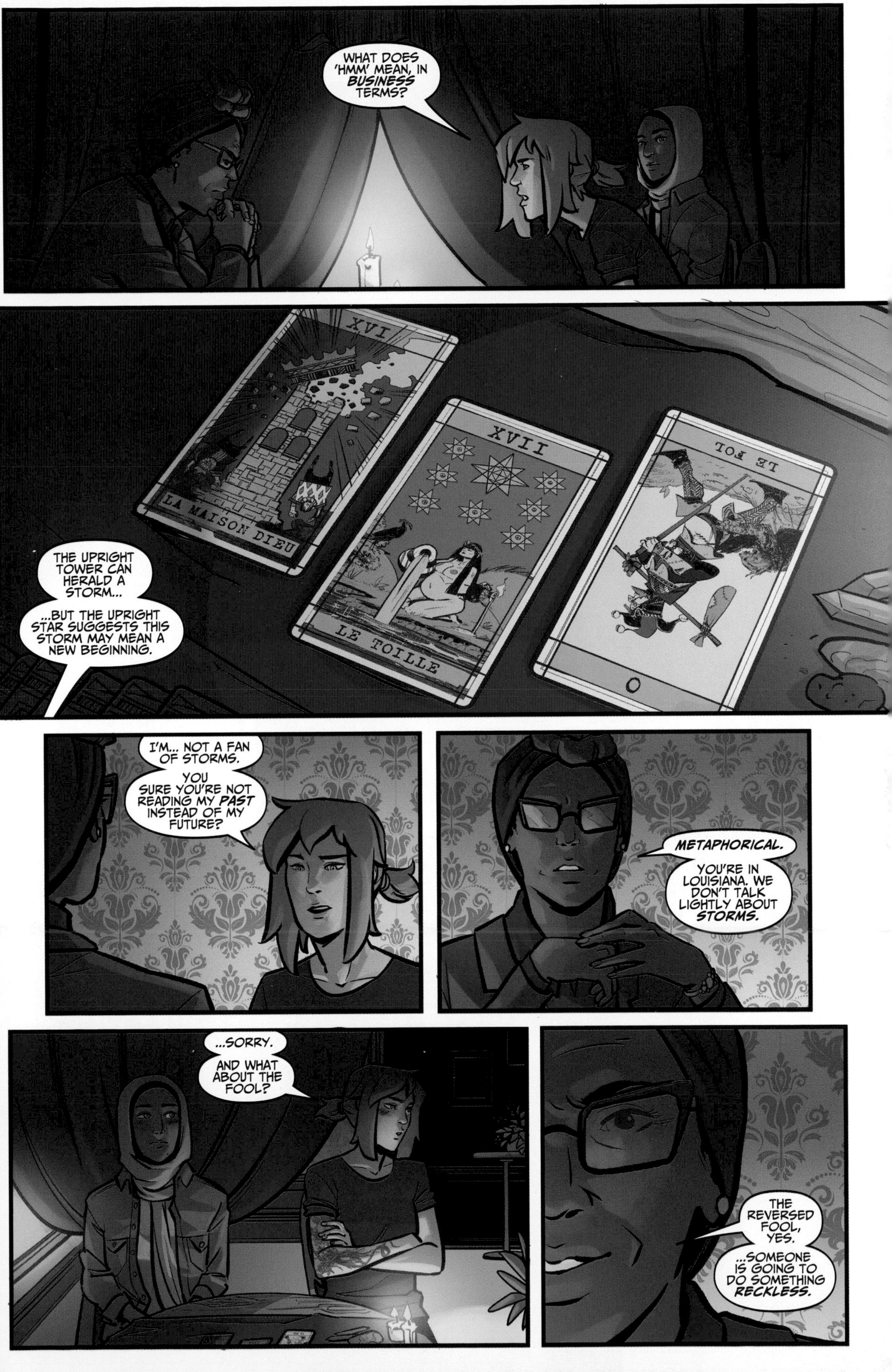
WHAT DOES 'HMM' MEAN, IN BUSINESS TERMS?
XVI
LA MAISON DIEU
XVII
LE TOILLE
LE FOL
0
THE UPRIGHT TOWER CAN HERALD A STORM...
...BUT THE UPRIGHT STAR SUGGESTS THIS STORM MAY MEAN A NEW BEGINNING.
I'M... NOT A FAN OF STORMS.
YOU SURE YOU'RE NOT READING MY PAST INSTEAD OF MY FUTURE?
METAPHORICAL.
YOU'RE IN LOUISIANA. WE DON'T TALK LIGHTLY ABOUT STORMS.
...SORRY.
AND WHAT ABOUT THE FOOL?
THE REVERSED FOOL, YES.
...SOMEONE IS GOING TO DO SOMETHING RECKLESS.

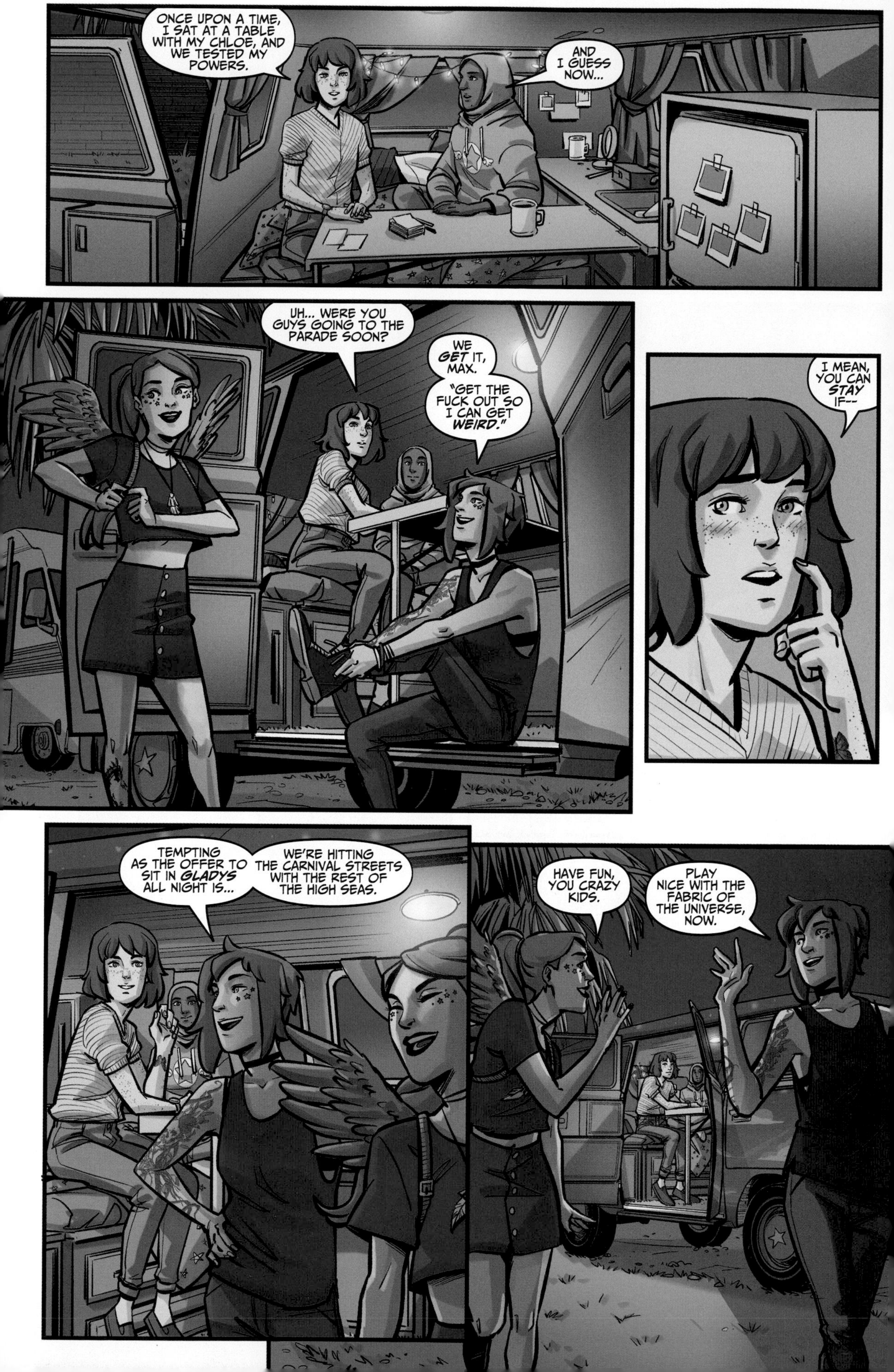
ONCE UPON A TIME, I SAT AT A TABLE WITH MY CHLOE, AND WE TESTED MY POWERS.
AND I GUESS NOW...
UH... WERE YOU GUYS GOING TO THE PARADE SOON?
WE GET IT, MAX.
"GET THE FUCK OUT SO I CAN GET WEIRD."
I MEAN, YOU CAN STAY IF--
TEMPTING AS THE OFFER TO SIT IN GLADYS ALL NIGHT IS...
WE'RE HITTING THE CARNIVAL STREETS WITH THE REST OF THE HIGH SEAS.
HAVE FUN, YOU CRAZY KIDS.
PLAY NICE WITH THE FABRIC OF THE UNIVERSE, NOW.

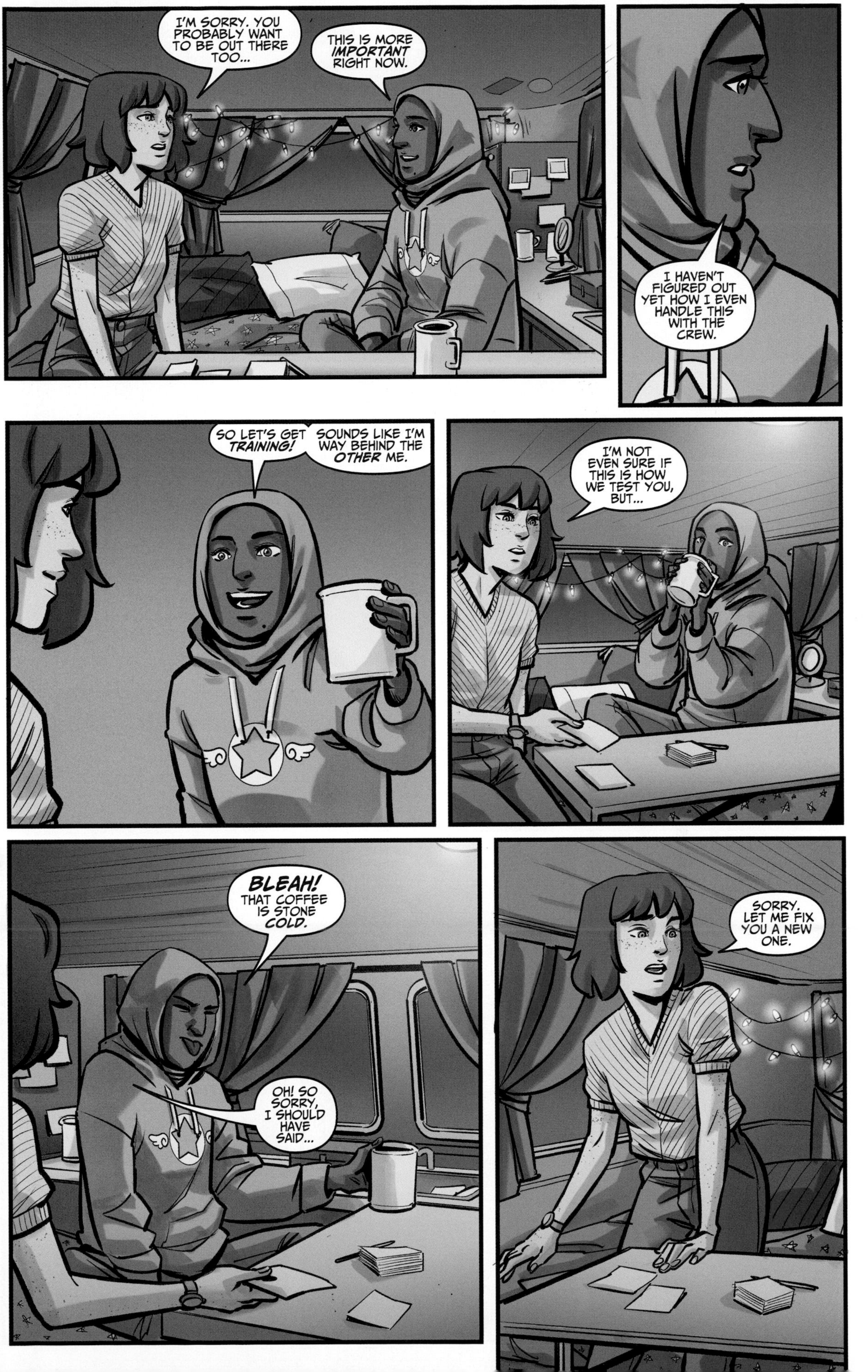
I'M SORRY. YOU PROBABLY WANT TO BE OUT THERE TOO...
THIS IS MORE *IMPORTANT* RIGHT NOW.
I HAVEN'T FIGURED OUT YET HOW I EVEN HANDLE THIS WITH THE CREW.
SO LET'S GET *TRAINING!*
SOUNDS LIKE I'M WAY BEHIND THE *OTHER* ME.
I'M NOT EVEN SURE IF THIS IS HOW WE TEST YOU, BUT...
BLEAH! THAT COFFEE IS STONE *COLD.*
OH! SO SORRY, I SHOULD HAVE SAID...
SORRY. LET ME FIX YOU A NEW ONE.

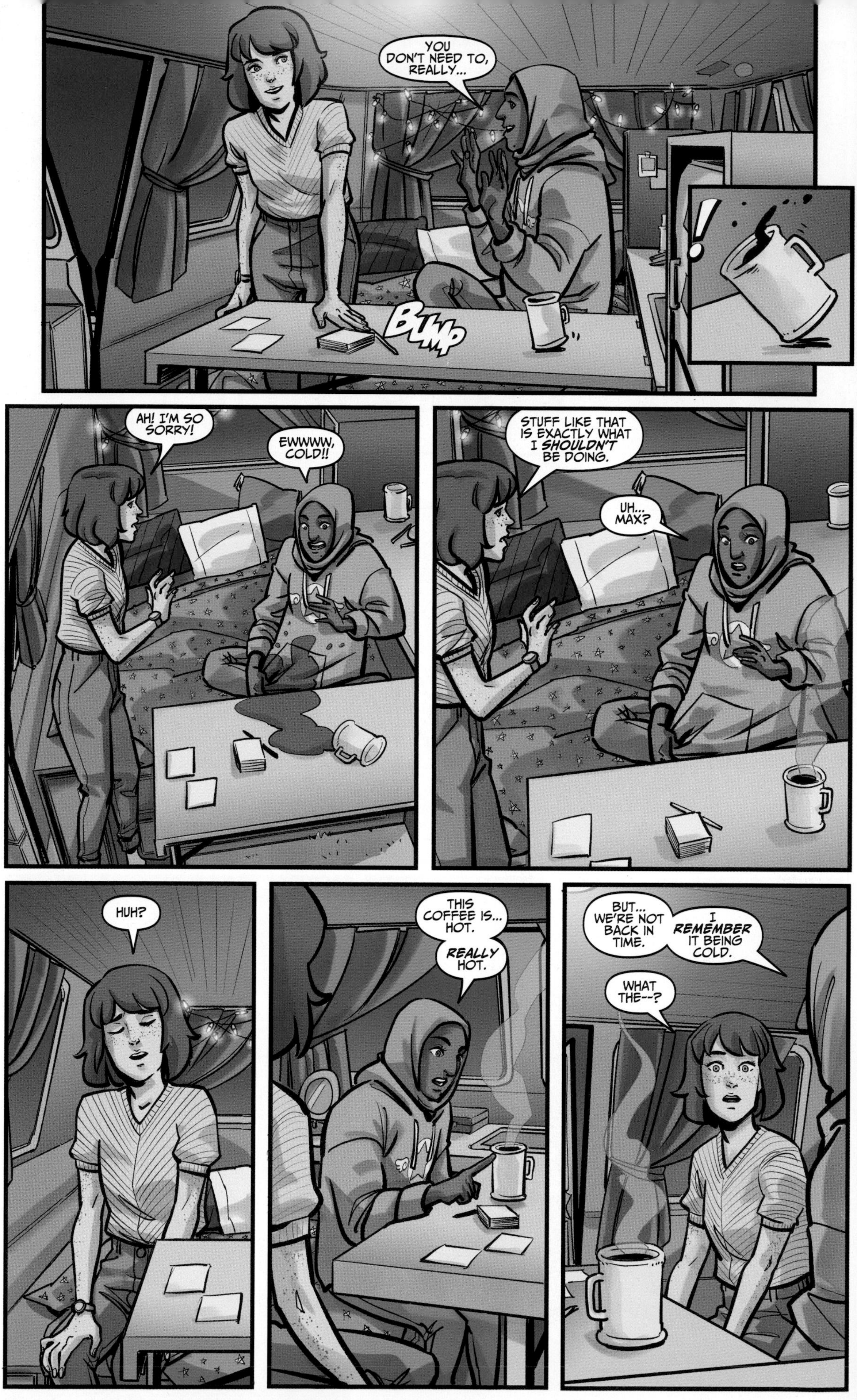
YOU DON'T NEED TO, REALLY...
BUMP
!
AH! I'M SO SORRY!
EWWWW, COLD!!
STUFF LIKE THAT IS EXACTLY WHAT I SHOULDN'T BE DOING.
UH... MAX?
HUH?
THIS COFFEE IS... HOT.
REALLY HOT.
BUT... WE'RE NOT BACK IN TIME.
I REMEMBER IT BEING COLD.
WHAT THE--?

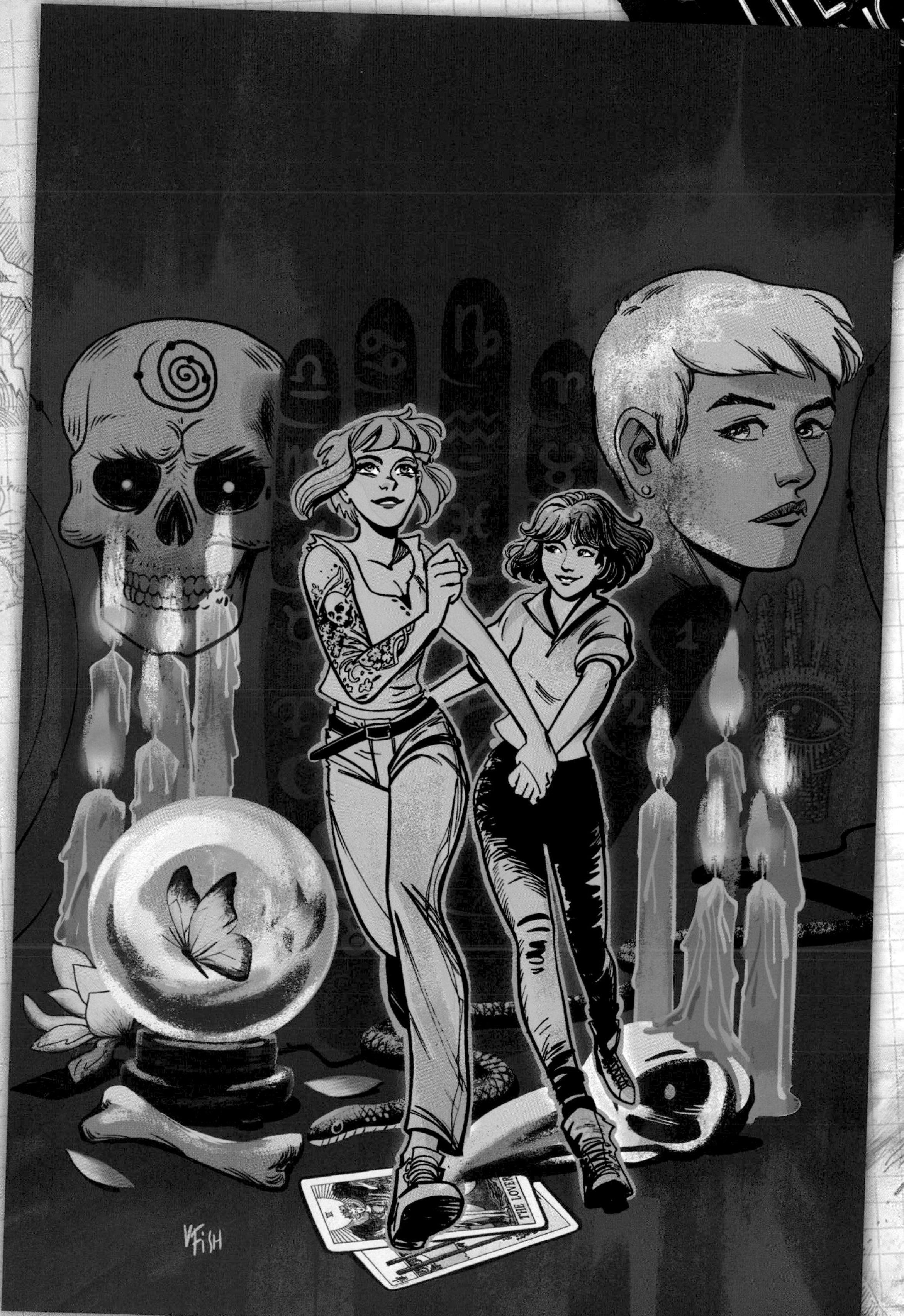
VFISH
THE LOVERS

COVER #1E
BY VERONICA FISH

CHAPTER 2

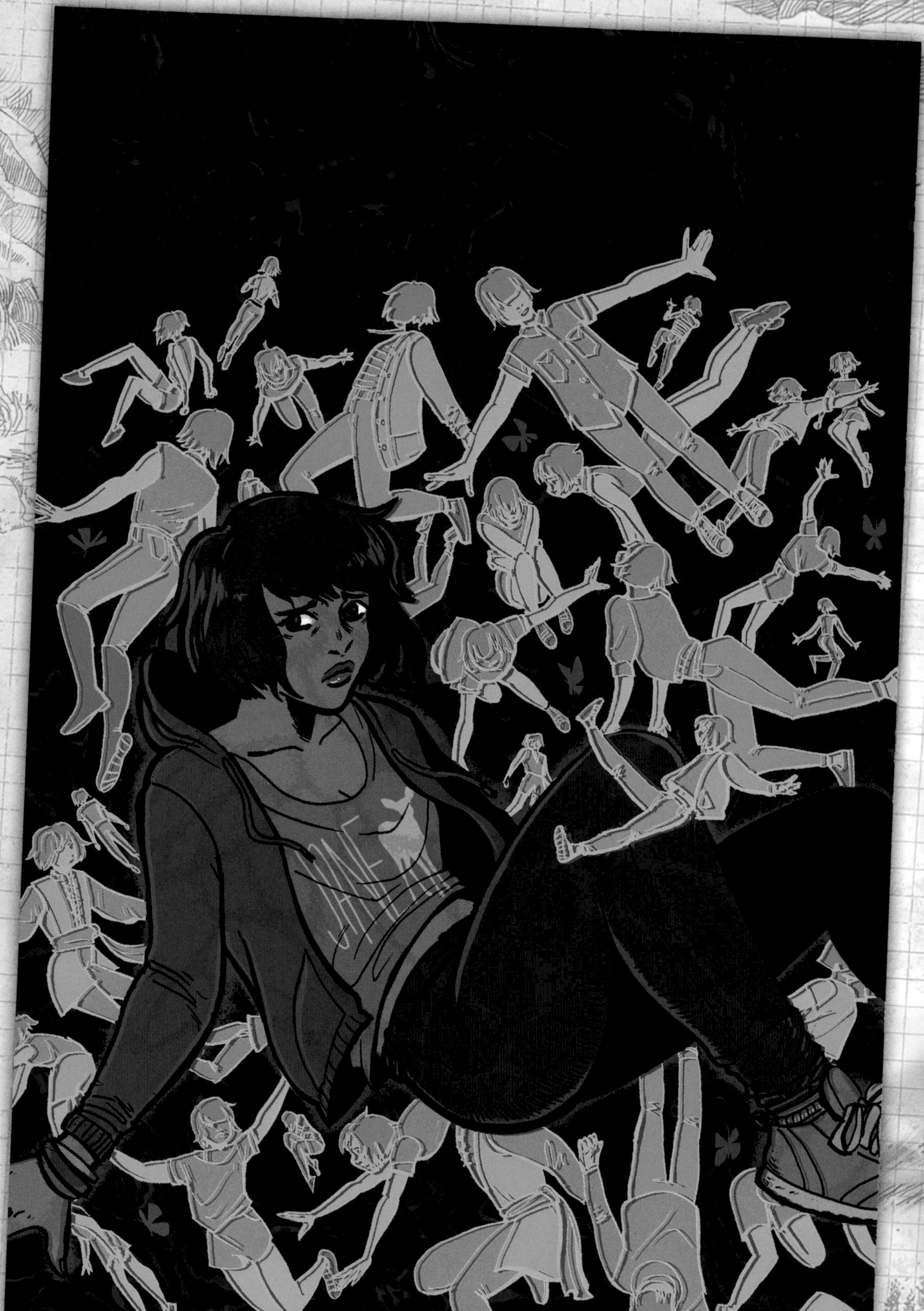

COVER #2A
BY SLOANE LEONG

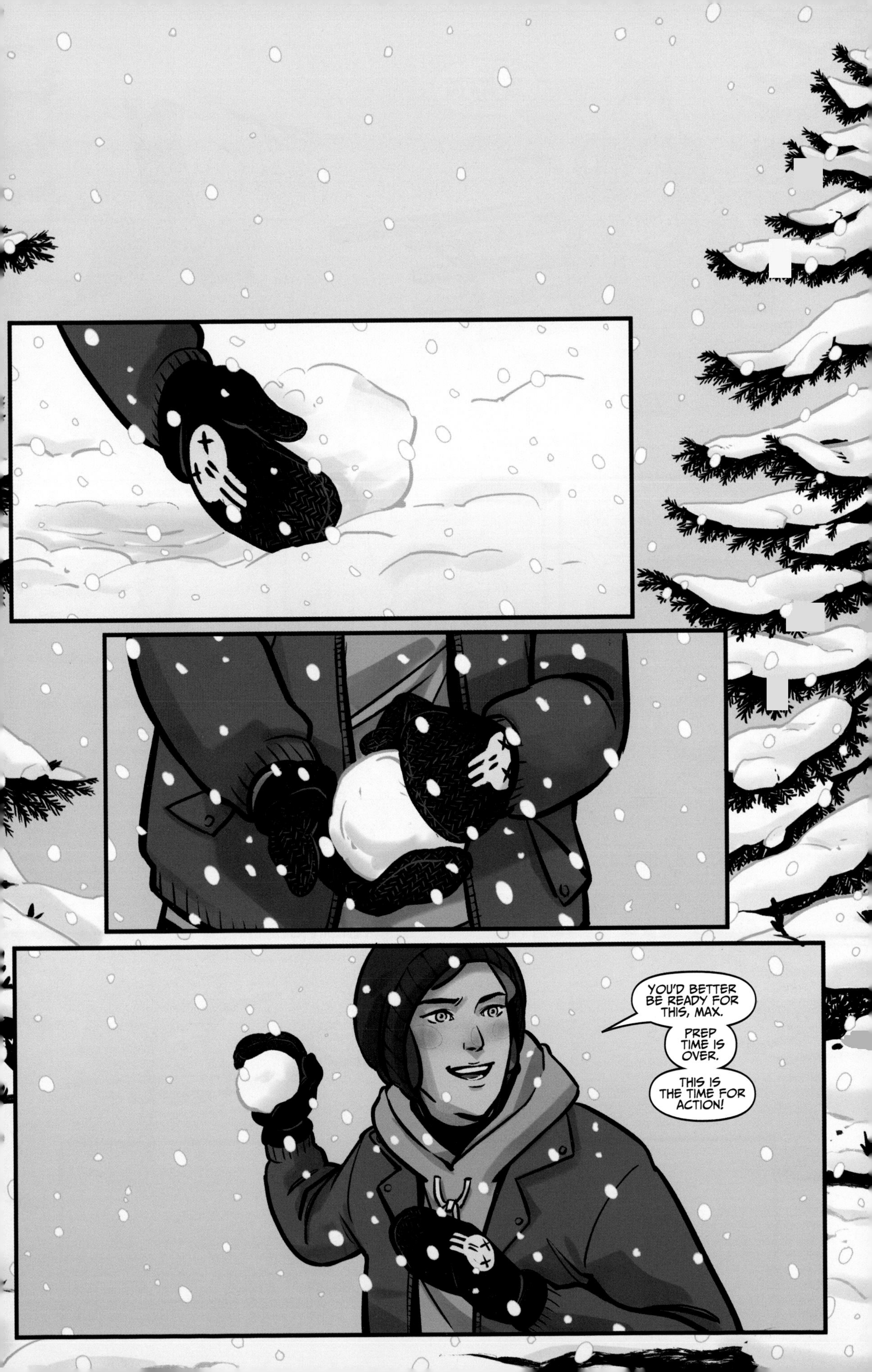
YOU'D BETTER BE READY FOR THIS, MAX.
PREP TIME IS OVER.
THIS IS THE TIME FOR ACTION!

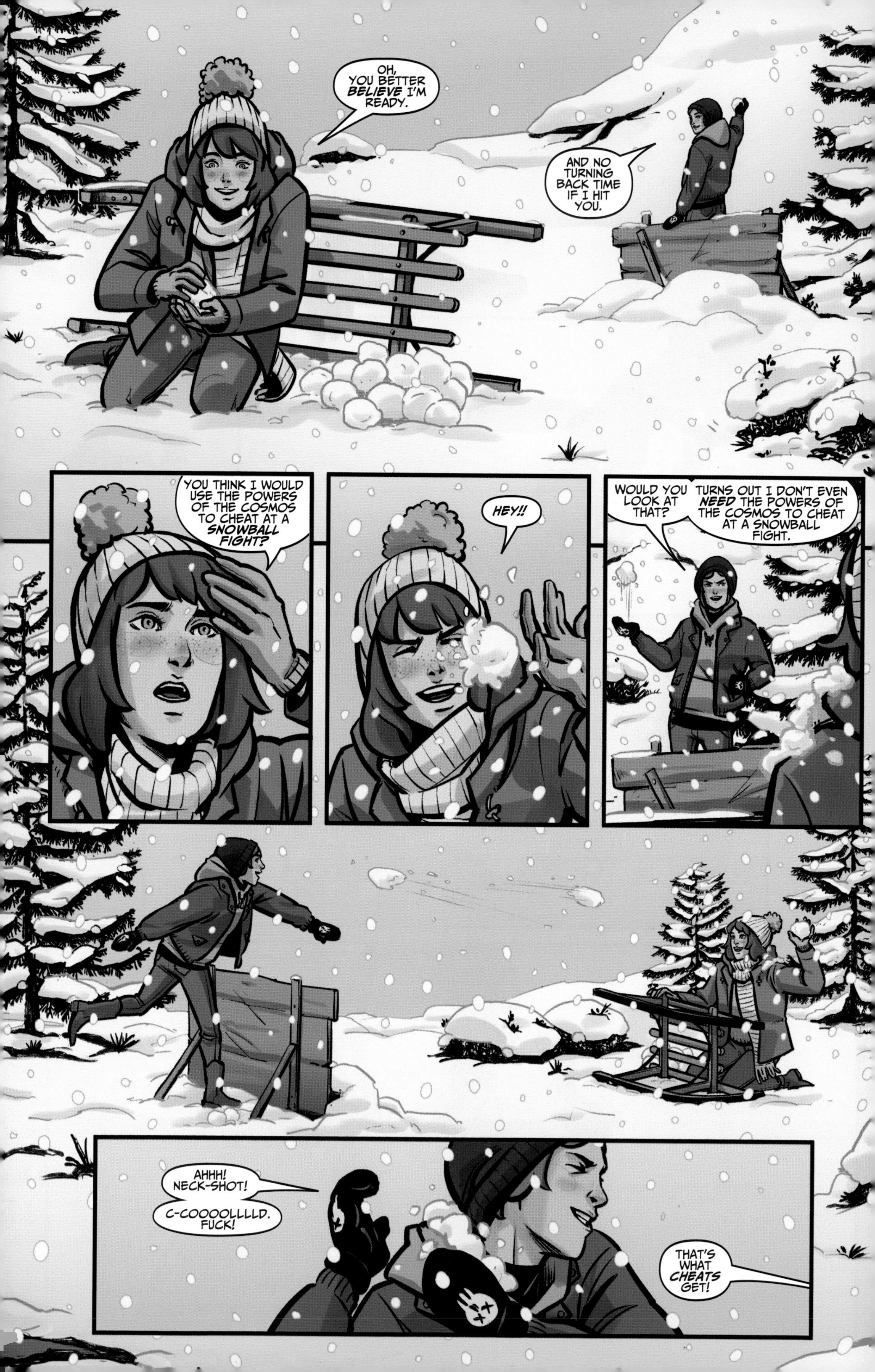
OH, YOU BETTER *BELIEVE* I'M READY.
AND NO TURNING BACK TIME IF I HIT YOU.
YOU THINK I WOULD USE THE POWERS OF THE COSMOS TO CHEAT AT A *SNOWBALL FIGHT?*
HEY!!
WOULD YOU LOOK AT THAT?
TURNS OUT I DON'T EVEN *NEED* THE POWERS OF THE COSMOS TO CHEAT AT A SNOWBALL FIGHT.
AHHH! NECK-SHOT!
C-COOOOLLLLLD. FUCK!
THAT'S WHAT *CHEATS* GET!

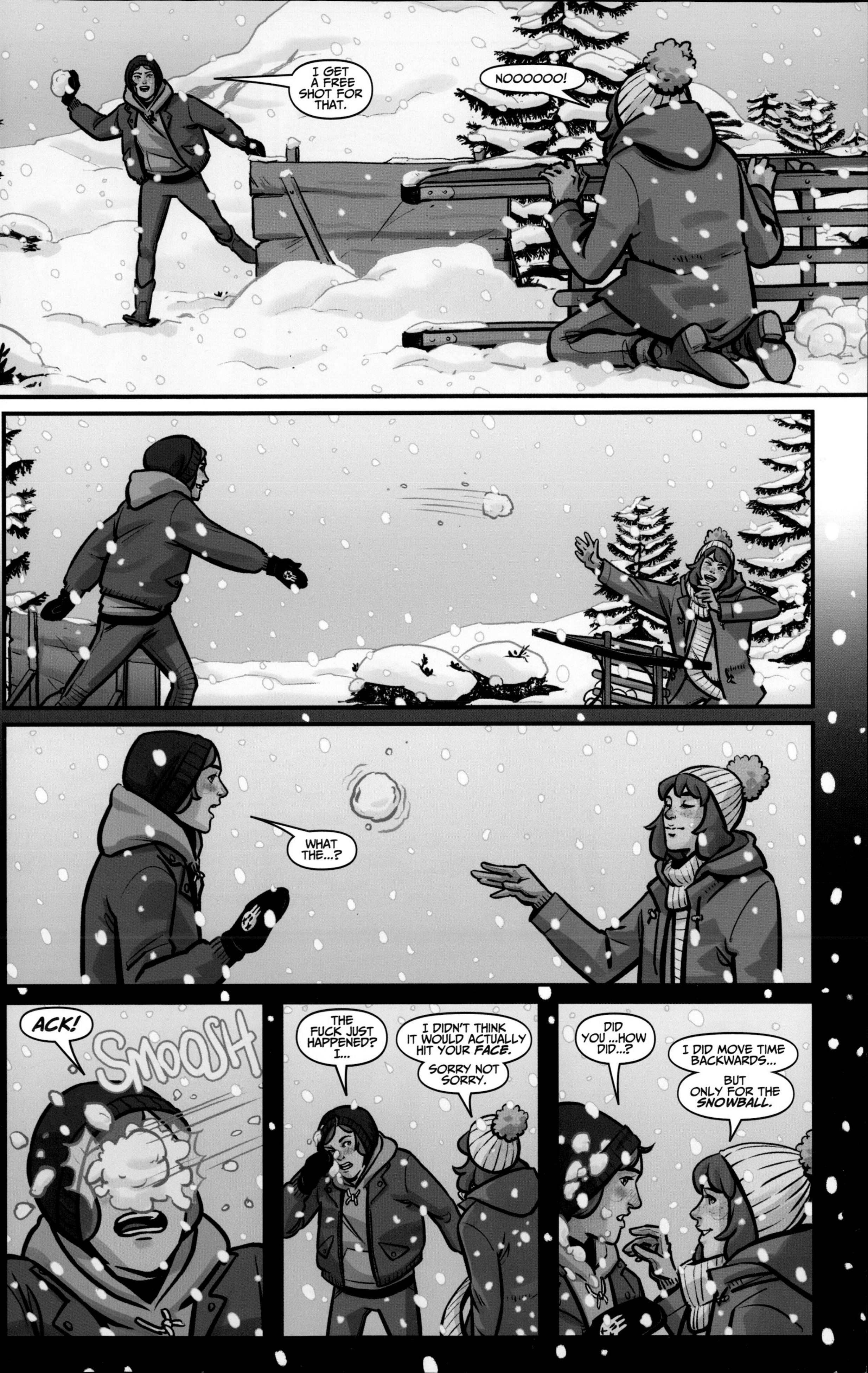
I GET A FREE SHOT FOR THAT.
NOOOOOO!
WHAT THE...?
ACK!
SMOOSH
THE FUCK JUST HAPPENED? I...
I DIDN'T THINK IT WOULD ACTUALLY HIT YOUR *FACE.*
SORRY NOT SORRY.
DID YOU ...HOW DID...?
I DID MOVE TIME BACKWARDS...
BUT ONLY FOR THE *SNOWBALL.*

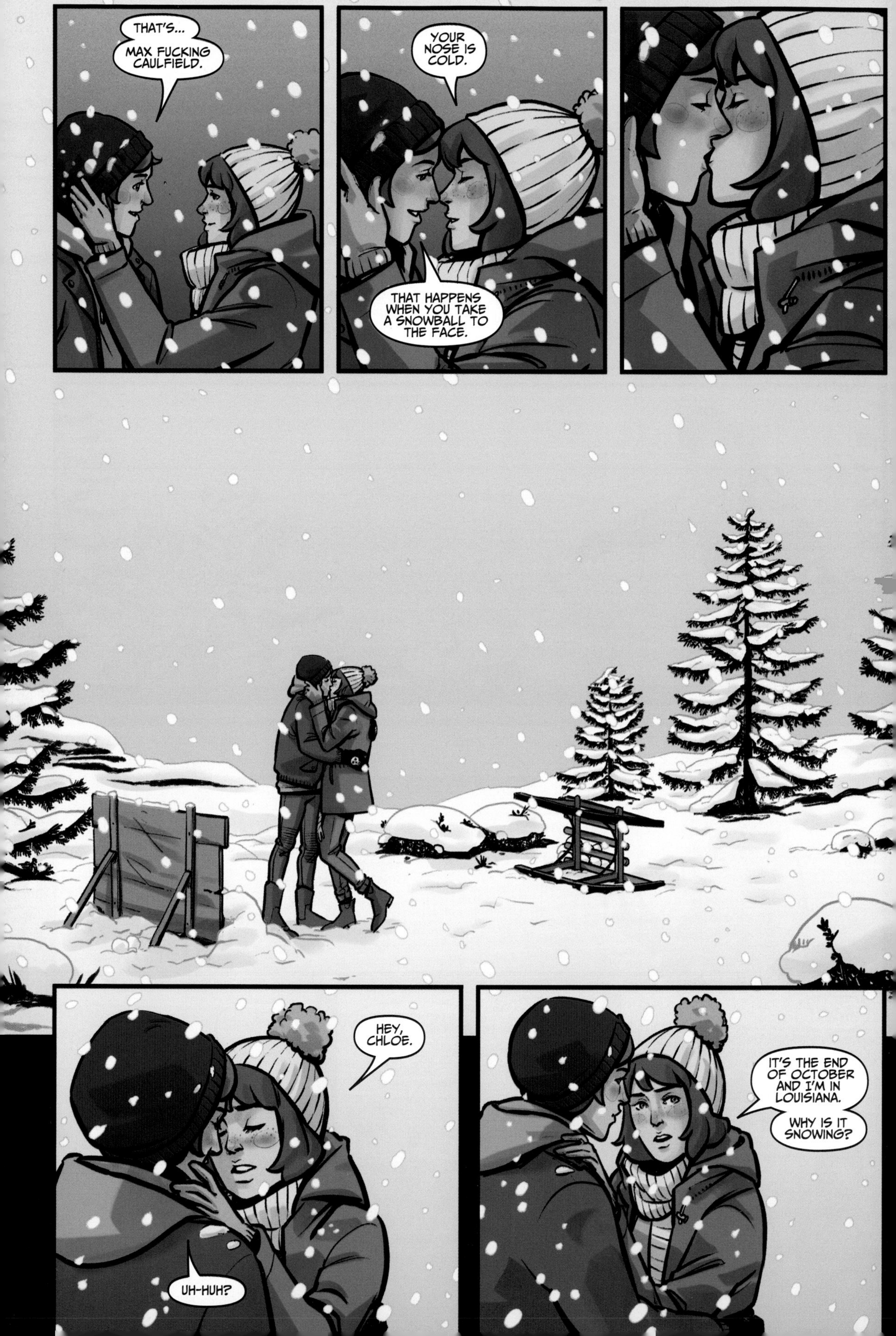
THAT'S... MAX FUCKING CAULFIELD.
YOUR NOSE IS COLD.
THAT HAPPENS WHEN YOU TAKE A SNOWBALL TO THE FACE.
HEY, CHLOE.
UH-HUH?
IT'S THE END OF OCTOBER AND I'M IN LOUISIANA.
WHY IS IT SNOWING?

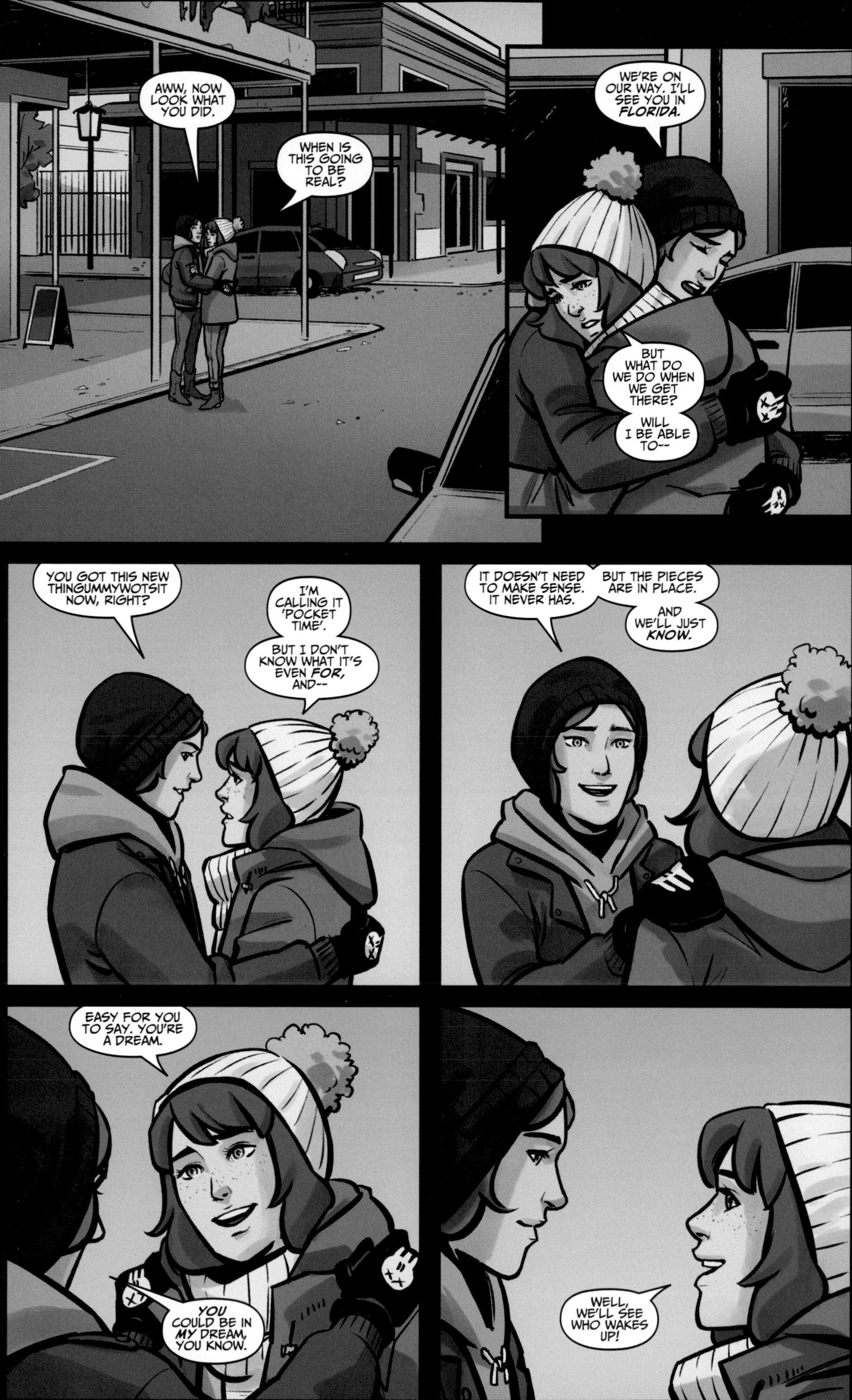
AWW, NOW LOOK WHAT YOU DID.
WHEN IS THIS GOING TO BE REAL?
WE'RE ON OUR WAY. I'LL SEE YOU IN *FLORIDA.*
BUT WHAT DO WE DO WHEN WE GET THERE?
WILL I BE ABLE TO--
YOU GOT THIS NEW THINGUMMYWOTSIT NOW, RIGHT?
I'M CALLING IT 'POCKET TIME'.
BUT I DON'T KNOW WHAT IT'S EVEN *FOR,* AND--
IT DOESN'T NEED TO MAKE SENSE. IT NEVER HAS.
BUT THE PIECES ARE IN PLACE.
AND WE'LL JUST *KNOW.*
EASY FOR YOU TO SAY. YOU'RE A DREAM.
YOU COULD BE IN *MY* DREAM, YOU KNOW.
WELL, WE'LL SEE WHO WAKES UP!

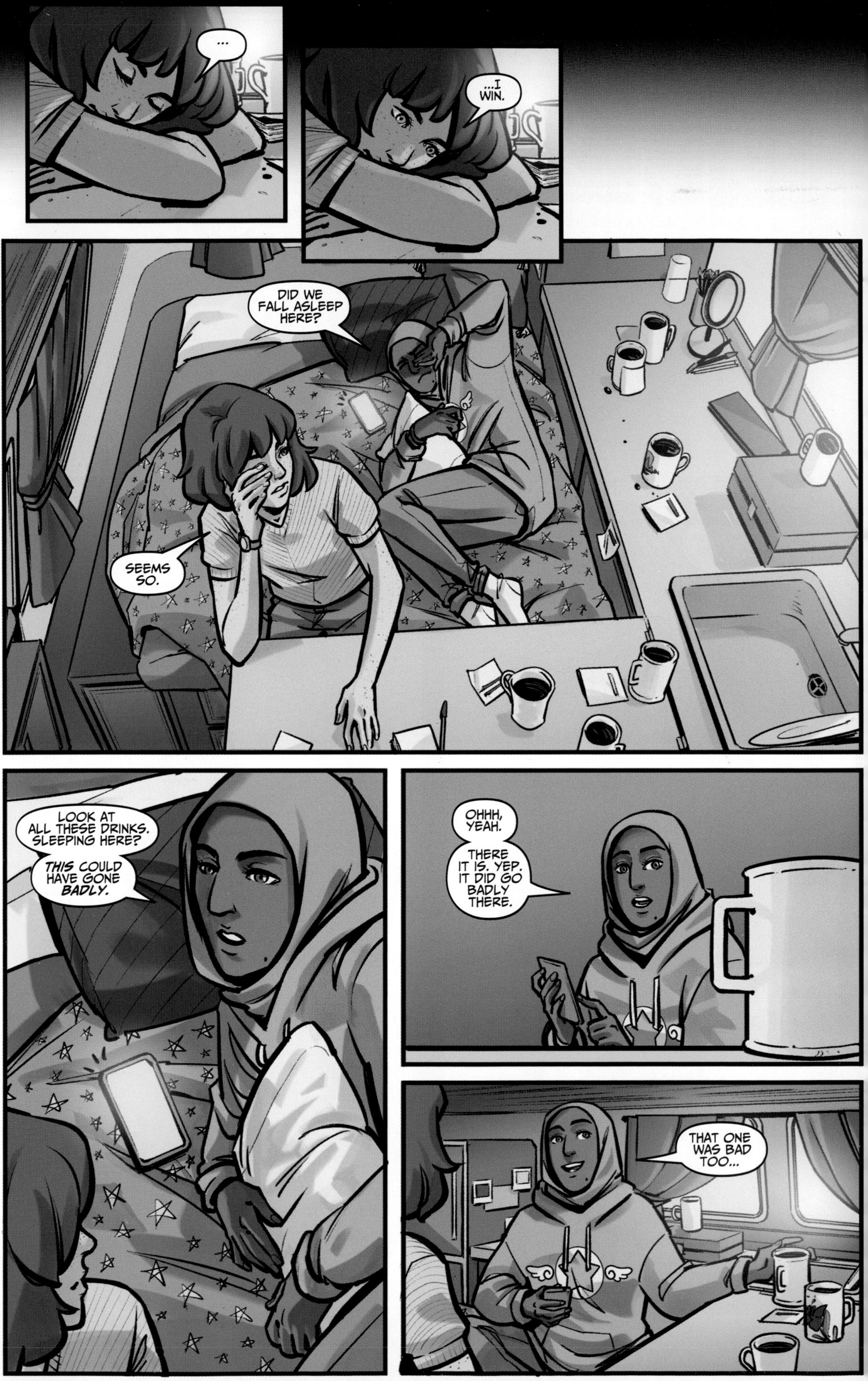
...
...I WIN.
DID WE FALL ASLEEP HERE?
SEEMS SO.
LOOK AT ALL THESE DRINKS. SLEEPING HERE?
THIS COULD HAVE GONE *BADLY*.
OHHH, YEAH.
THERE IT IS. YEP. IT DID GO BADLY THERE.
THAT ONE WAS BAD TOO...

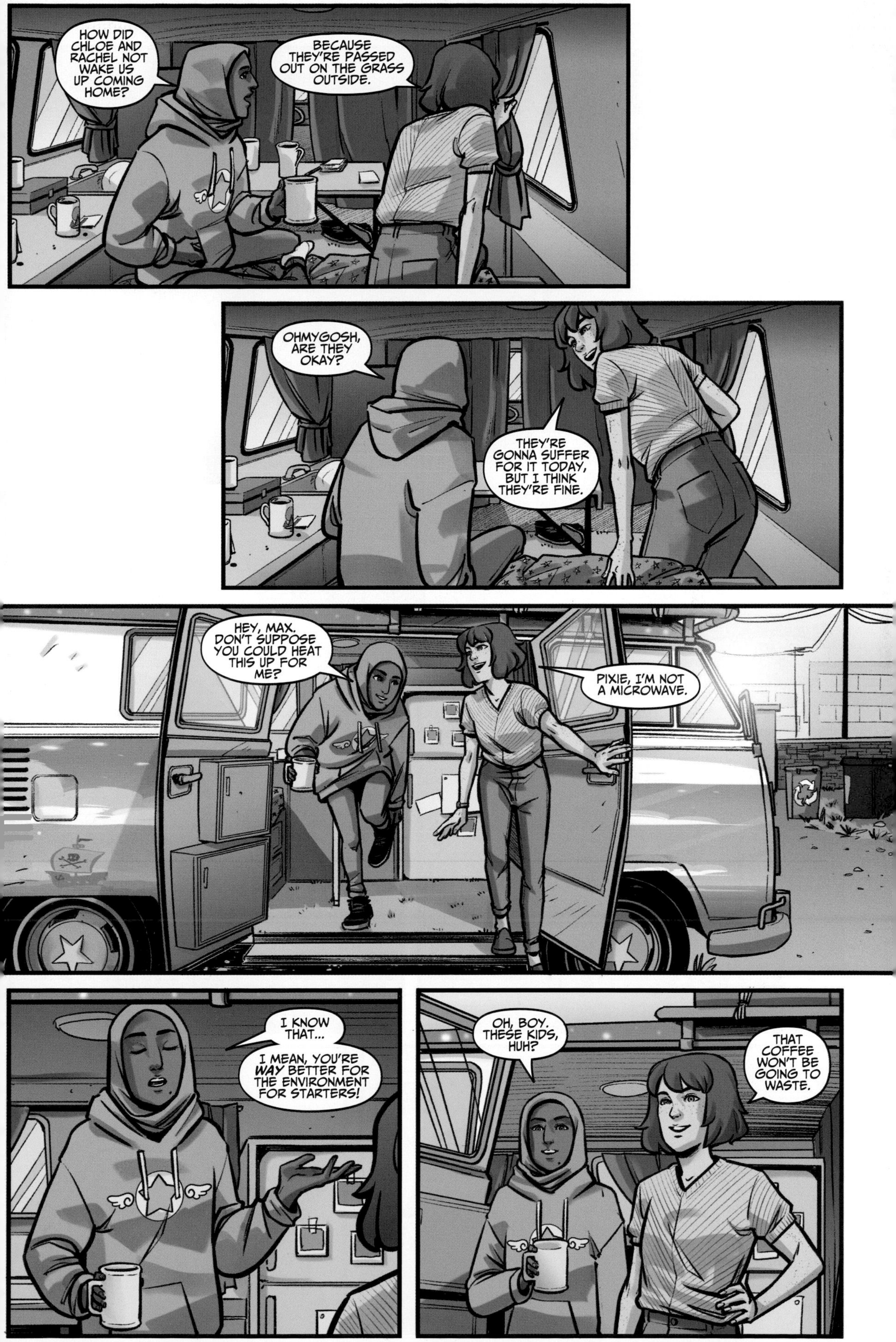
HOW DID CHLOE AND RACHEL NOT WAKE US UP COMING HOME?
BECAUSE THEY'RE PASSED OUT ON THE GRASS OUTSIDE.
OHMYGOSH, ARE THEY OKAY?
THEY'RE GONNA SUFFER FOR IT TODAY, BUT I THINK THEY'RE FINE.
HEY, MAX. DON'T SUPPOSE YOU COULD HEAT THIS UP FOR ME?
PIXIE, I'M NOT A MICROWAVE.
I KNOW THAT...
I MEAN, YOU'RE *WAY* BETTER FOR THE ENVIRONMENT FOR STARTERS!
OH, BOY. THESE KIDS, HUH?
THAT COFFEE WON'T BE GOING TO WASTE.

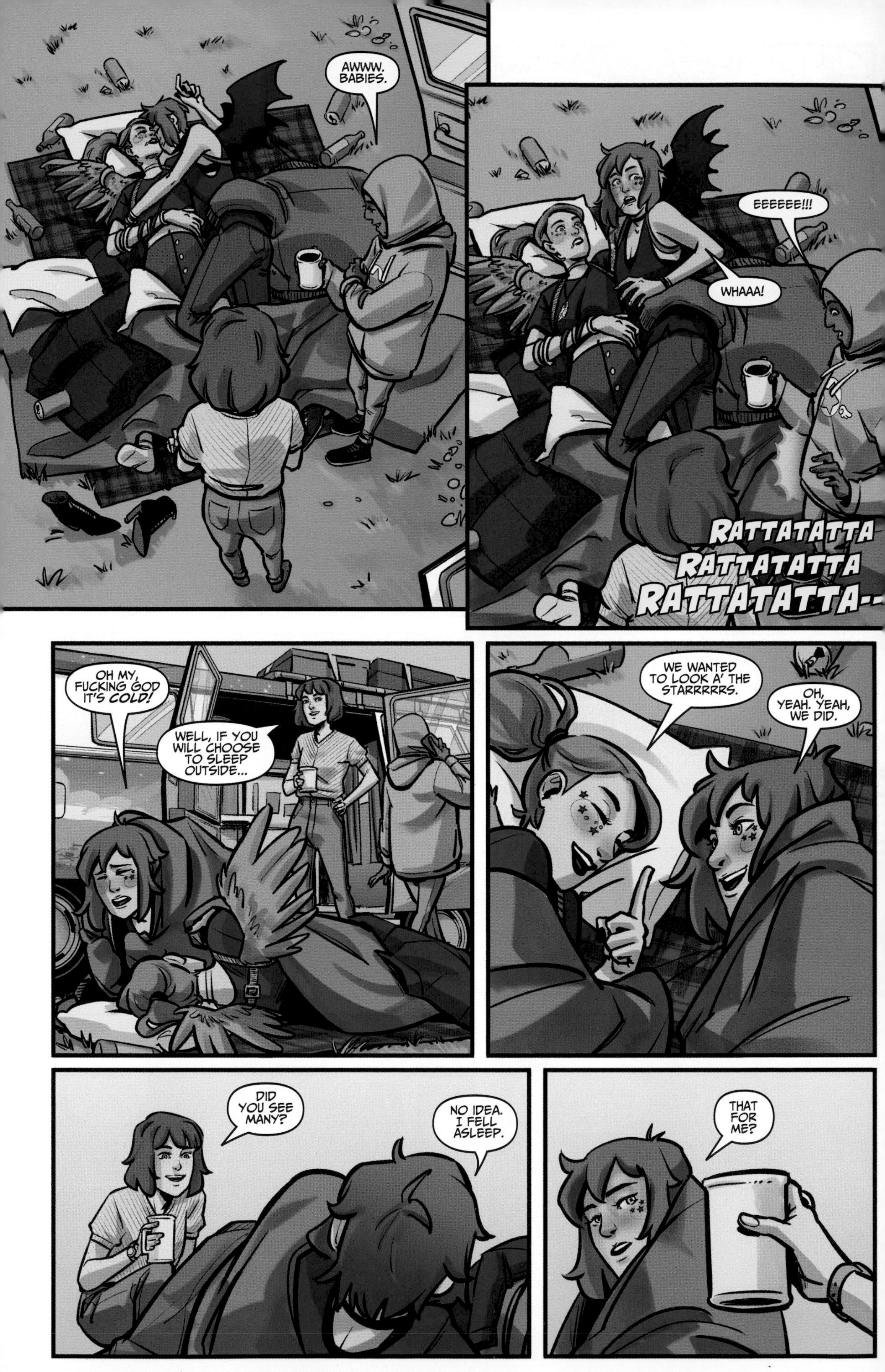
AWWW. BABIES.
EEEEEE!!!
WHAAA!
RATTATATTA RATTATATTA RATTATATTA...
OH MY, FUCKING GOD IT'S COLD!
WELL, IF YOU WILL CHOOSE TO SLEEP OUTSIDE...
WE WANTED TO LOOK A' THE STARRRRRS.
OH, YEAH. YEAH, WE DID.
DID YOU SEE MANY?
NO IDEA. I FELL ASLEEP.
THAT FOR ME?

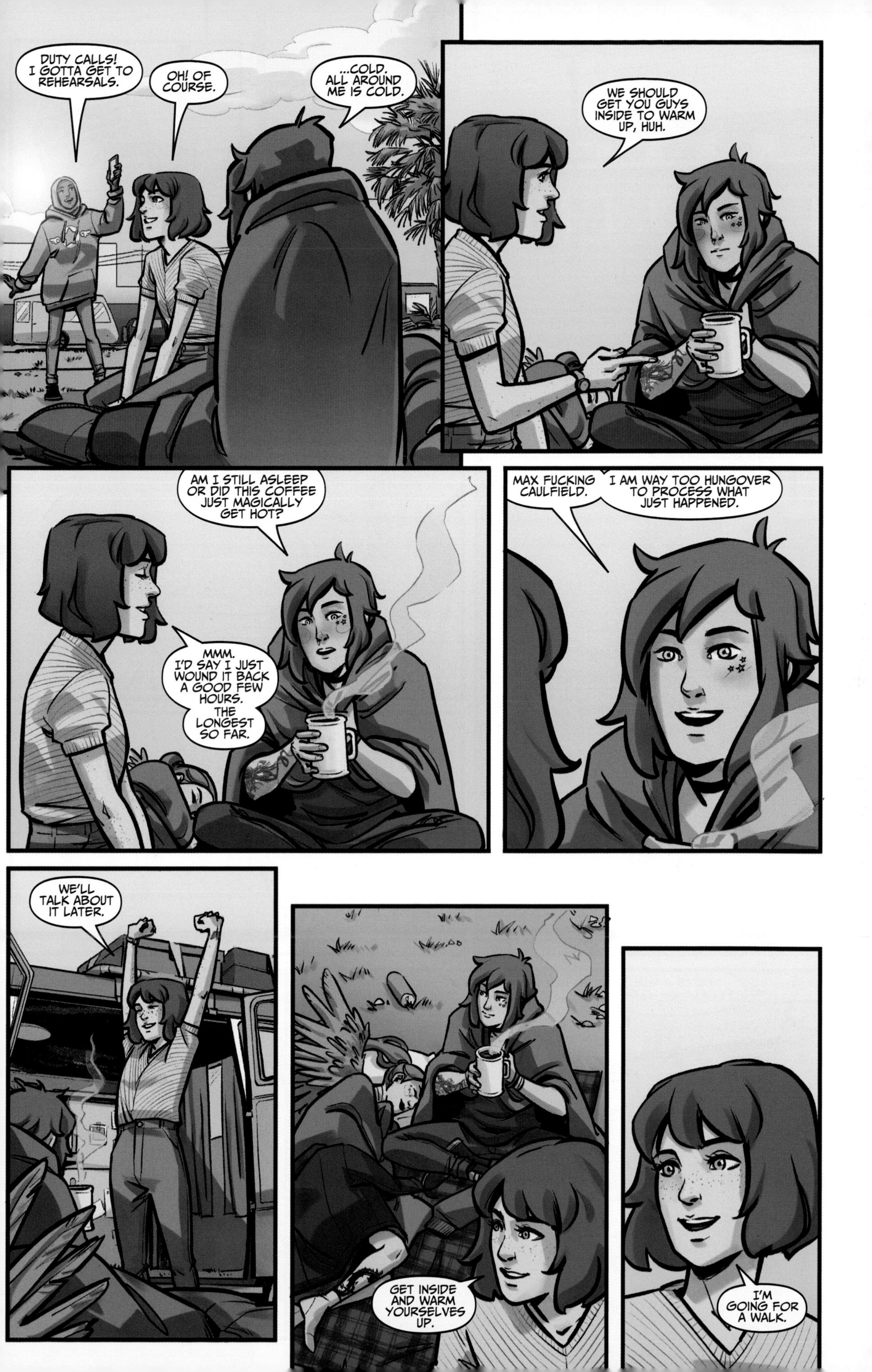
DUTY CALLS! I GOTTA GET TO REHEARSALS.
OH! OF COURSE.
...COLD. ALL AROUND ME IS COLD.
WE SHOULD GET YOU GUYS INSIDE TO WARM UP, HUH.
AM I STILL ASLEEP OR DID THIS COFFEE JUST MAGICALLY GET HOT?
MMM. I'D SAY I JUST WOUND IT BACK A GOOD FEW HOURS.
THE LONGEST SO FAR.
MAX FUCKING CAULFIELD.
I AM WAY TOO HUNGOVER TO PROCESS WHAT JUST HAPPENED.
WE'LL TALK ABOUT IT LATER.
GET INSIDE AND WARM YOURSELVES UP.
I'M GOING FOR A WALK.

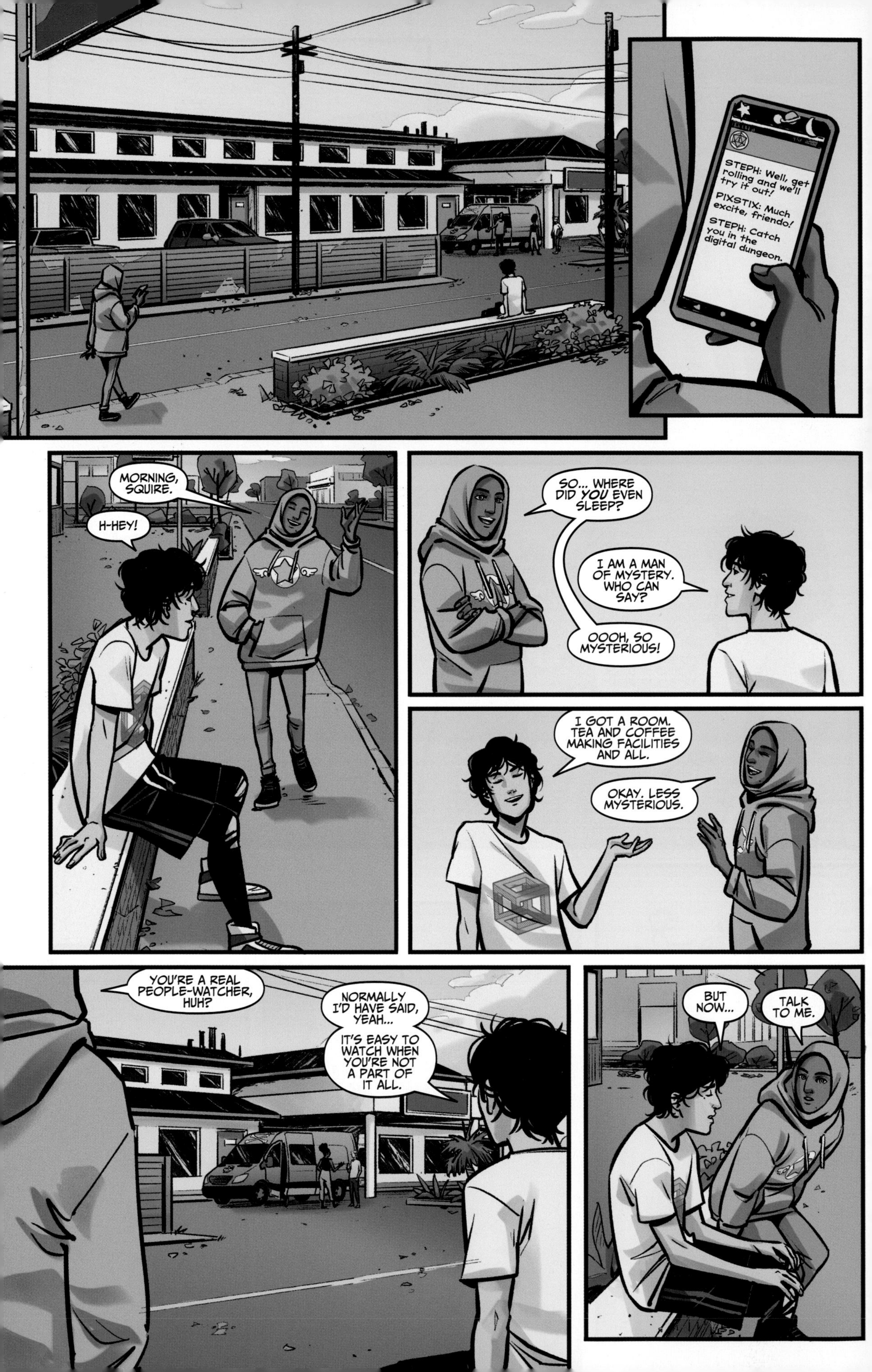
STEPH: Well, get rolling and we'll try it out!
PIXSTIX: Much excite, friendo!
STEPH: Catch you in the digital dungeon.
MORNING, SQUIRE.
H-HEY!
SO... WHERE DID YOU EVEN SLEEP?
I AM A MAN OF MYSTERY. WHO CAN SAY?
OOOH, SO MYSTERIOUS!
I GOT A ROOM. TEA AND COFFEE MAKING FACILITIES AND ALL.
OKAY. LESS MYSTERIOUS.
YOU'RE A REAL PEOPLE-WATCHER, HUH?
NORMALLY I'D HAVE SAID, YEAH...
IT'S EASY TO WATCH WHEN YOU'RE NOT A PART OF IT ALL.
BUT NOW...
TALK TO ME.

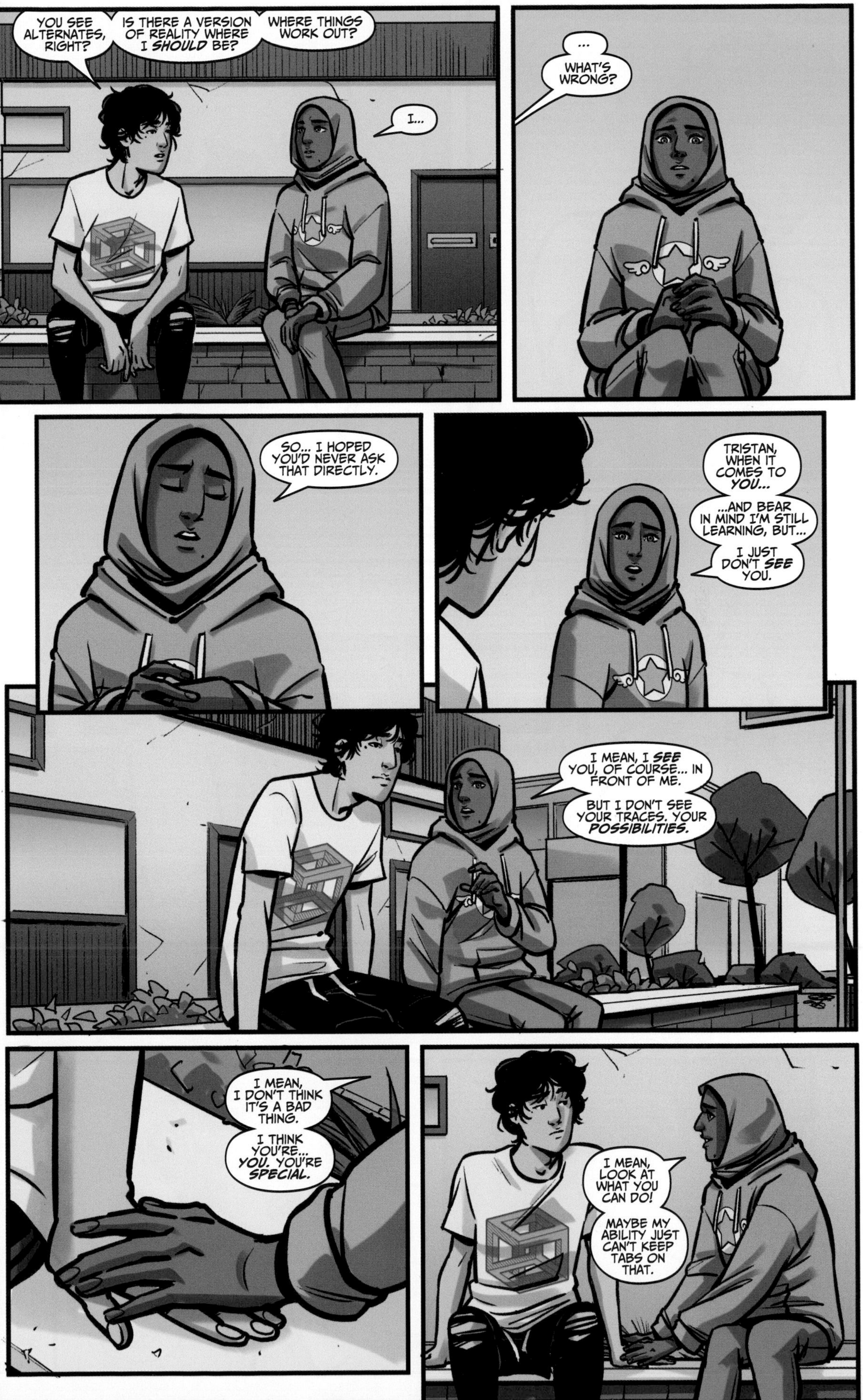
YOU SEE ALTERNATES, RIGHT?
IS THERE A VERSION OF REALITY WHERE I SHOULD BE?
WHERE THINGS WORK OUT?
I...
...
WHAT'S WRONG?
SO... I HOPED YOU'D NEVER ASK THAT DIRECTLY.
TRISTAN, WHEN IT COMES TO YOU...
...AND BEAR IN MIND I'M STILL LEARNING, BUT...
I JUST DON'T SEE YOU.
I MEAN, I SEE YOU, OF COURSE... IN FRONT OF ME.
BUT I DON'T SEE YOUR TRACES. YOUR POSSIBILITIES.
I MEAN, I DON'T THINK IT'S A BAD THING.
I THINK YOU'RE... YOU. YOU'RE SPECIAL.
I MEAN, LOOK AT WHAT YOU CAN DO!
MAYBE MY ABILITY JUST CAN'T KEEP TABS ON THAT.

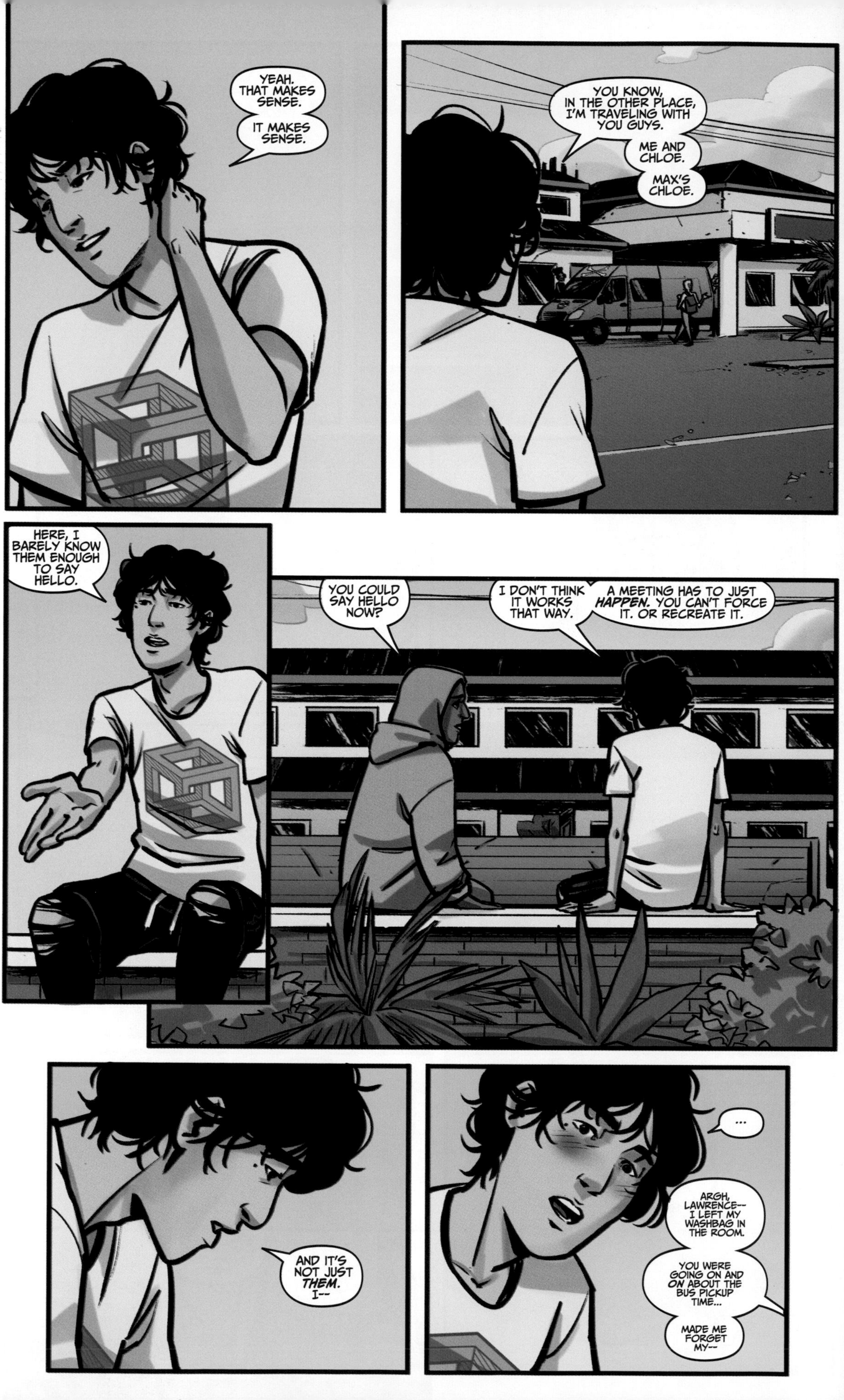
YEAH. THAT MAKES SENSE.
IT MAKES SENSE.
YOU KNOW, IN THE OTHER PLACE, I'M TRAVELING WITH YOU GUYS.
ME AND CHLOE.
MAX'S CHLOE.
HERE, I BARELY KNOW THEM ENOUGH TO SAY HELLO.
YOU COULD SAY HELLO NOW?
I DON'T THINK IT WORKS THAT WAY.
A MEETING HAS TO JUST HAPPEN. YOU CAN'T FORCE IT. OR RECREATE IT.
AND IT'S NOT JUST THEM. I--
...
ARGH, LAWRENCE-- I LEFT MY WASHBAG IN THE ROOM.
YOU WERE GOING ON AND ON ABOUT THE BUS PICKUP TIME...
MADE ME FORGET MY--

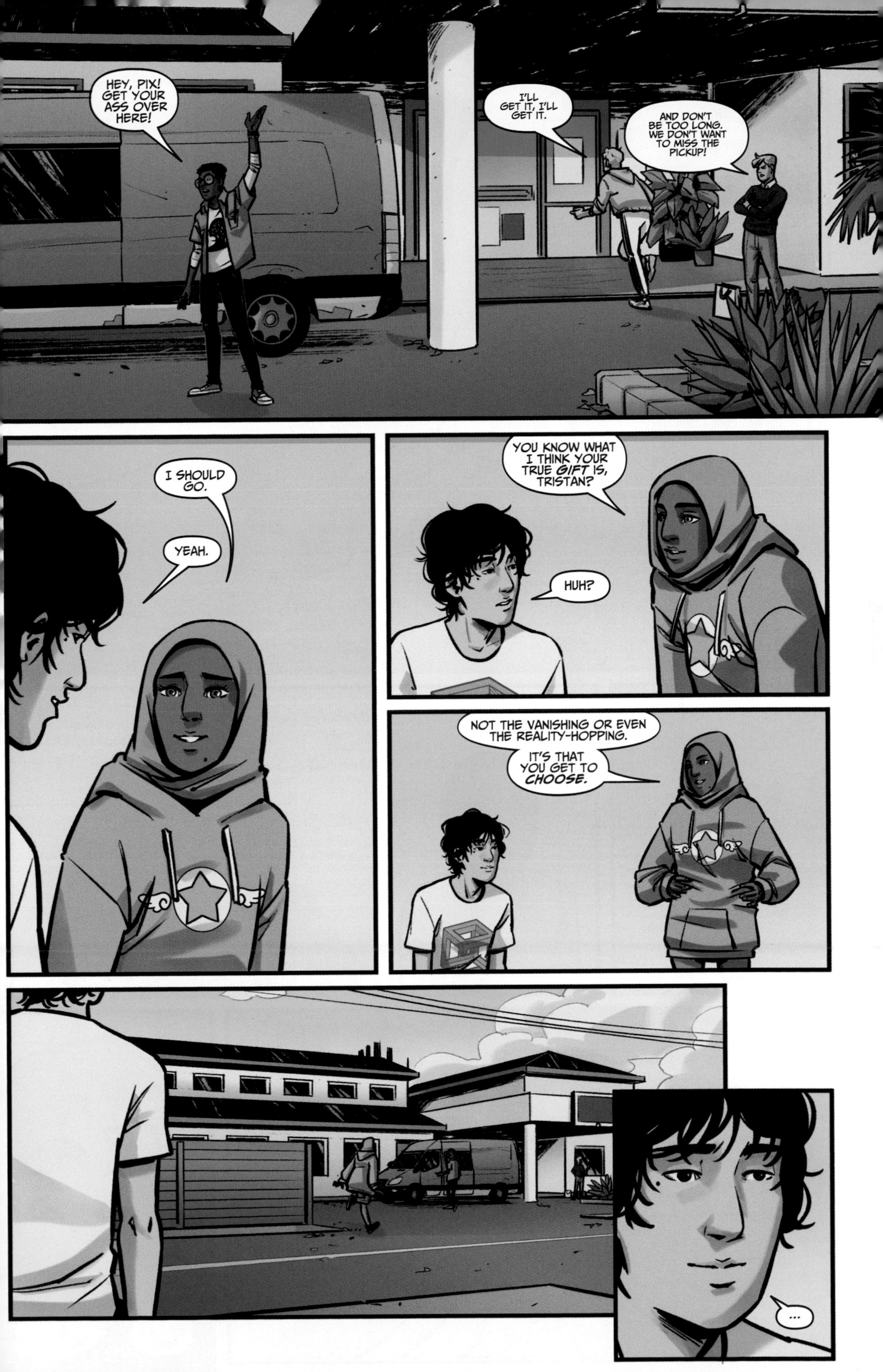
HEY, PIX! GET YOUR ASS OVER HERE!
I'LL GET IT, I'LL GET IT.
AND DON'T BE TOO LONG. WE DON'T WANT TO MISS THE PICKUP!
I SHOULD GO.
YEAH.
YOU KNOW WHAT I THINK YOUR TRUE GIFT IS, TRISTAN?
HUH?
NOT THE VANISHING OR EVEN THE REALITY-HOPPING.
IT'S THAT YOU GET TO CHOOSE.
...

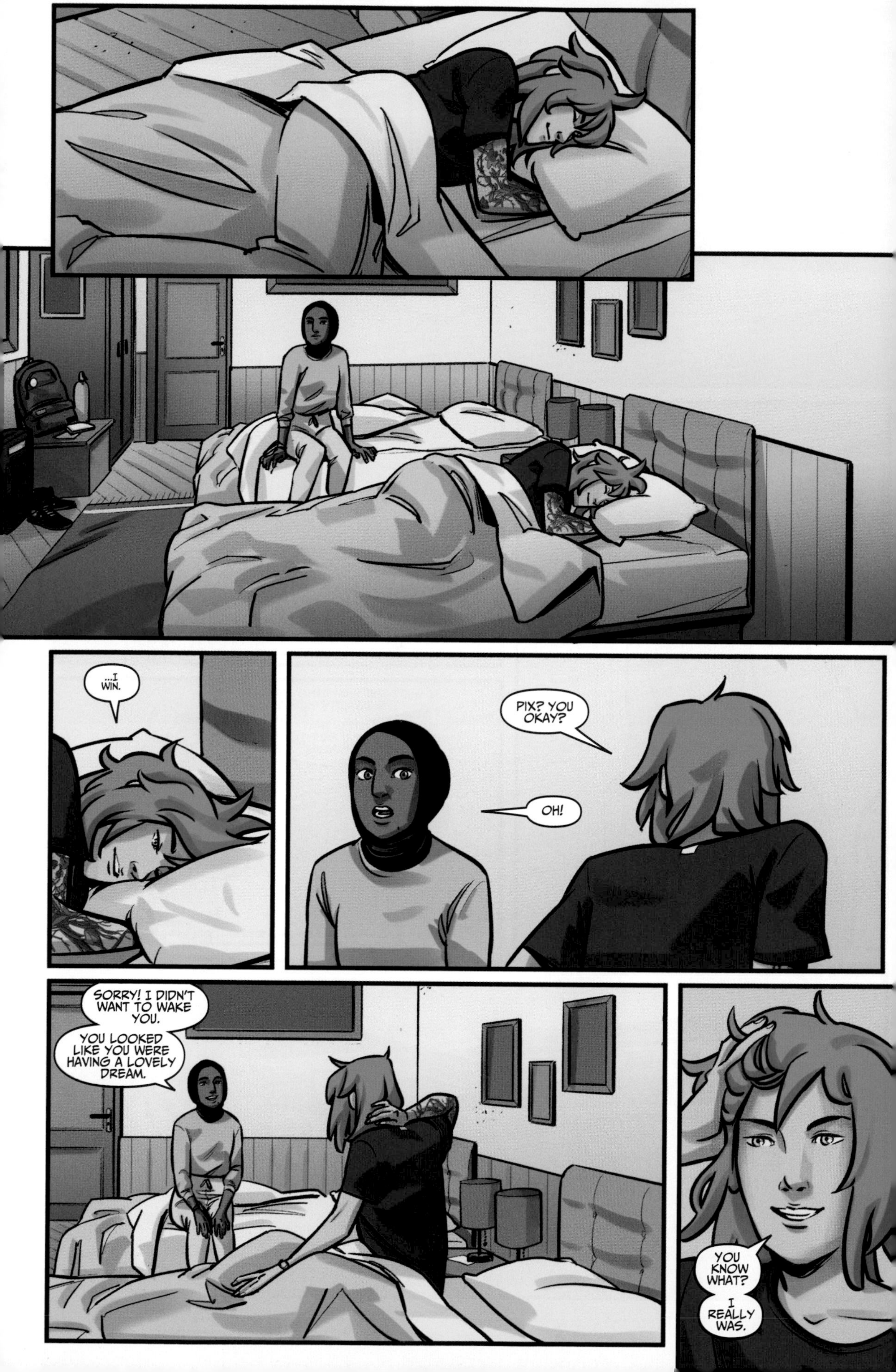
...I WIN.
PIX? YOU OKAY?
OH!
SORRY! I DIDN'T WANT TO WAKE YOU.
YOU LOOKED LIKE YOU WERE HAVING A LOVELY DREAM.
YOU KNOW WHAT?
I REALLY WAS.

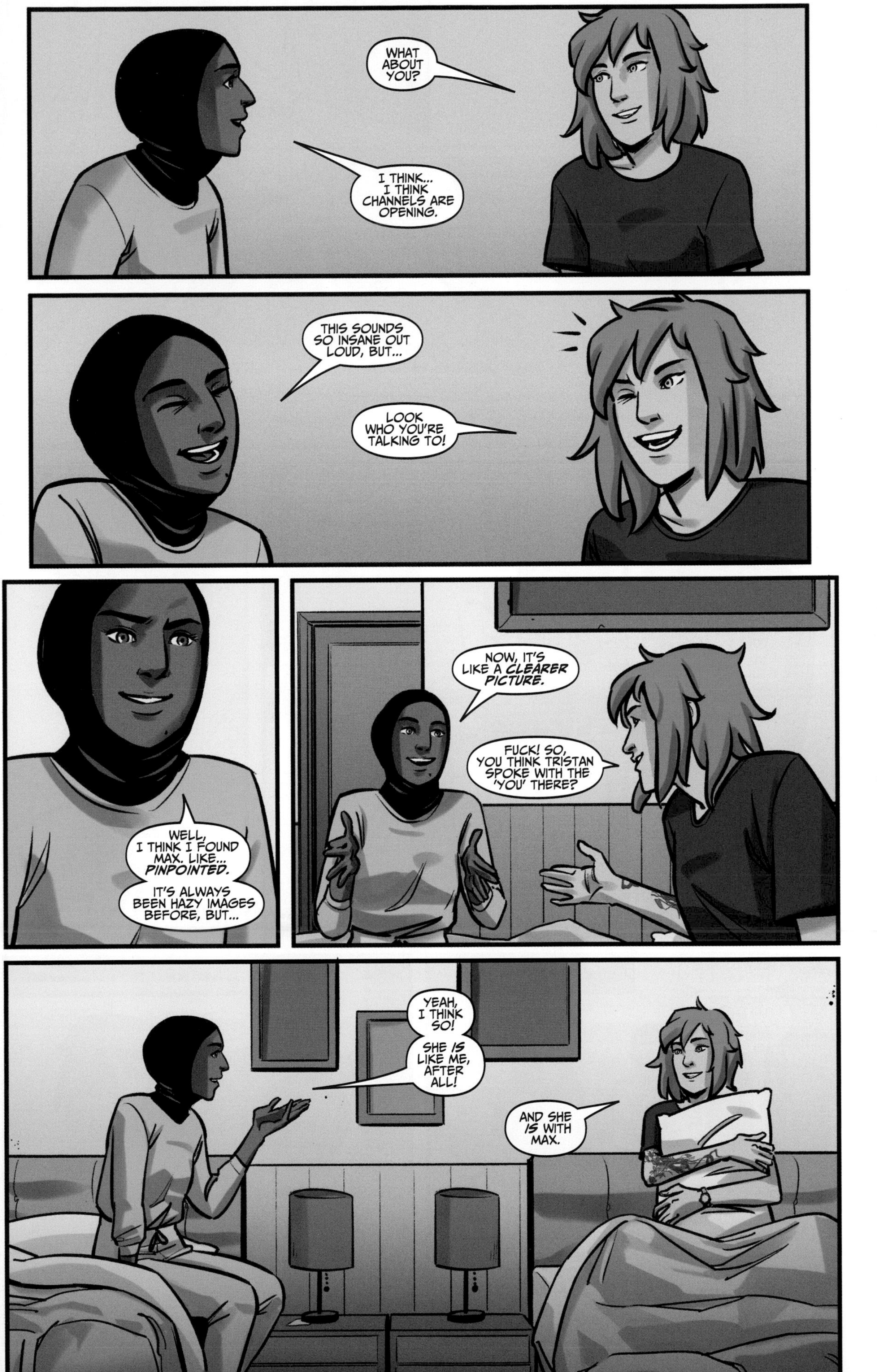

WHAT ABOUT YOU?
I THINK... I THINK CHANNELS ARE OPENING.
THIS SOUNDS SO INSANE OUT LOUD, BUT...
LOOK WHO YOU'RE TALKING TO!
WELL, I THINK I FOUND MAX. LIKE... *PINPOINTED.*
IT'S ALWAYS BEEN HAZY IMAGES BEFORE, BUT...
NOW, IT'S LIKE A *CLEARER PICTURE.*
FUCK! SO, YOU THINK TRISTAN SPOKE WITH THE 'YOU' THERE?
YEAH, I THINK SO!
SHE *IS* LIKE ME, AFTER ALL!
AND SHE *IS* WITH MAX.

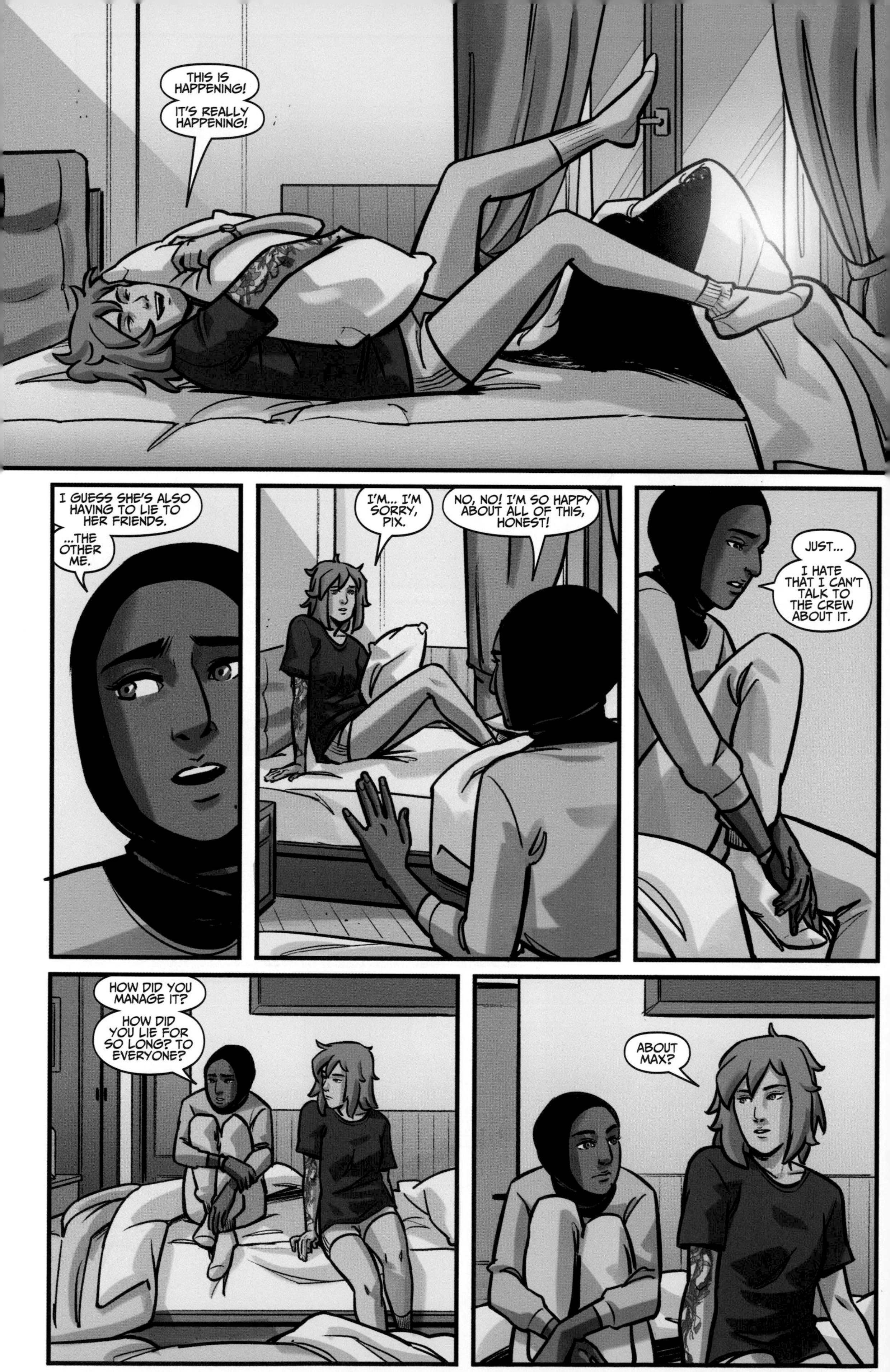
THIS IS HAPPENING!
IT'S REALLY HAPPENING!
I GUESS SHE'S ALSO HAVING TO LIE TO HER FRIENDS.
...THE OTHER ME.
I'M... I'M SORRY, PIX.
NO, NO! I'M SO HAPPY ABOUT ALL OF THIS, HONEST!
JUST...
I HATE THAT I CAN'T TALK TO THE CREW ABOUT IT.
HOW DID YOU MANAGE IT?
HOW DID YOU LIE FOR SO LONG? TO EVERYONE?
ABOUT MAX?

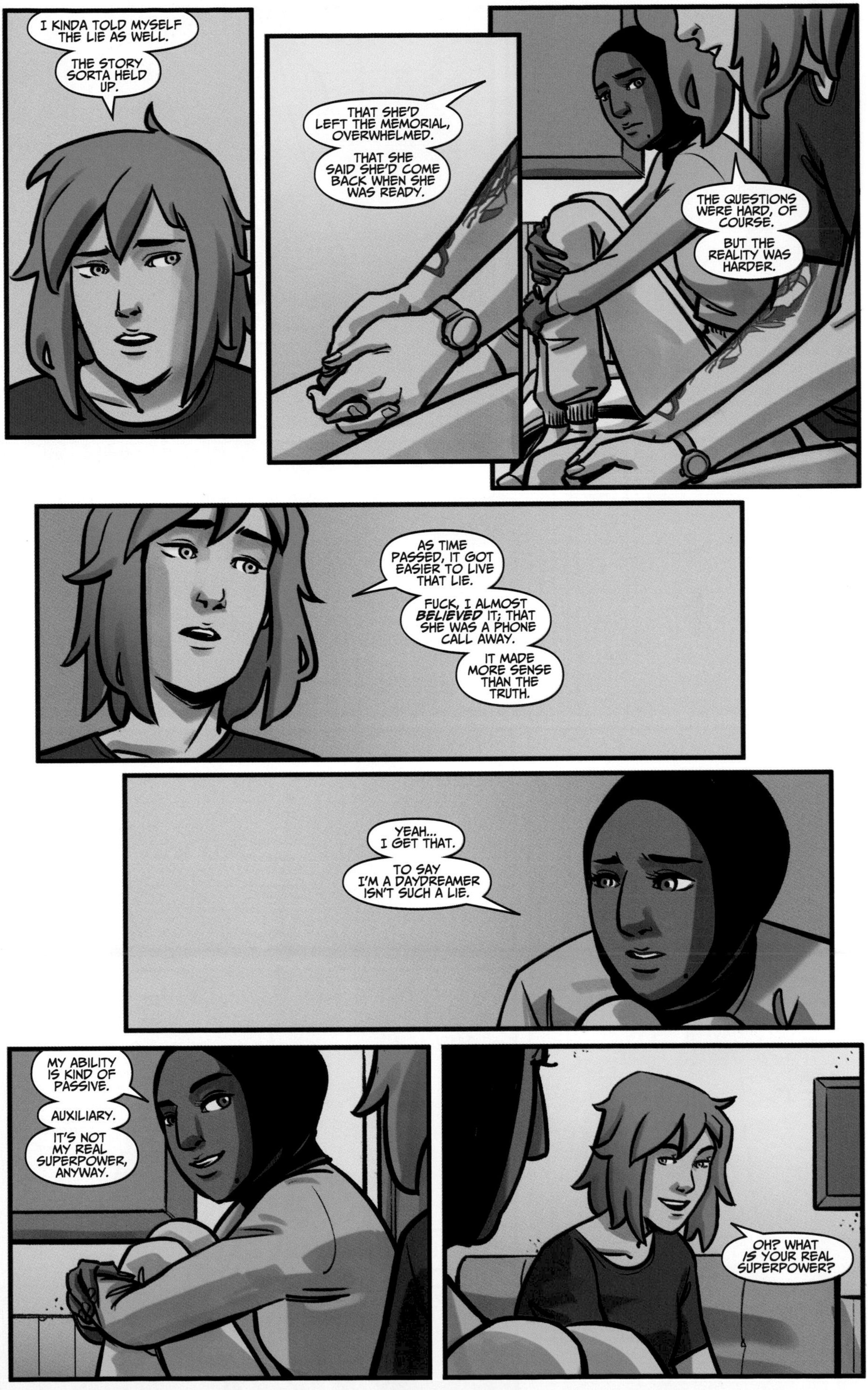
I KINDA TOLD MYSELF THE LIE AS WELL.
THE STORY SORTA HELD UP.
THAT SHE'D LEFT THE MEMORIAL, OVERWHELMED.
THAT SHE SAID SHE'D COME BACK WHEN SHE WAS READY.
THE QUESTIONS WERE HARD, OF COURSE.
BUT THE REALITY WAS HARDER.
AS TIME PASSED, IT GOT EASIER TO LIVE THAT LIE.
FUCK, I ALMOST *BELIEVED* IT; THAT SHE WAS A PHONE CALL AWAY.
IT MADE MORE SENSE THAN THE TRUTH.
YEAH... I GET THAT.
TO SAY I'M A DAYDREAMER ISN'T SUCH A LIE.
MY ABILITY IS KIND OF PASSIVE.
AUXILIARY.
IT'S NOT MY REAL SUPERPOWER, ANYWAY.
OH? WHAT *IS* YOUR REAL SUPERPOWER?

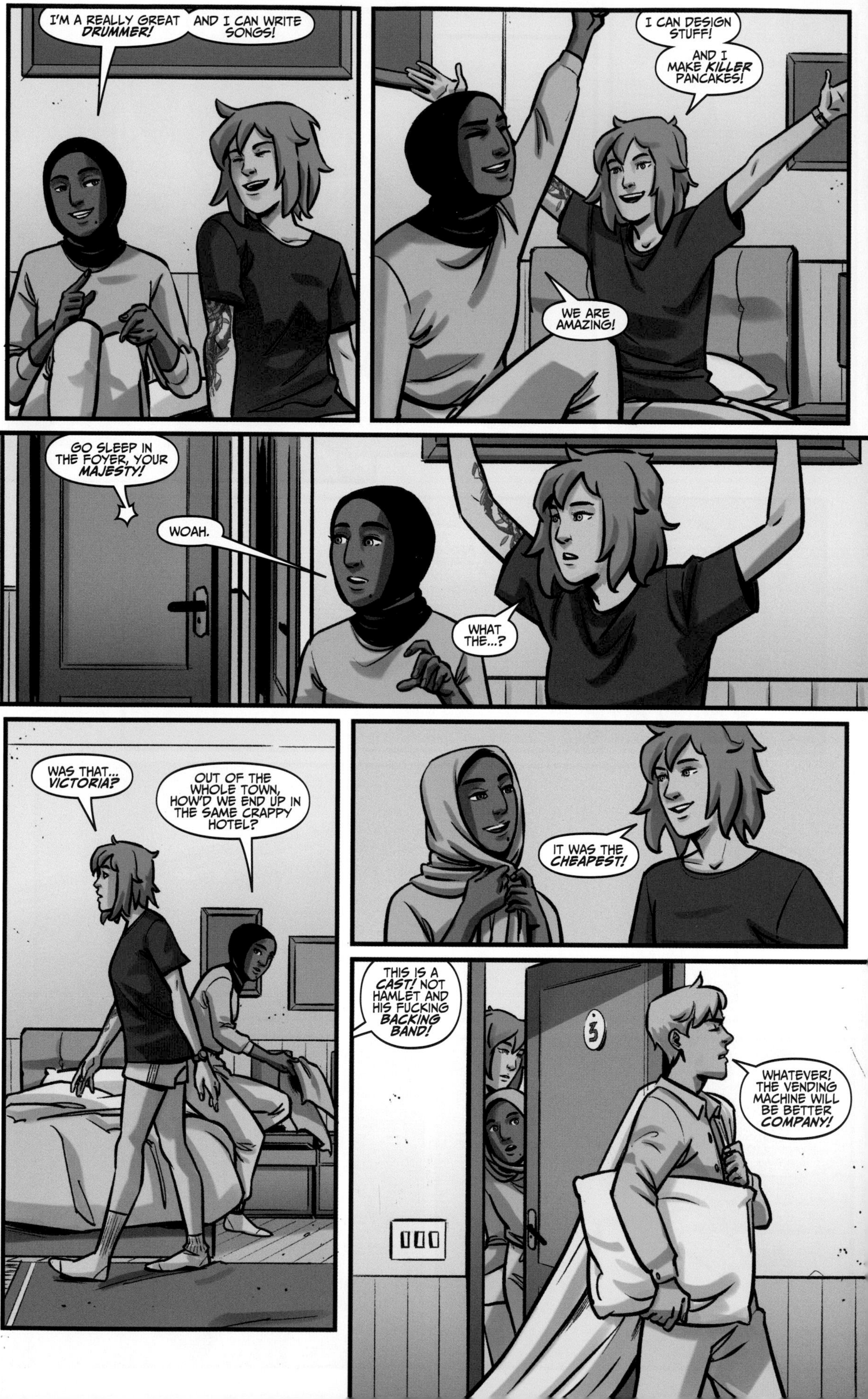
I'M A REALLY GREAT DRUMMER!
AND I CAN WRITE SONGS!
I CAN DESIGN STUFF!
AND I MAKE KILLER PANCAKES!
WE ARE AMAZING!
GO SLEEP IN THE FOYER, YOUR MAJESTY!
WOAH.
WHAT THE...?
WAS THAT... VICTORIA?
OUT OF THE WHOLE TOWN, HOW'D WE END UP IN THE SAME CRAPPY HOTEL?
IT WAS THE CHEAPEST!
THIS IS A CAST! NOT HAMLET AND HIS FUCKING BACKING BAND!
3
WHATEVER! THE VENDING MACHINE WILL BE BETTER COMPANY!

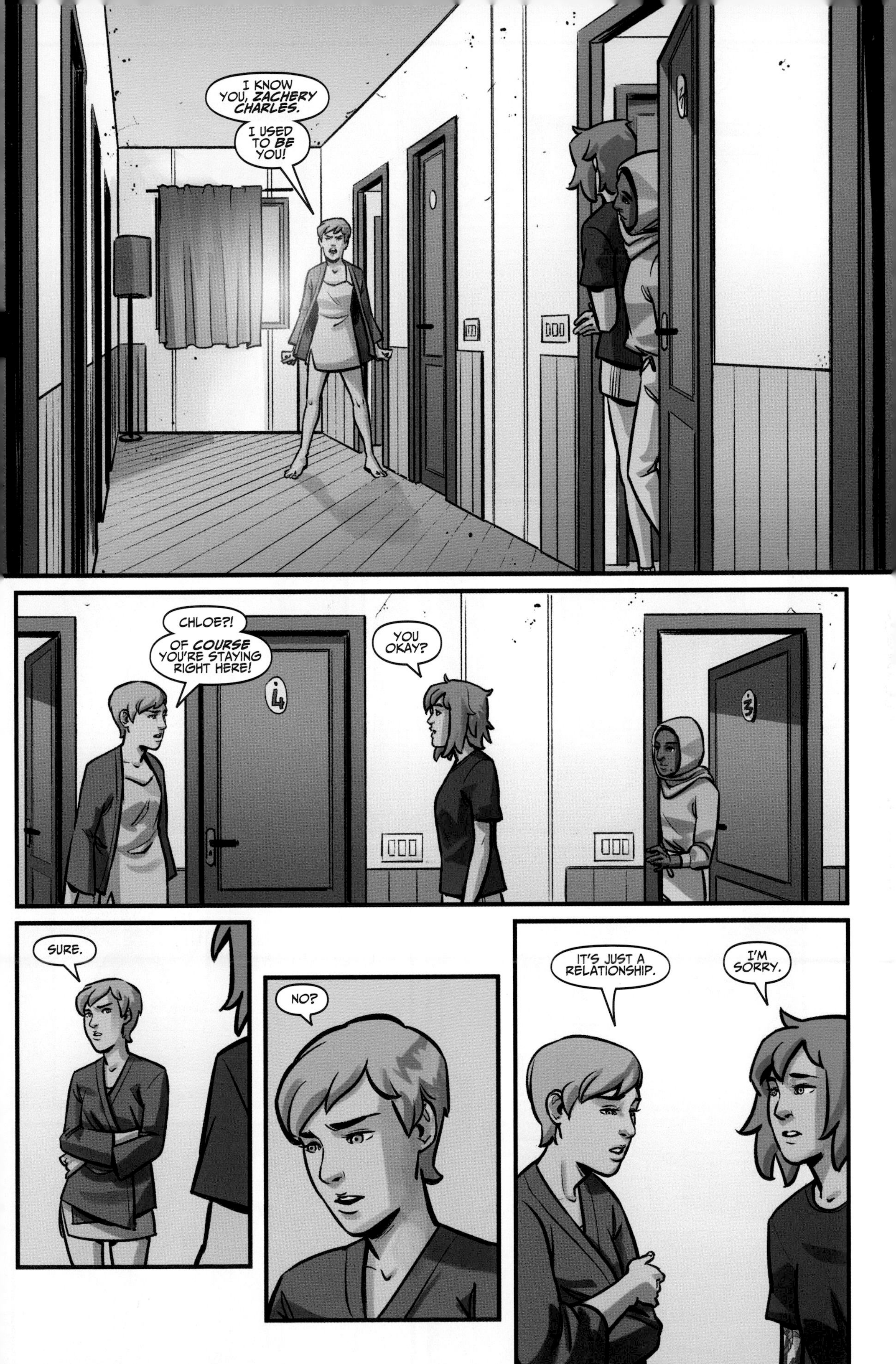
I KNOW YOU, ZACHERY CHARLES.
I USED TO BE YOU!
CHLOE?!
OF COURSE YOU'RE STAYING RIGHT HERE!
YOU OKAY?
SURE.
NO?
IT'S JUST A RELATIONSHIP.
I'M SORRY.

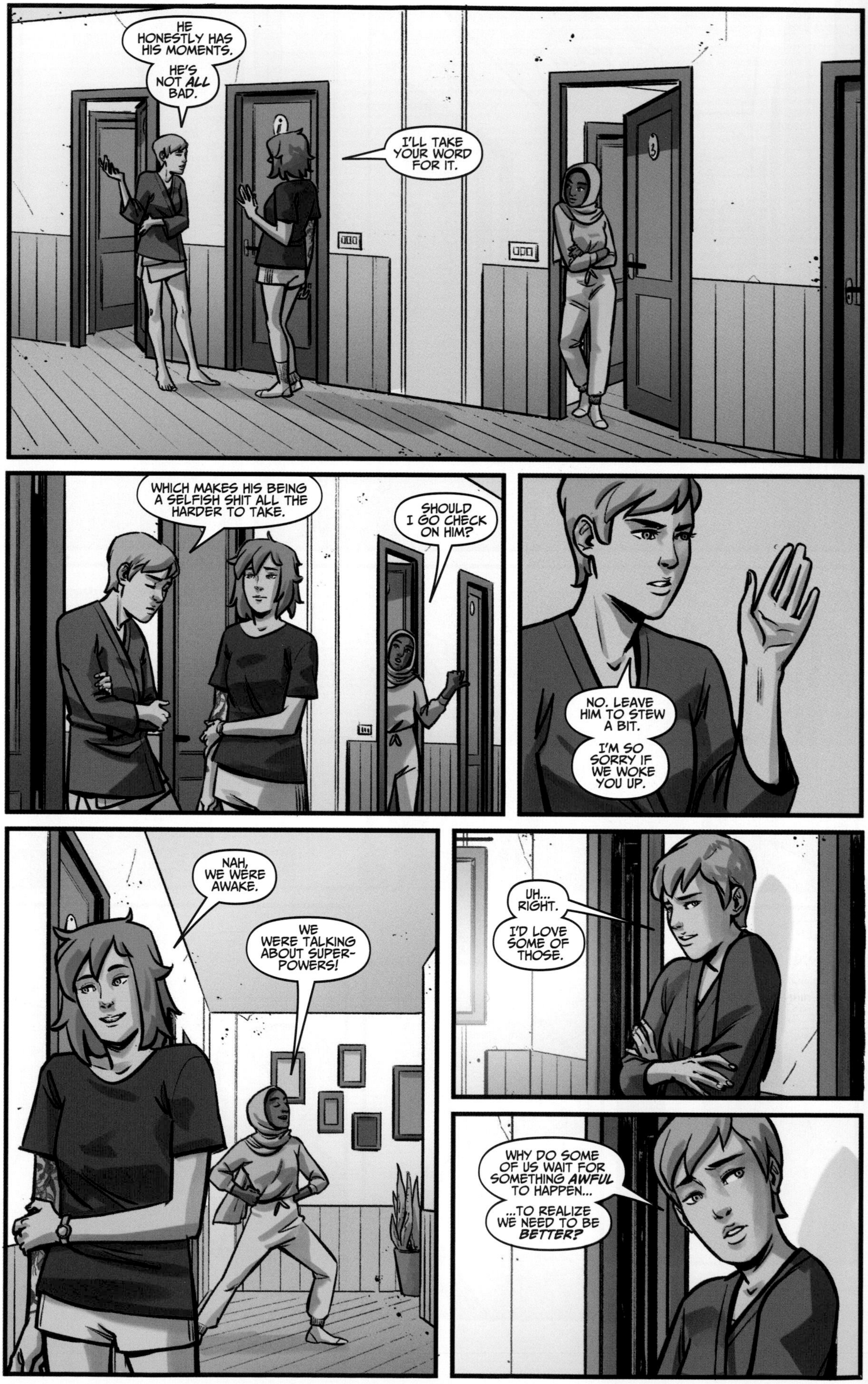
HE HONESTLY HAS HIS MOMENTS.
HE'S NOT *ALL* BAD.
I'LL TAKE YOUR WORD FOR IT.
WHICH MAKES HIS BEING A SELFISH SHIT ALL THE HARDER TO TAKE.
SHOULD I GO CHECK ON HIM?
NO. LEAVE HIM TO STEW A BIT.
I'M SO SORRY IF WE WOKE YOU UP.
NAH, WE WERE AWAKE.
WE WERE TALKING ABOUT SUPER-POWERS!
UH... RIGHT.
I'D LOVE SOME OF THOSE.
WHY DO SOME OF US WAIT FOR SOMETHING *AWFUL* TO HAPPEN...
...TO REALIZE WE NEED TO BE *BETTER?*

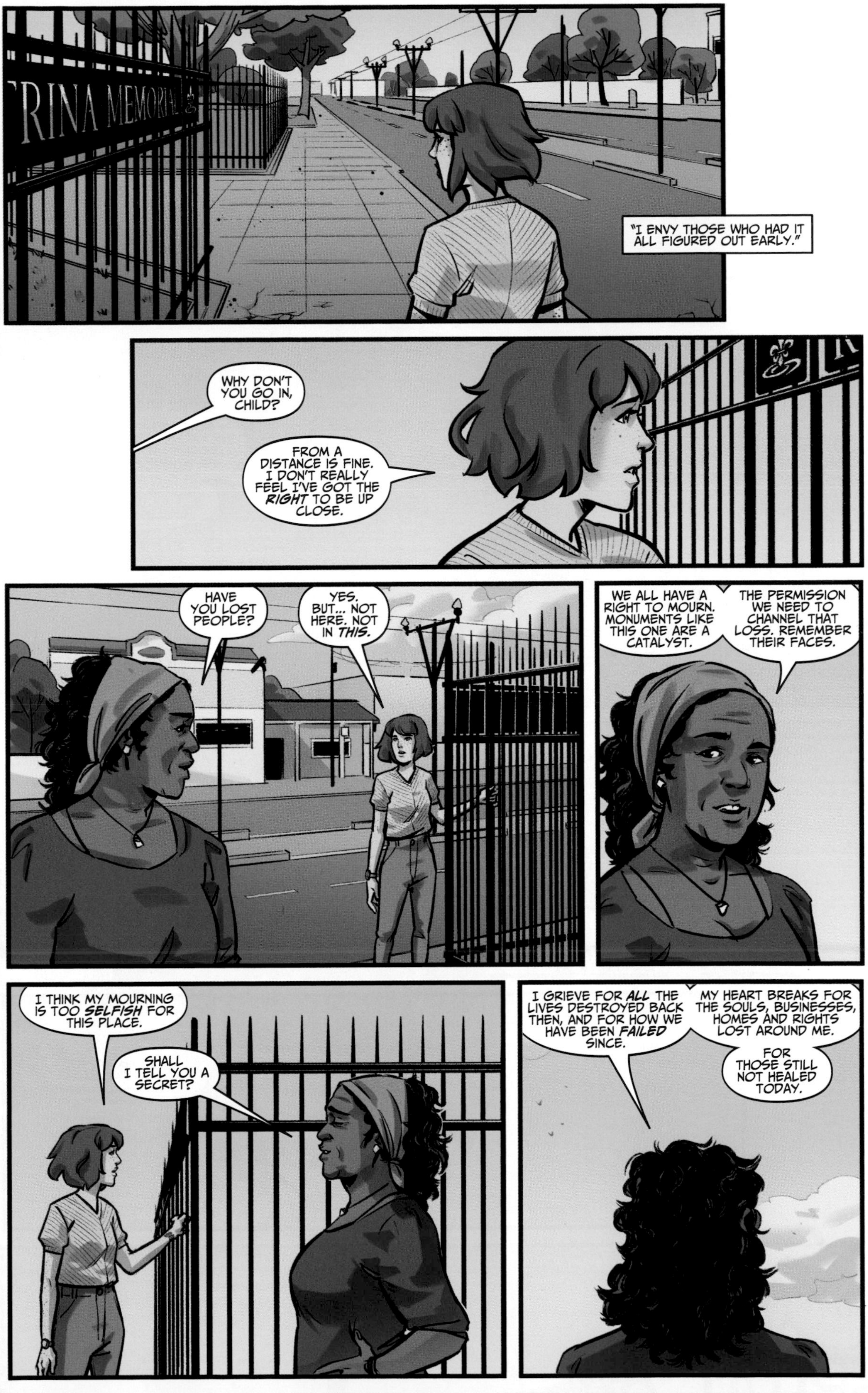
TRINA MEMORIAL
"I ENVY THOSE WHO HAD IT ALL FIGURED OUT EARLY."
WHY DON'T YOU GO IN, CHILD?
FROM A DISTANCE IS FINE. I DON'T REALLY FEEL I'VE GOT THE RIGHT TO BE UP CLOSE.
HAVE YOU LOST PEOPLE?
YES. BUT... NOT HERE. NOT IN THIS.
WE ALL HAVE A RIGHT TO MOURN. MONUMENTS LIKE THIS ONE ARE A CATALYST.
THE PERMISSION WE NEED TO CHANNEL THAT LOSS. REMEMBER THEIR FACES.
I THINK MY MOURNING IS TOO SELFISH FOR THIS PLACE.
SHALL I TELL YOU A SECRET?
I GRIEVE FOR ALL THE LIVES DESTROYED BACK THEN, AND FOR HOW WE HAVE BEEN FAILED SINCE.
MY HEART BREAKS FOR THE SOULS, BUSINESSES, HOMES AND RIGHTS LOST AROUND ME.
FOR THOSE STILL NOT HEALED TODAY.

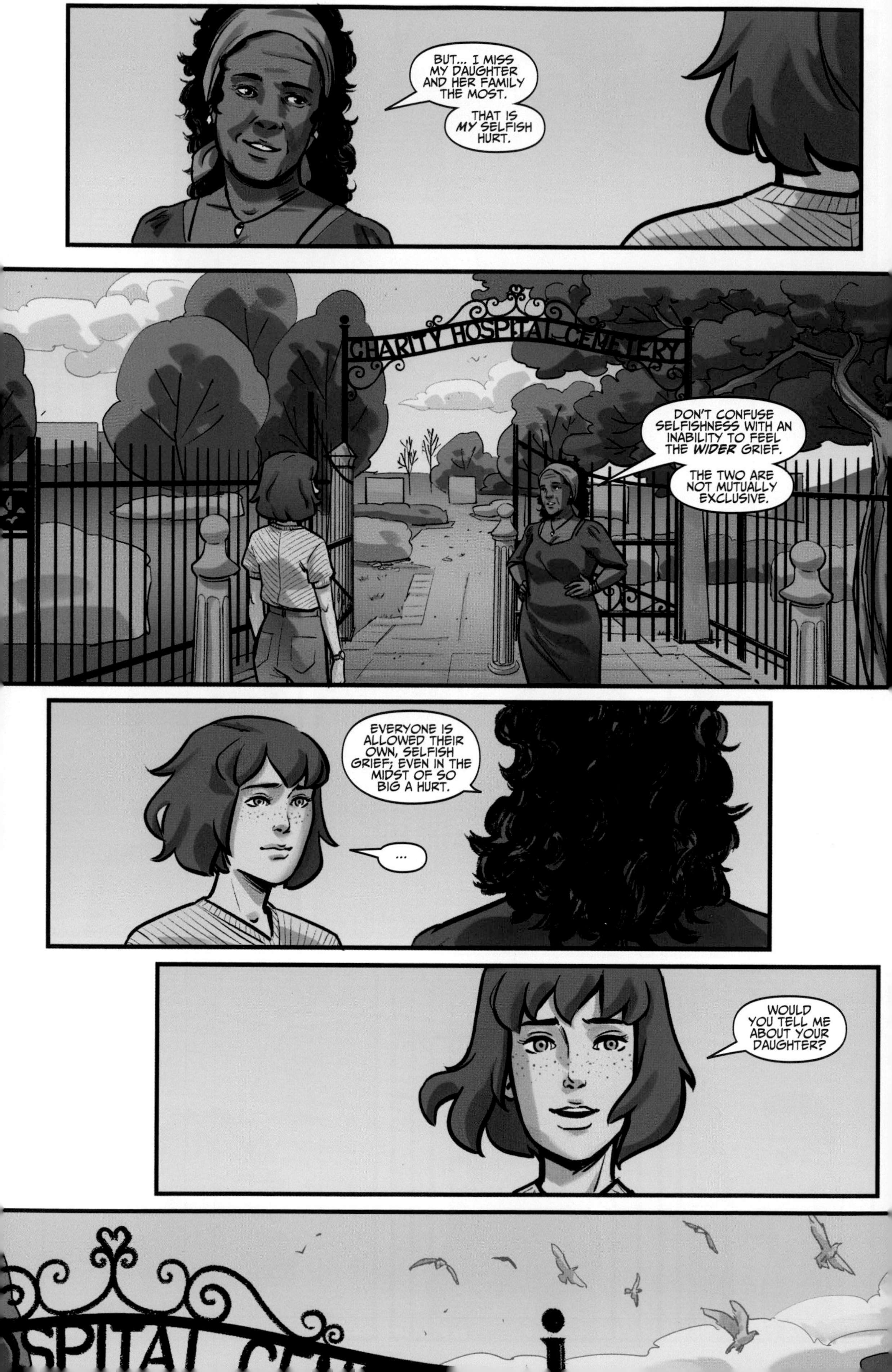
BUT... I MISS MY DAUGHTER AND HER FAMILY THE MOST.
THAT IS MY SELFISH HURT.
CHARITY HOSPITAL CEMETERY
DON'T CONFUSE SELFISHNESS WITH AN INABILITY TO FEEL THE WIDER GRIEF.
THE TWO ARE NOT MUTUALLY EXCLUSIVE.
EVERYONE IS ALLOWED THEIR OWN, SELFISH GRIEF; EVEN IN THE MIDST OF SO BIG A HURT.
...
WOULD YOU TELL ME ABOUT YOUR DAUGHTER?

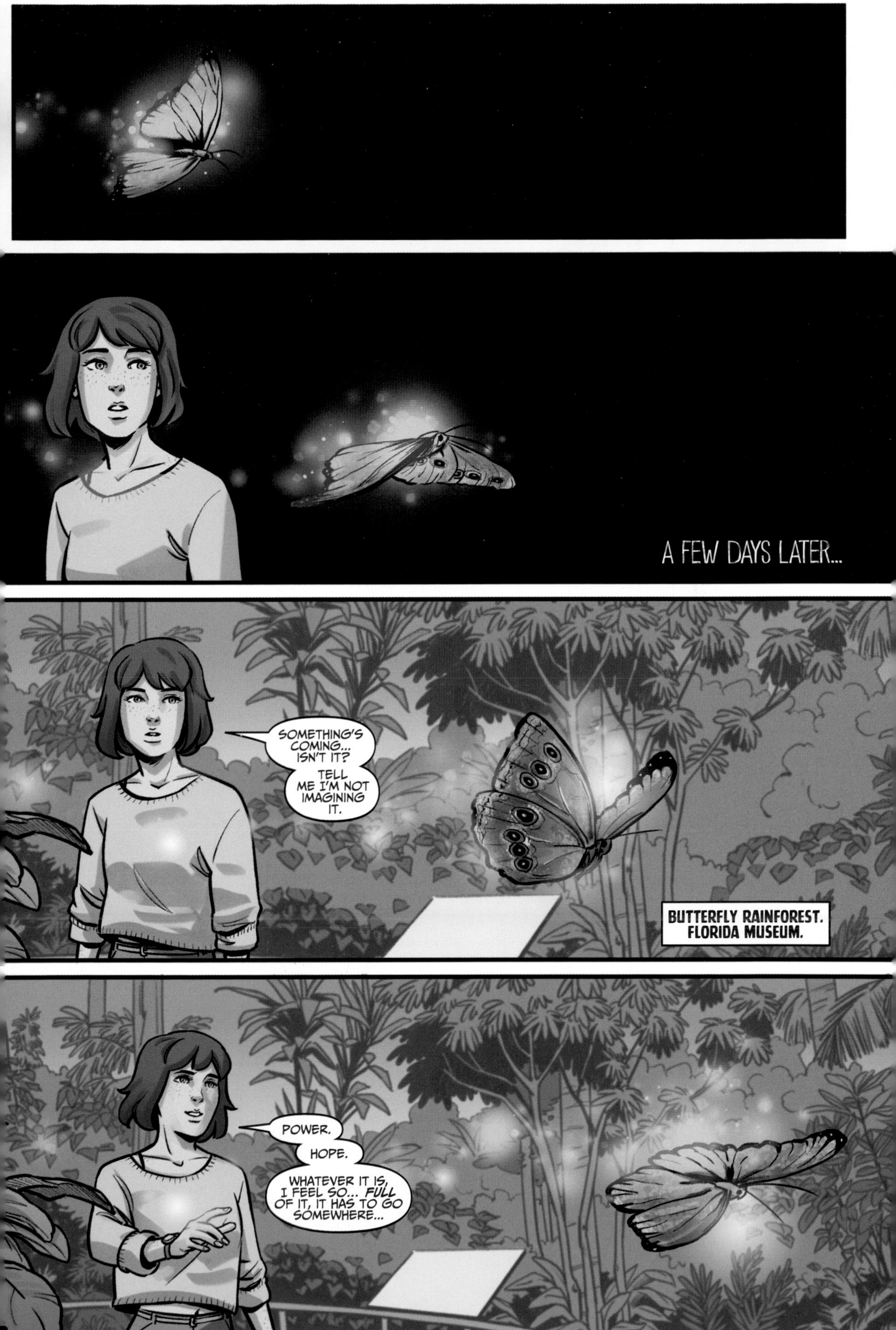
A FEW DAYS LATER...
BUTTERFLY RAINFOREST. FLORIDA MUSEUM.
SOMETHING'S COMING... ISN'T IT?
TELL ME I'M NOT IMAGINING IT.
POWER.
HOPE.
WHATEVER IT IS, I FEEL SO... FULL OF IT, IT HAS TO GO SOMEWHERE...

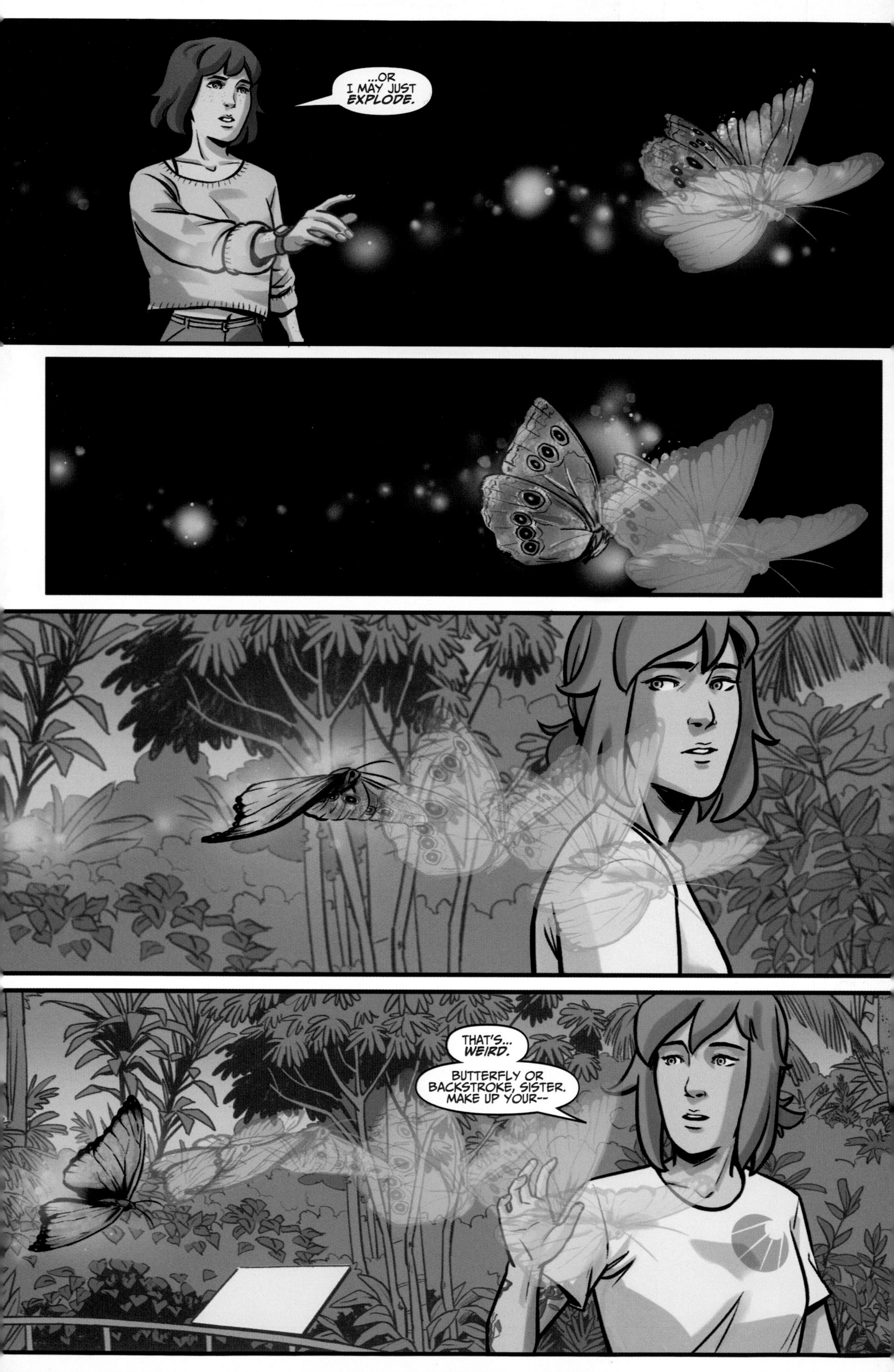
...OR I MAY JUST *EXPLODE.*
THAT'S... *WEIRD.*
BUTTERFLY OR BACKSTROKE, SISTER. MAKE UP YOUR--

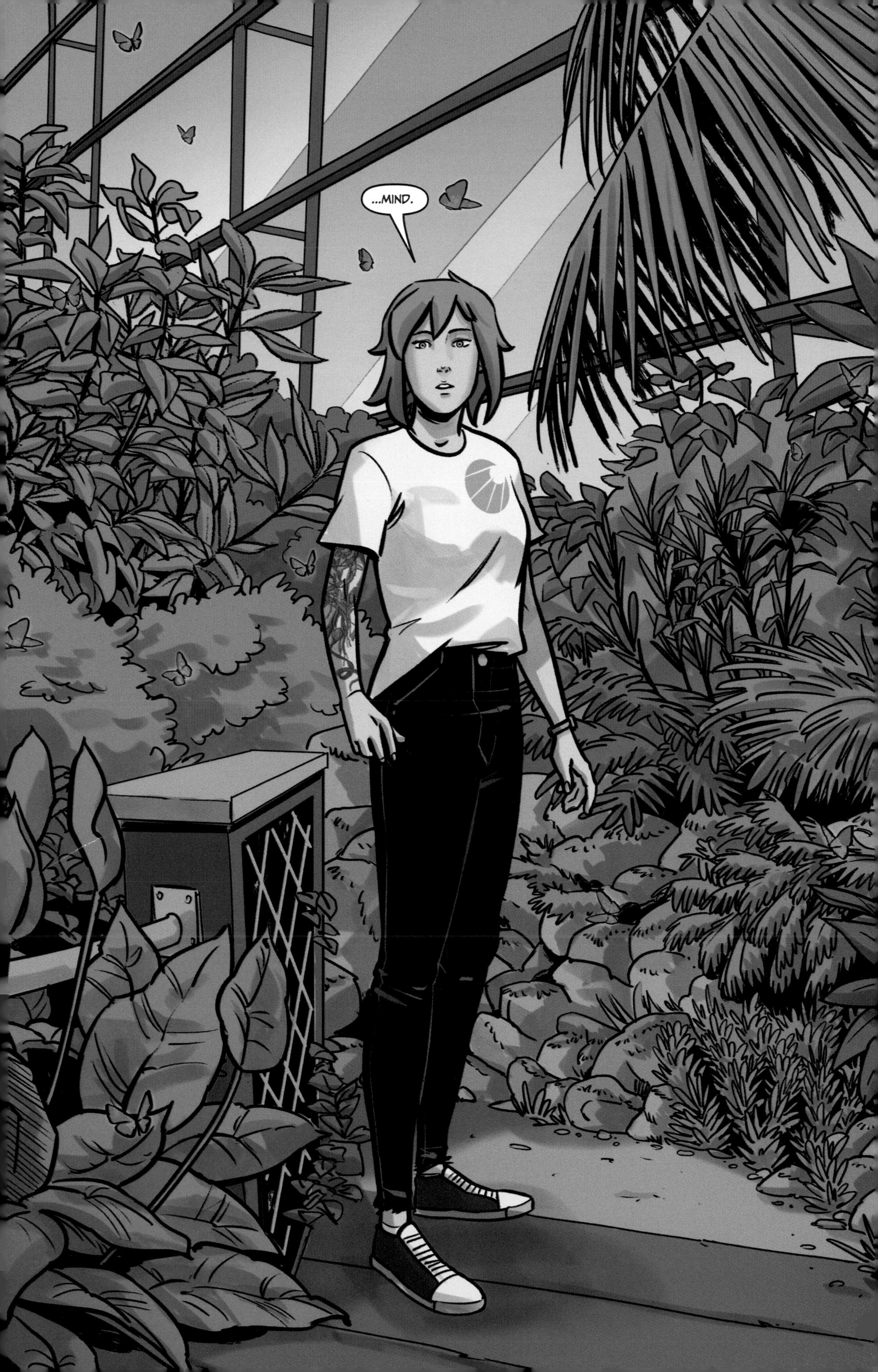
...MIND.

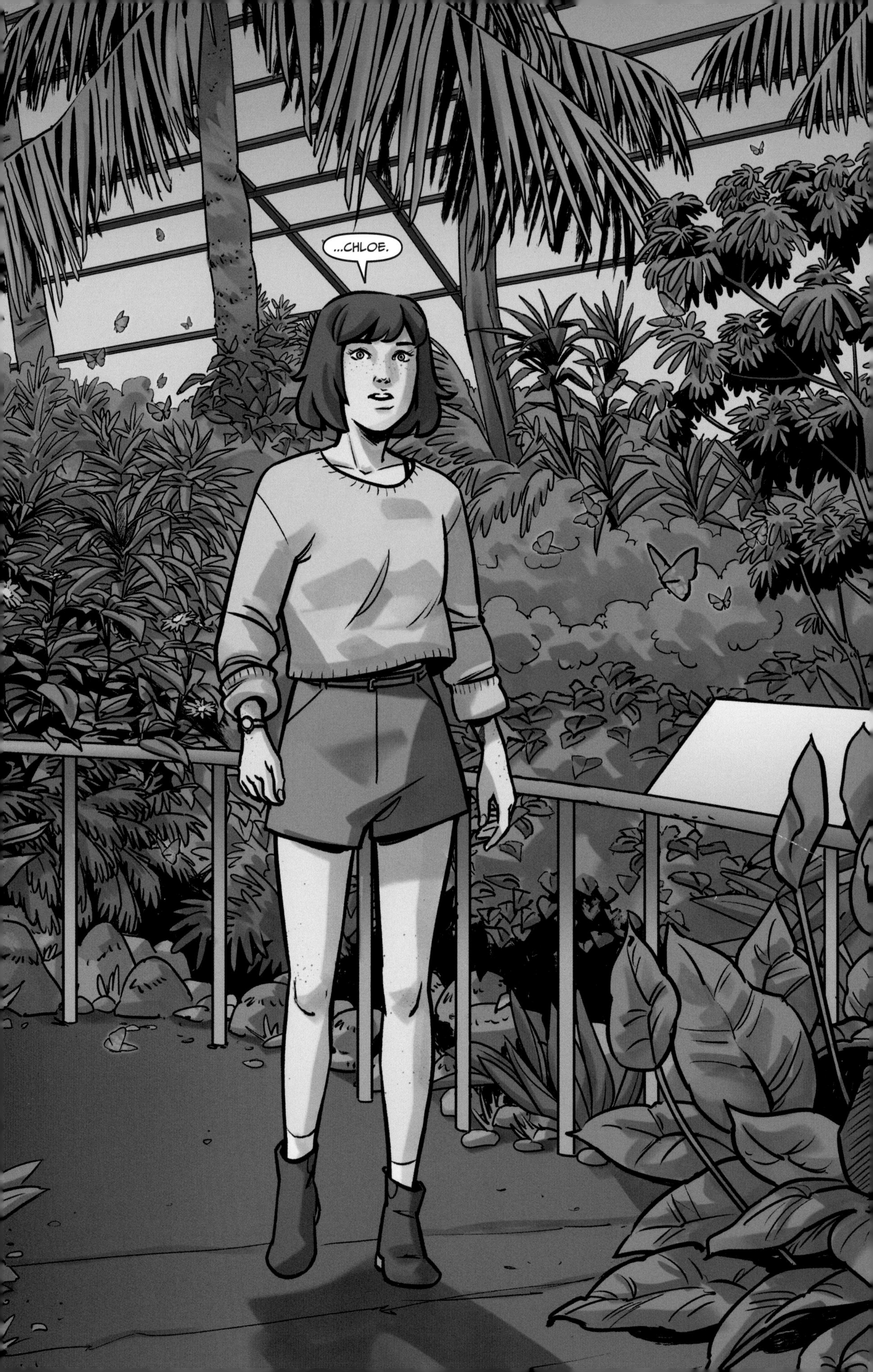
...CHLOE.

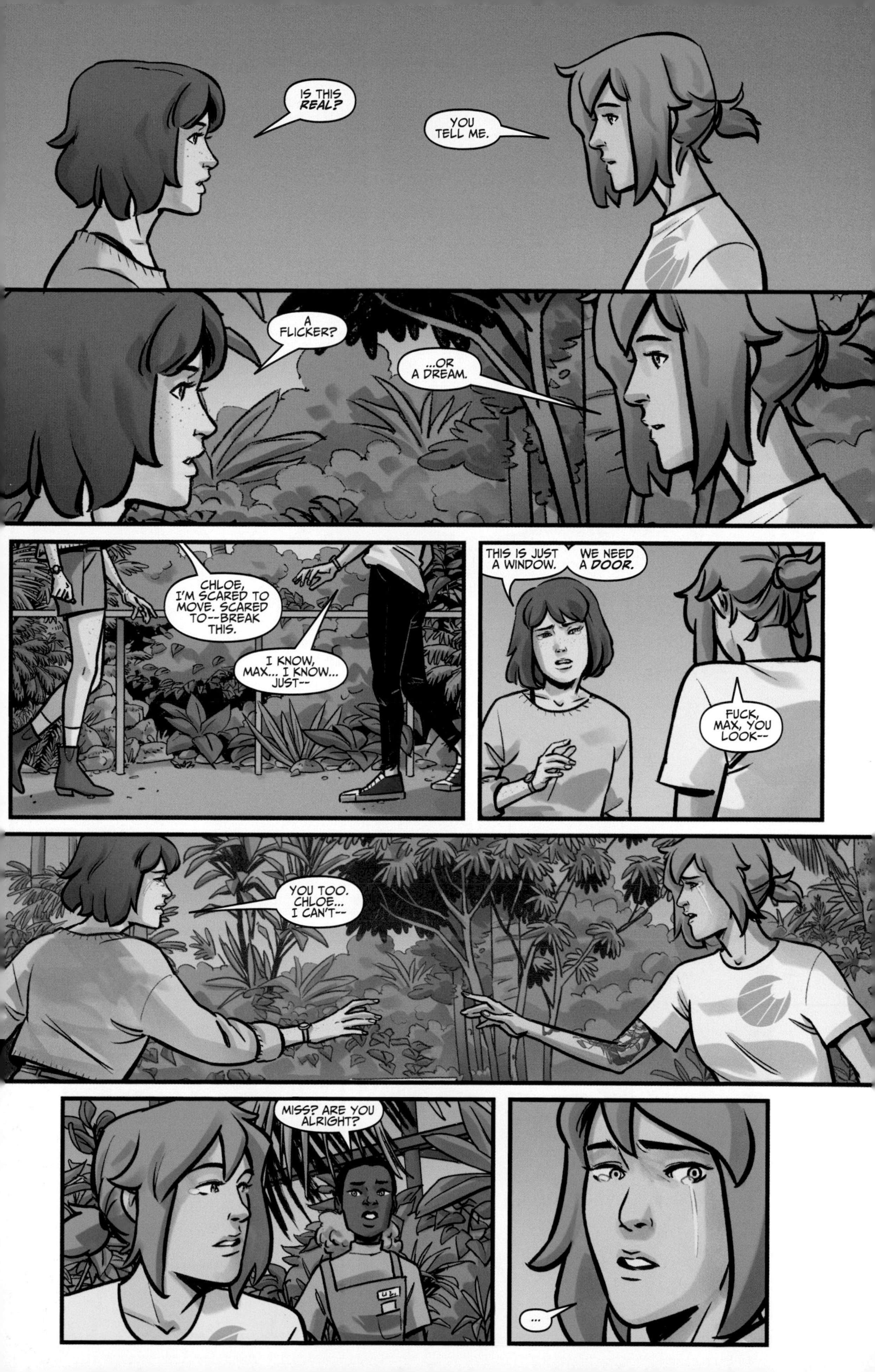
IS THIS *REAL?*
YOU TELL ME.
A FLICKER?
...OR A DREAM.
CHLOE, I'M SCARED TO MOVE. SCARED TO--BREAK THIS.
I KNOW, MAX... I KNOW... JUST--
THIS IS JUST A WINDOW.
WE NEED A *DOOR.*
FUCK, MAX, YOU LOOK--
YOU TOO. CHLOE... I CAN'T--
MISS? ARE YOU ALRIGHT?
...

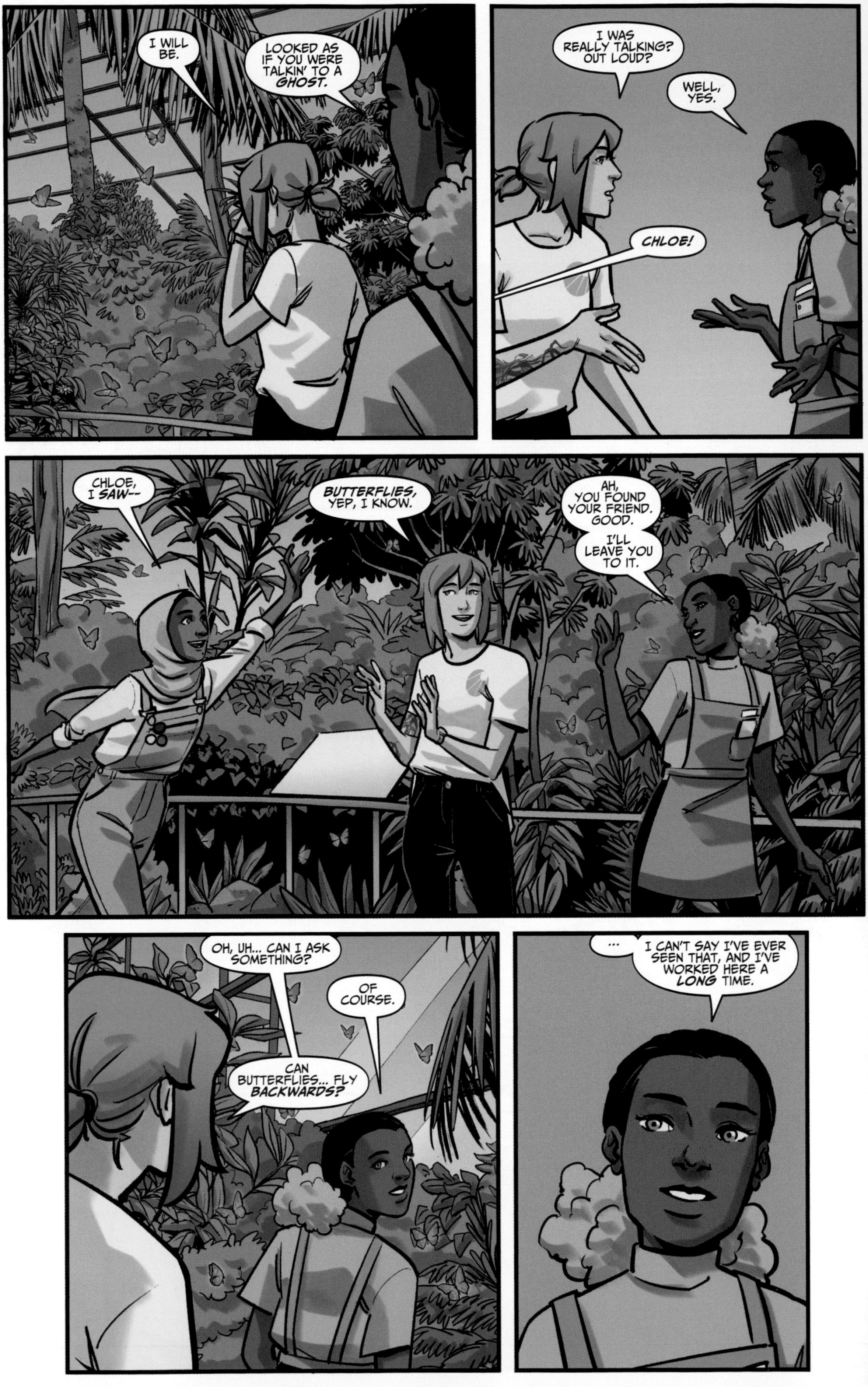
I WILL BE.
LOOKED AS IF YOU WERE TALKIN' TO A GHOST.
I WAS REALLY TALKING? OUT LOUD?
WELL, YES.
CHLOE!
CHLOE, I SAW--
BUTTERFLIES, YEP, I KNOW.
AH, YOU FOUND YOUR FRIEND. GOOD.
I'LL LEAVE YOU TO IT.
OH, UH... CAN I ASK SOMETHING?
OF COURSE.
CAN BUTTERFLIES... FLY BACKWARDS?
...
I CAN'T SAY I'VE EVER SEEN THAT, AND I'VE WORKED HERE A LONG TIME.

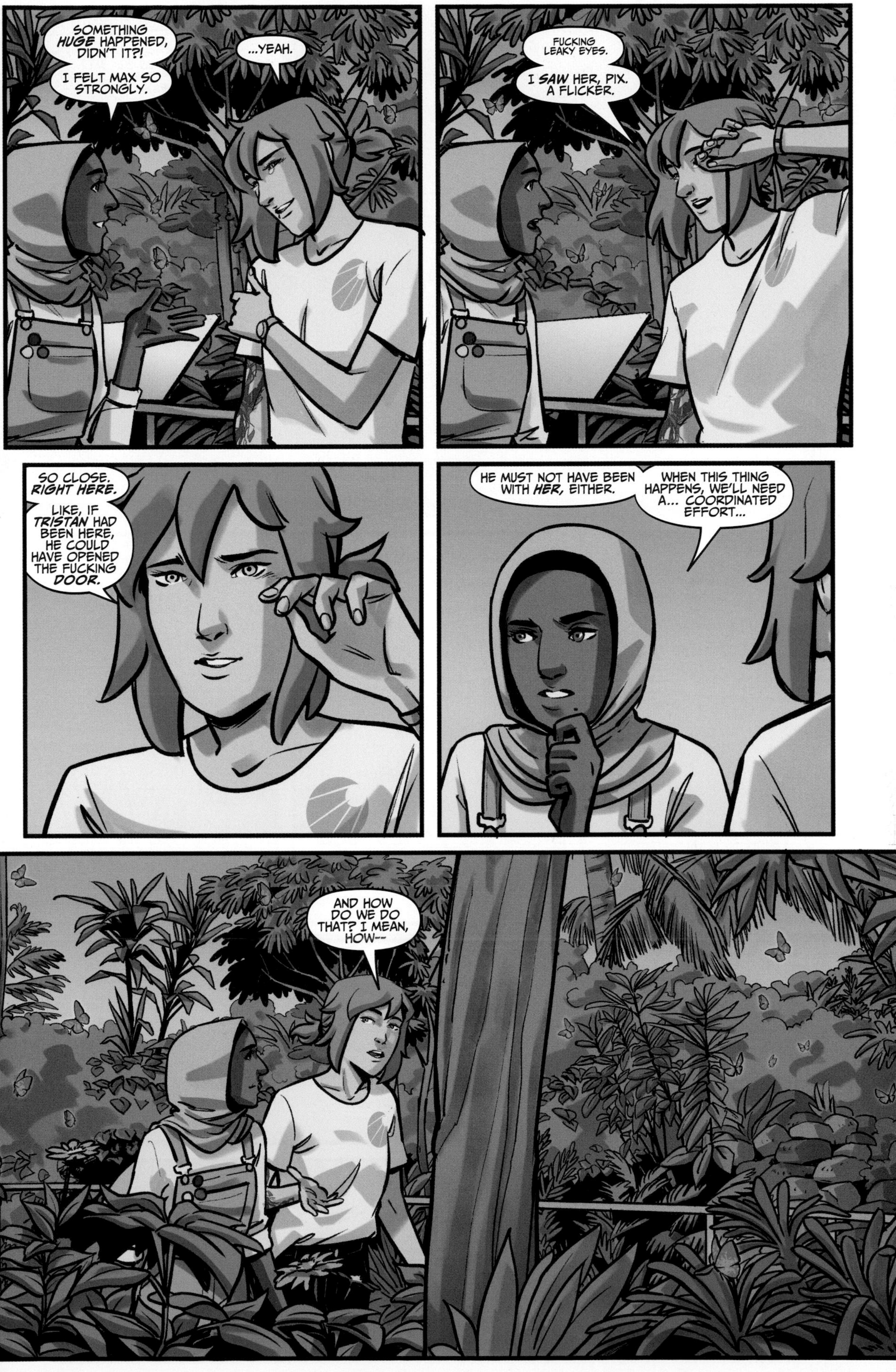
SOMETHING *HUGE* HAPPENED, DIDN'T IT?!
I FELT MAX SO STRONGLY.
...YEAH.
FUCKING LEAKY EYES.
I *SAW* HER, PIX. A FLICKER.
SO CLOSE. *RIGHT HERE.*
LIKE, IF *TRISTAN* HAD BEEN HERE, HE COULD HAVE OPENED THE FUCKING *DOOR.*
HE MUST NOT HAVE BEEN WITH *HER,* EITHER.
WHEN THIS THING HAPPENS, WE'LL NEED A... COORDINATED EFFORT...
AND HOW DO WE DO THAT? I MEAN, HOW--

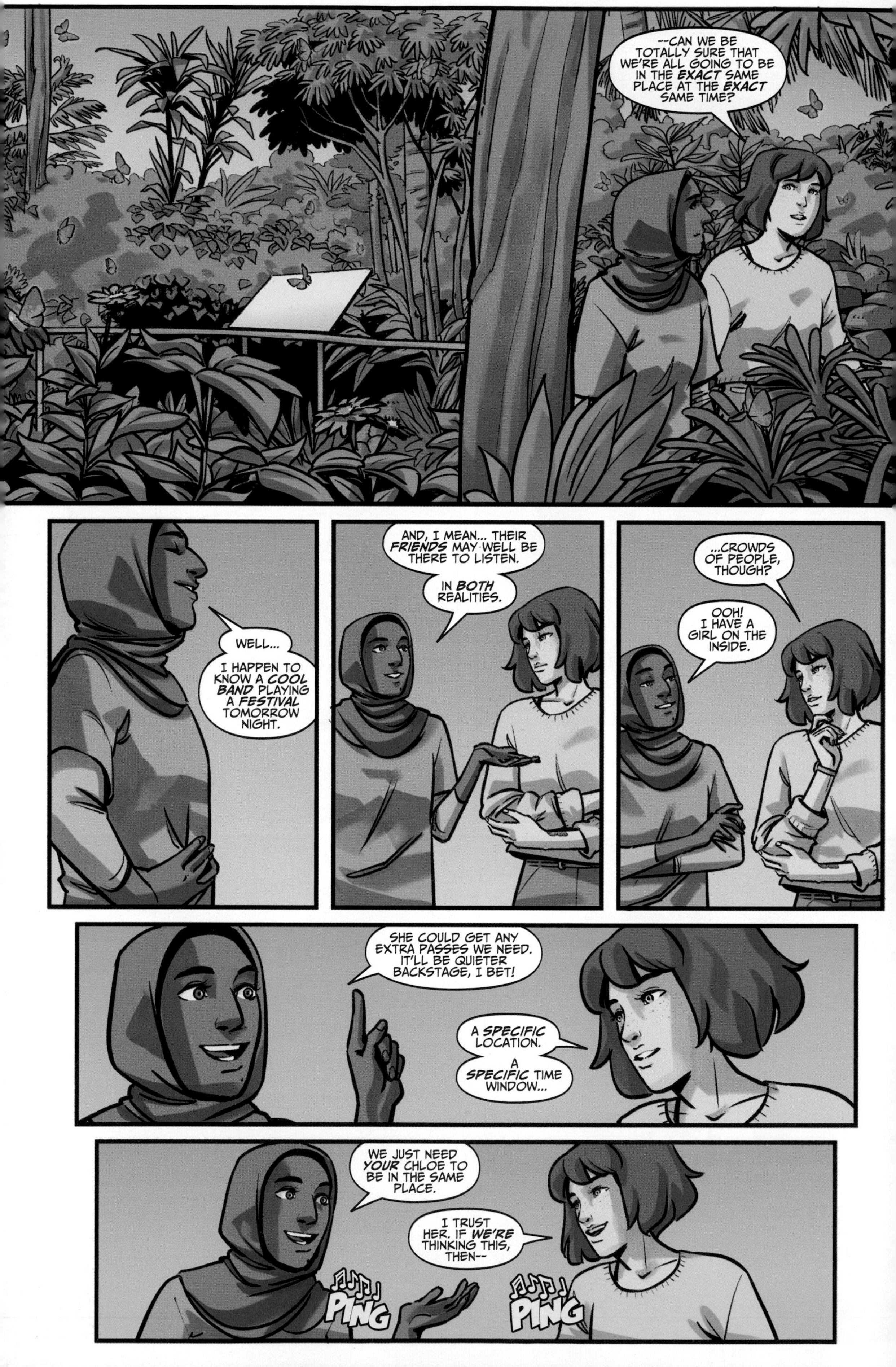
--CAN WE BE TOTALLY SURE THAT WE'RE ALL GOING TO BE IN THE *EXACT* SAME PLACE AT THE *EXACT* SAME TIME?
WELL...
I HAPPEN TO KNOW A *COOL BAND* PLAYING A *FESTIVAL* TOMORROW NIGHT.
AND, I MEAN... THEIR *FRIENDS* MAY WELL BE THERE TO LISTEN.
IN *BOTH* REALITIES.
...CROWDS OF PEOPLE, THOUGH?
OOH! I HAVE A GIRL ON THE INSIDE.
SHE COULD GET ANY EXTRA PASSES WE NEED. IT'LL BE QUIETER BACKSTAGE, I BET!
A *SPECIFIC* LOCATION.
A *SPECIFIC* TIME WINDOW...
WE JUST NEED *YOUR* CHLOE TO BE IN THE SAME PLACE.
I TRUST HER. IF *WE'RE* THINKING THIS, THEN--
PING
PING

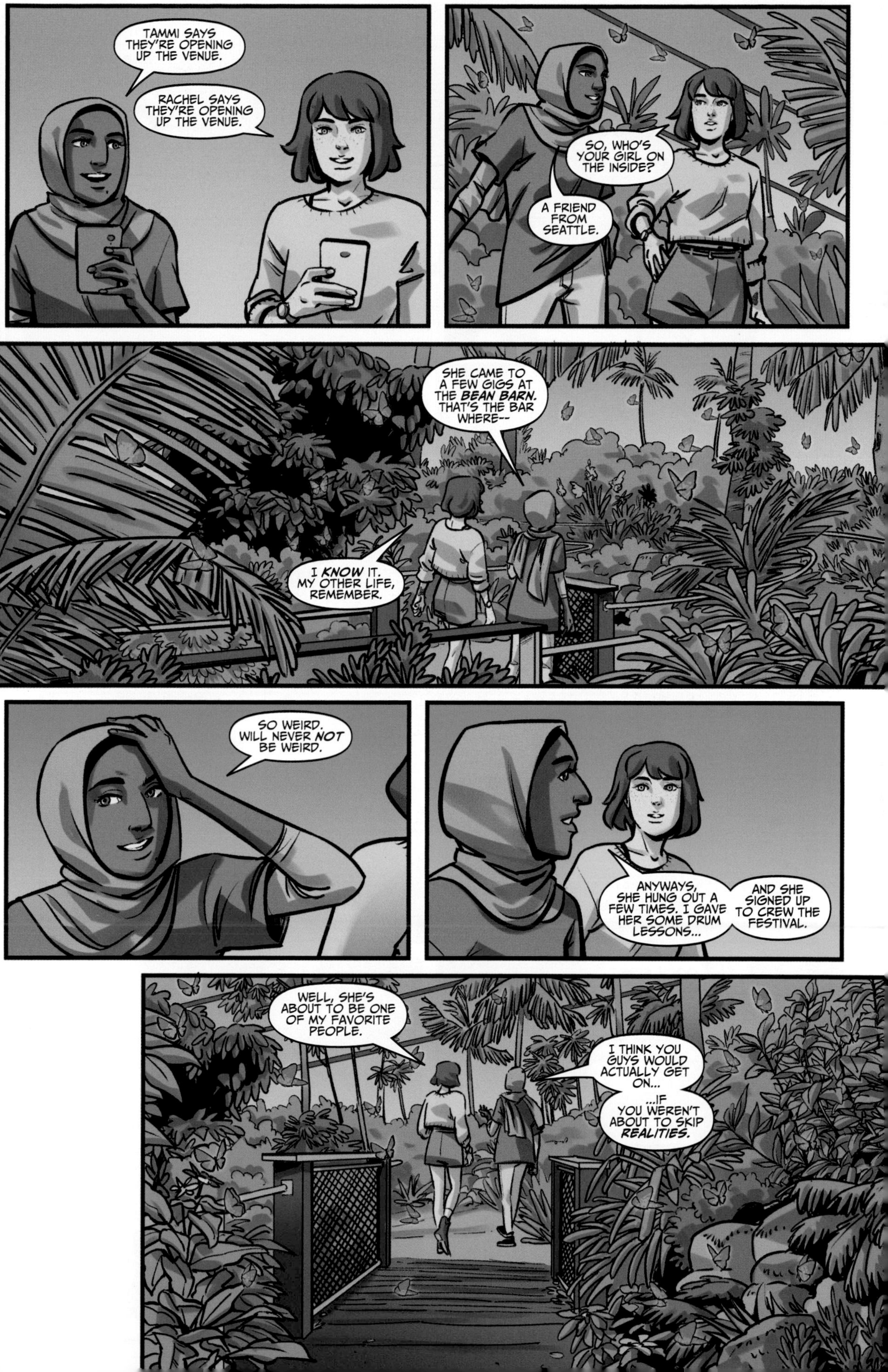
TAMMI SAYS THEY'RE OPENING UP THE VENUE.
RACHEL SAYS THEY'RE OPENING UP THE VENUE.
SO, WHO'S YOUR GIRL ON THE INSIDE?
A FRIEND FROM SEATTLE.
SHE CAME TO A FEW GIGS AT THE **BEAN BARN.** THAT'S THE BAR WHERE--
I **KNOW** IT. MY OTHER LIFE, REMEMBER.
SO WEIRD. WILL NEVER **NOT** BE WEIRD.
ANYWAYS, SHE HUNG OUT A FEW TIMES. I GAVE HER SOME DRUM LESSONS...
AND SHE SIGNED UP TO CREW THE FESTIVAL.
WELL, SHE'S ABOUT TO BE ONE OF MY FAVORITE PEOPLE.
I THINK YOU GUYS WOULD ACTUALLY GET ON...
...IF YOU WEREN'T ABOUT TO SKIP **REALITIES.**

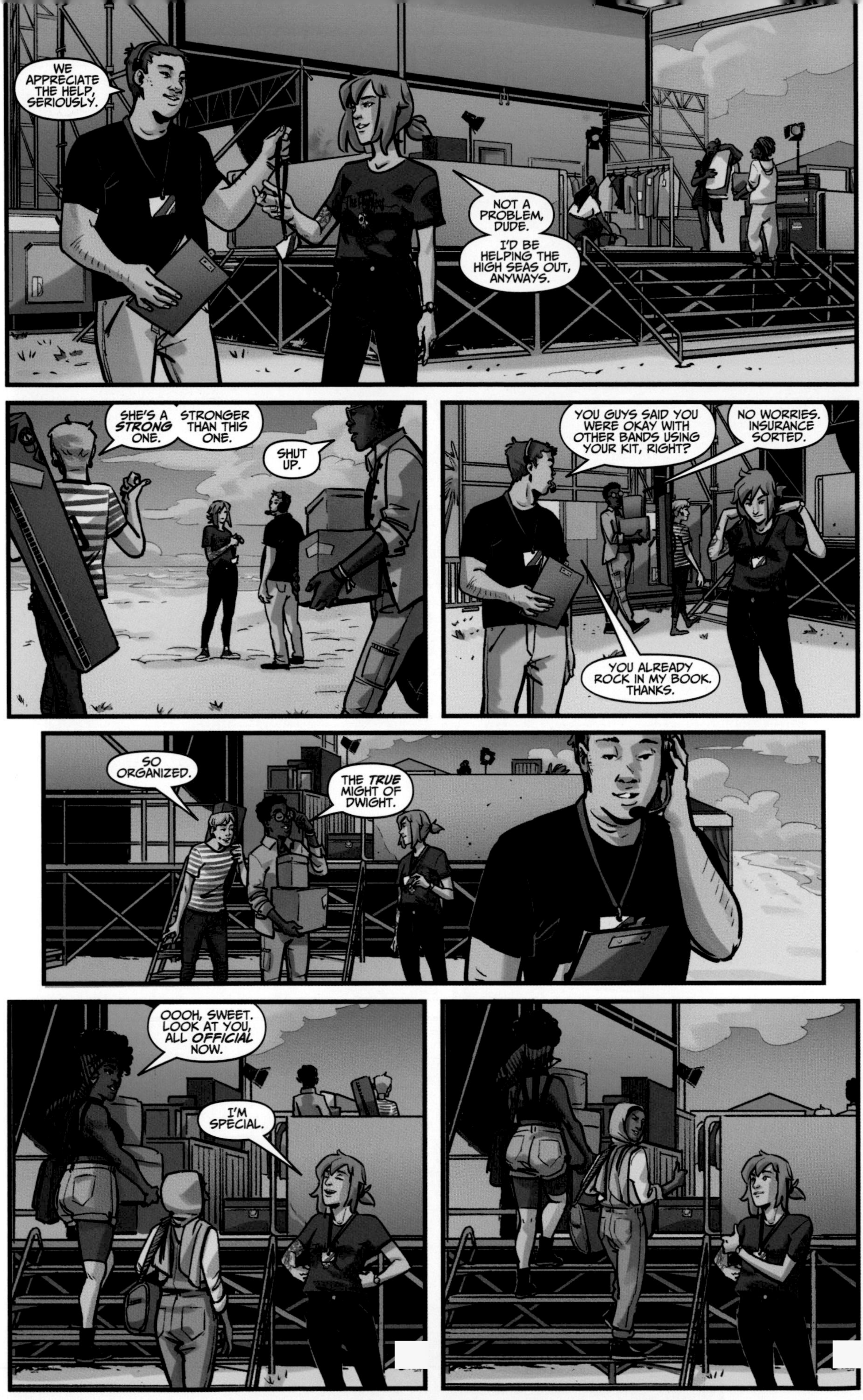
WE APPRECIATE THE HELP, SERIOUSLY.
NOT A PROBLEM, DUDE.
I'D BE HELPING THE HIGH SEAS OUT, ANYWAYS.
SHE'S A STRONG ONE.
STRONGER THAN THIS ONE.
SHUT UP.
YOU GUYS SAID YOU WERE OKAY WITH OTHER BANDS USING YOUR KIT, RIGHT?
NO WORRIES. INSURANCE SORTED.
YOU ALREADY ROCK IN MY BOOK. THANKS.
SO ORGANIZED.
THE TRUE MIGHT OF DWIGHT.
OOOH, SWEET. LOOK AT YOU, ALL OFFICIAL NOW.
I'M SPECIAL.

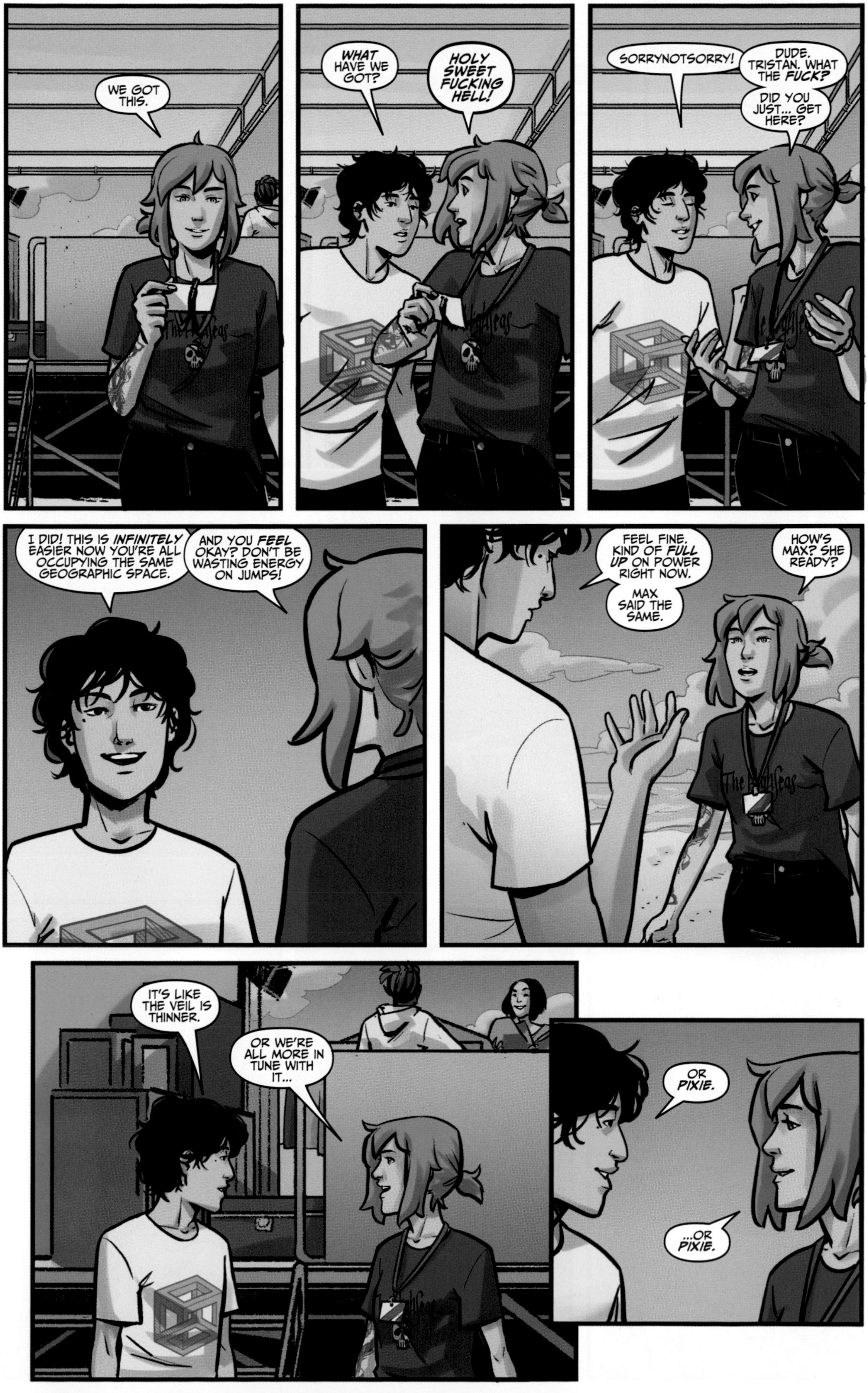
WE GOT THIS.
WHAT HAVE WE GOT?
HOLY SWEET FUCKING HELL!
SORRYNOTSORRY!
DUDE. TRISTAN. WHAT THE FUCK?
DID YOU JUST... GET HERE?
I DID! THIS IS INFINITELY EASIER NOW YOU'RE ALL OCCUPYING THE SAME GEOGRAPHIC SPACE.
AND YOU FEEL OKAY? DON'T BE WASTING ENERGY ON JUMPS!
FEEL FINE. KIND OF FULL UP ON POWER RIGHT NOW.
MAX SAID THE SAME.
HOW'S MAX? SHE READY?
IT'S LIKE THE VEIL IS THINNER.
OR WE'RE ALL MORE IN TUNE WITH IT...
OR PIXIE.
...OR PIXIE.

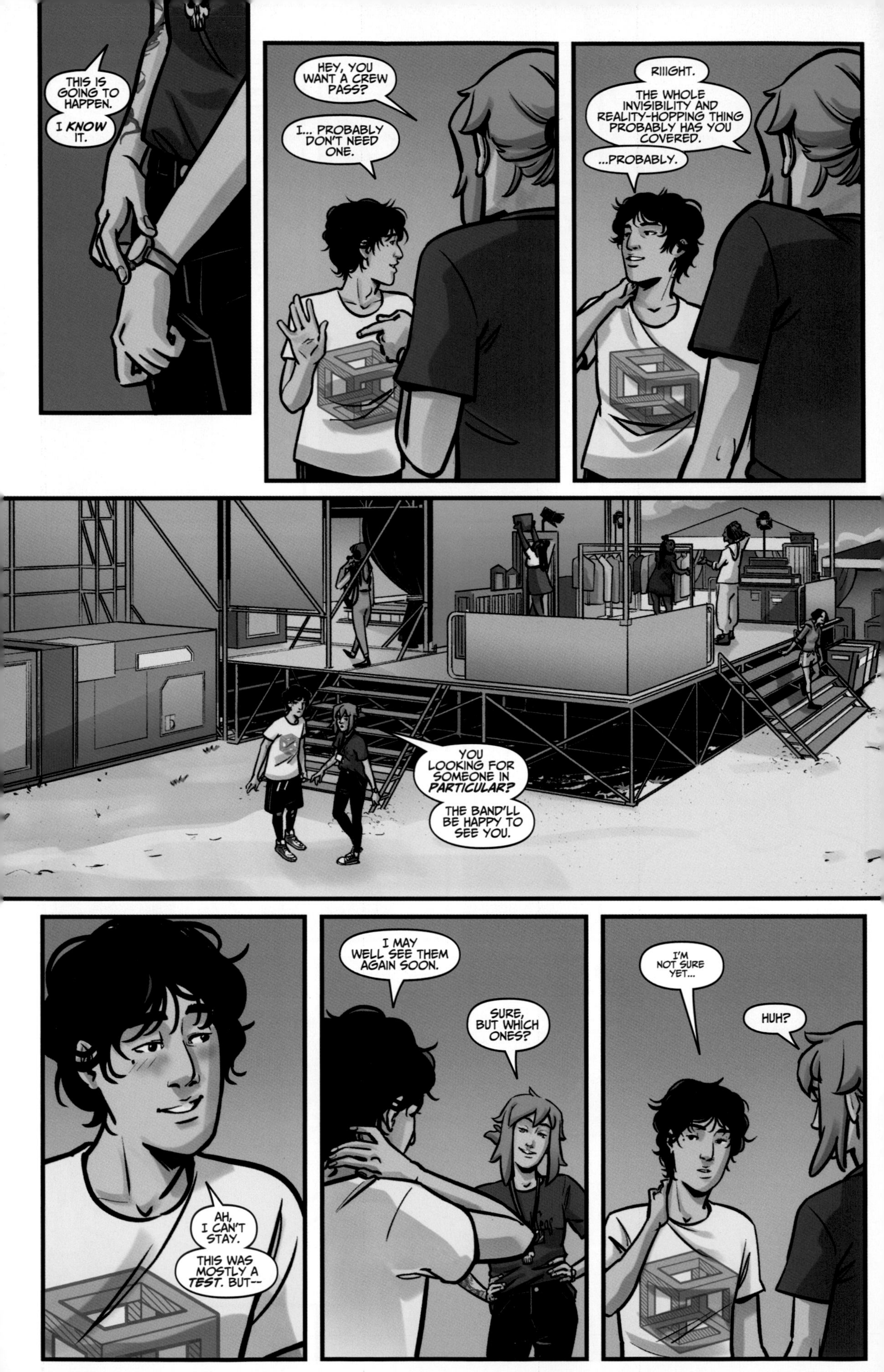

THIS IS GOING TO HAPPEN.
I *KNOW* IT.
HEY, YOU WANT A CREW PASS?
I... PROBABLY DON'T NEED ONE.
RIIIGHT.
THE WHOLE INVISIBILITY AND REALITY-HOPPING THING PROBABLY HAS YOU COVERED.
...PROBABLY.
YOU LOOKING FOR SOMEONE IN *PARTICULAR?*
THE BAND'LL BE HAPPY TO SEE YOU.
AH, I CAN'T STAY.
THIS WAS MOSTLY A *TEST.* BUT--
I MAY WELL SEE THEM AGAIN SOON.
SURE, BUT WHICH ONES?
I'M NOT SURE YET...
HUH?

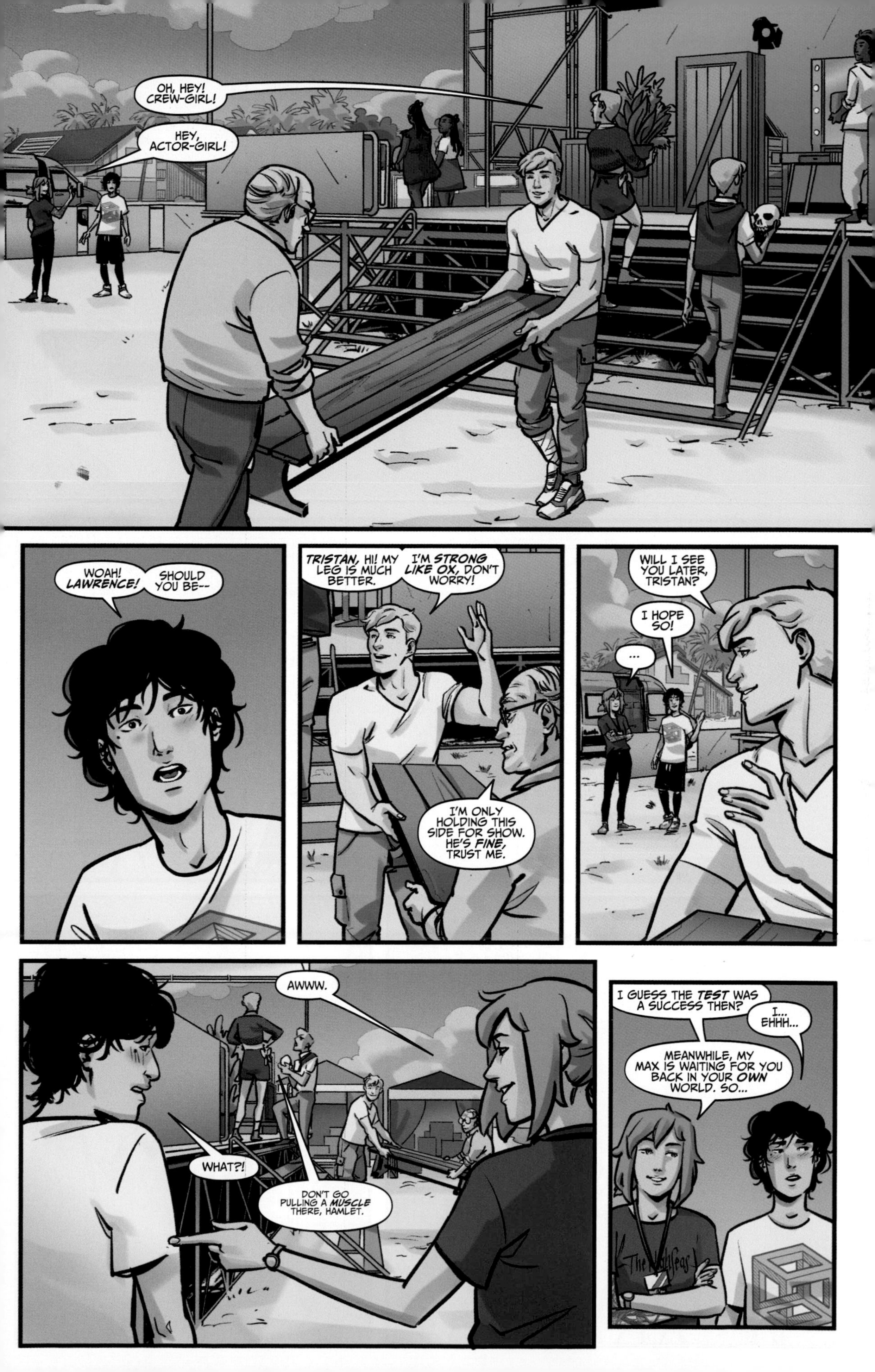
OH, HEY! CREW-GIRL!
HEY, ACTOR-GIRL!
WOAH! LAWRENCE!
SHOULD YOU BE--
TRISTAN, HI! MY LEG IS MUCH BETTER.
I'M STRONG LIKE OX, DON'T WORRY!
I'M ONLY HOLDING THIS SIDE FOR SHOW. HE'S FINE, TRUST ME.
WILL I SEE YOU LATER, TRISTAN?
I HOPE SO!
...
AWWW.
WHAT?!
DON'T GO PULLING A MUSCLE THERE, HAMLET.
I GUESS THE TEST WAS A SUCCESS THEN?
I... EHHH...
MEANWHILE, MY MAX IS WAITING FOR YOU BACK IN YOUR OWN WORLD. SO...

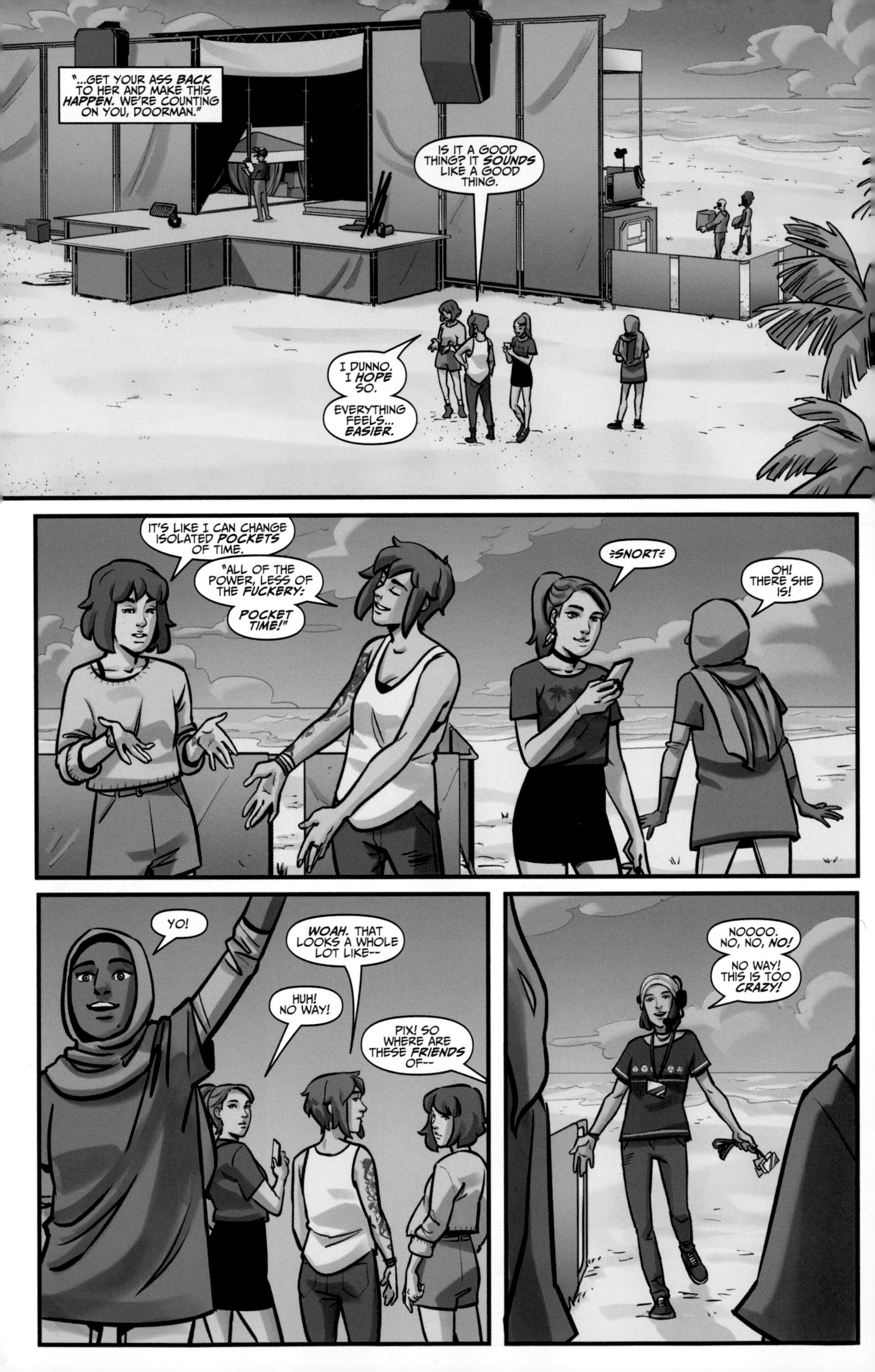
"...GET YOUR ASS BACK TO HER AND MAKE THIS HAPPEN. WE'RE COUNTING ON YOU, DOORMAN."
IS IT A GOOD THING? IT SOUNDS LIKE A GOOD THING.
I DUNNO. I HOPE SO.
EVERYTHING FEELS... EASIER.
IT'S LIKE I CAN CHANGE ISOLATED POCKETS OF TIME.
"ALL OF THE POWER, LESS OF THE FUCKERY:
POCKET TIME!"
SNORT
OH! THERE SHE IS!
YO!
WOAH. THAT LOOKS A WHOLE LOT LIKE--
HUH! NO WAY!
PIX! SO WHERE ARE THESE FRIENDS OF--
NOOOO. NO, NO, NO!
NO WAY! THIS IS TOO CRAZY!

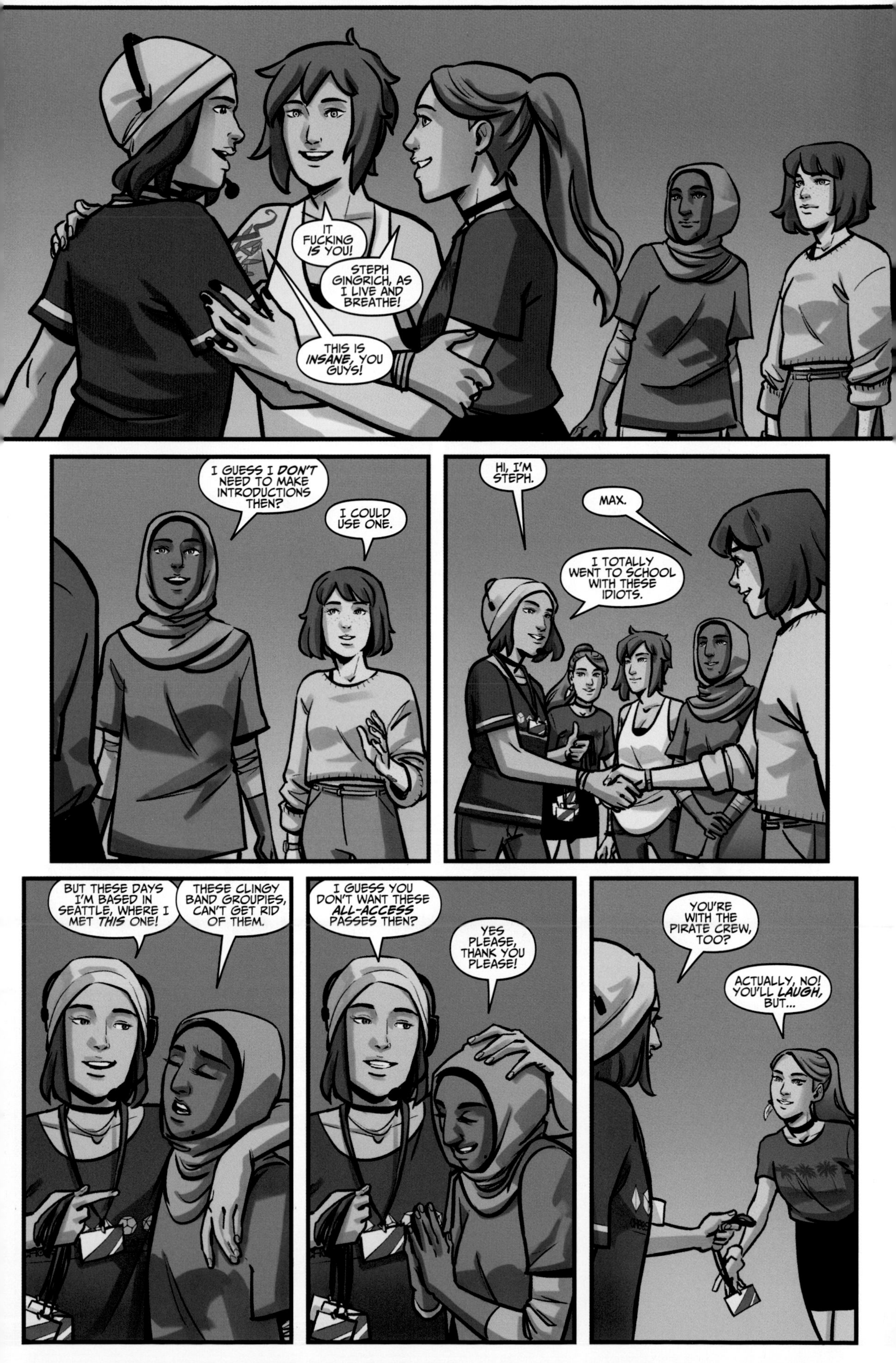
IT FUCKING IS YOU!
STEPH GINGRICH, AS I LIVE AND BREATHE!
THIS IS INSANE, YOU GUYS!
I GUESS I DON'T NEED TO MAKE INTRODUCTIONS THEN?
I COULD USE ONE.
HI, I'M STEPH.
MAX.
I TOTALLY WENT TO SCHOOL WITH THESE IDIOTS.
BUT THESE DAYS I'M BASED IN SEATTLE, WHERE I MET THIS ONE!
THESE CLINGY BAND GROUPIES, CAN'T GET RID OF THEM.
I GUESS YOU DON'T WANT THESE ALL-ACCESS PASSES THEN?
YES PLEASE, THANK YOU PLEASE!
YOU'RE WITH THE PIRATE CREW, TOO?
ACTUALLY, NO! YOU'LL LAUGH, BUT...

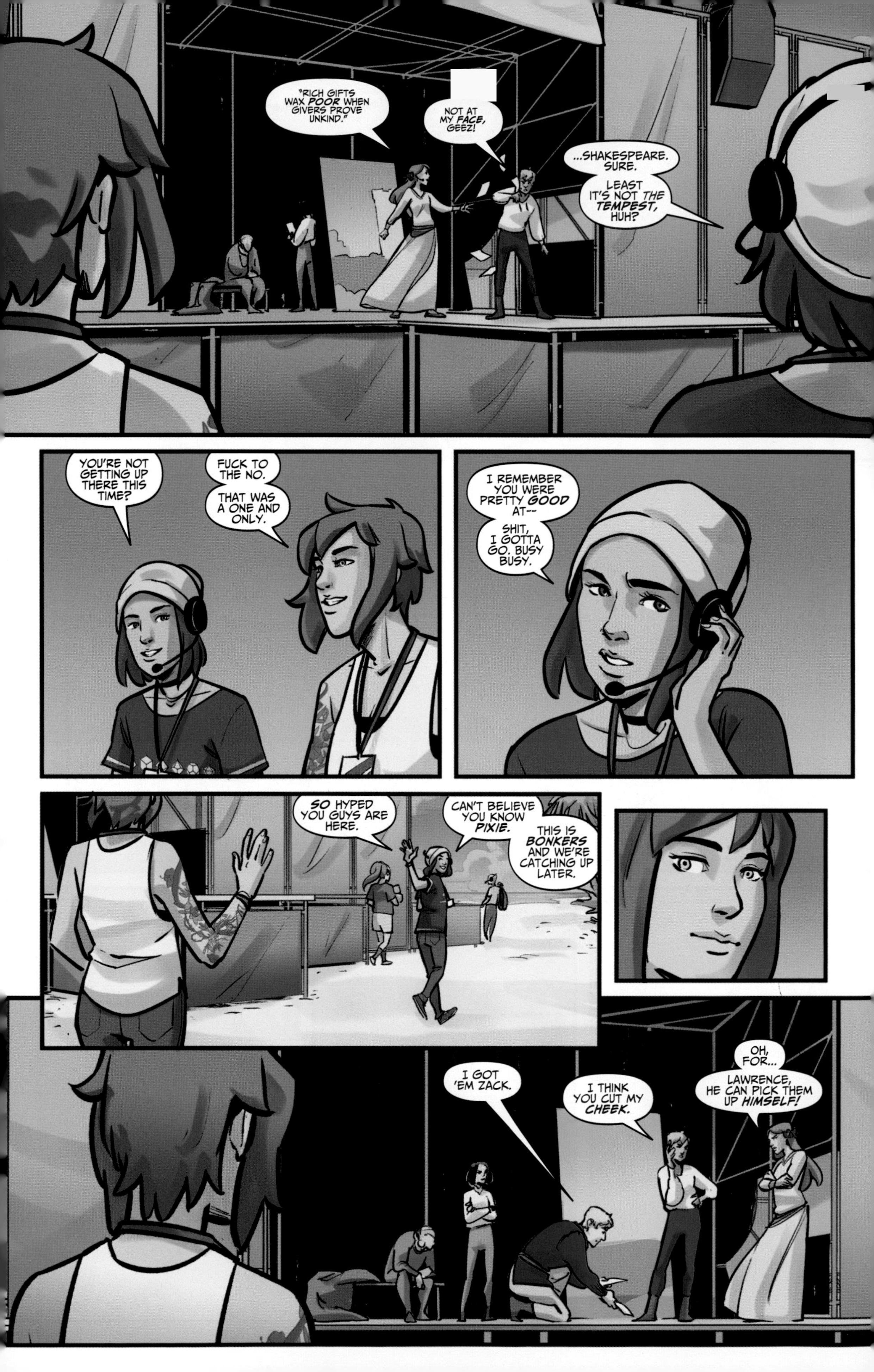

"RICH GIFTS WAX POOR WHEN GIVERS PROVE UNKIND."
NOT AT MY FACE, GEEZ!
...SHAKESPEARE. SURE.
LEAST IT'S NOT THE TEMPEST, HUH?
YOU'RE NOT GETTING UP THERE THIS TIME?
FUCK TO THE NO.
THAT WAS A ONE AND ONLY.
I REMEMBER YOU WERE PRETTY GOOD AT--
SHIT, I GOTTA GO. BUSY BUSY.
SO HYPED YOU GUYS ARE HERE.
CAN'T BELIEVE YOU KNOW PIXIE.
THIS IS BONKERS AND WE'RE CATCHING UP LATER.
I GOT 'EM ZACK.
I THINK YOU CUT MY CHEEK.
OH, FOR...
LAWRENCE, HE CAN PICK THEM UP HIMSELF!

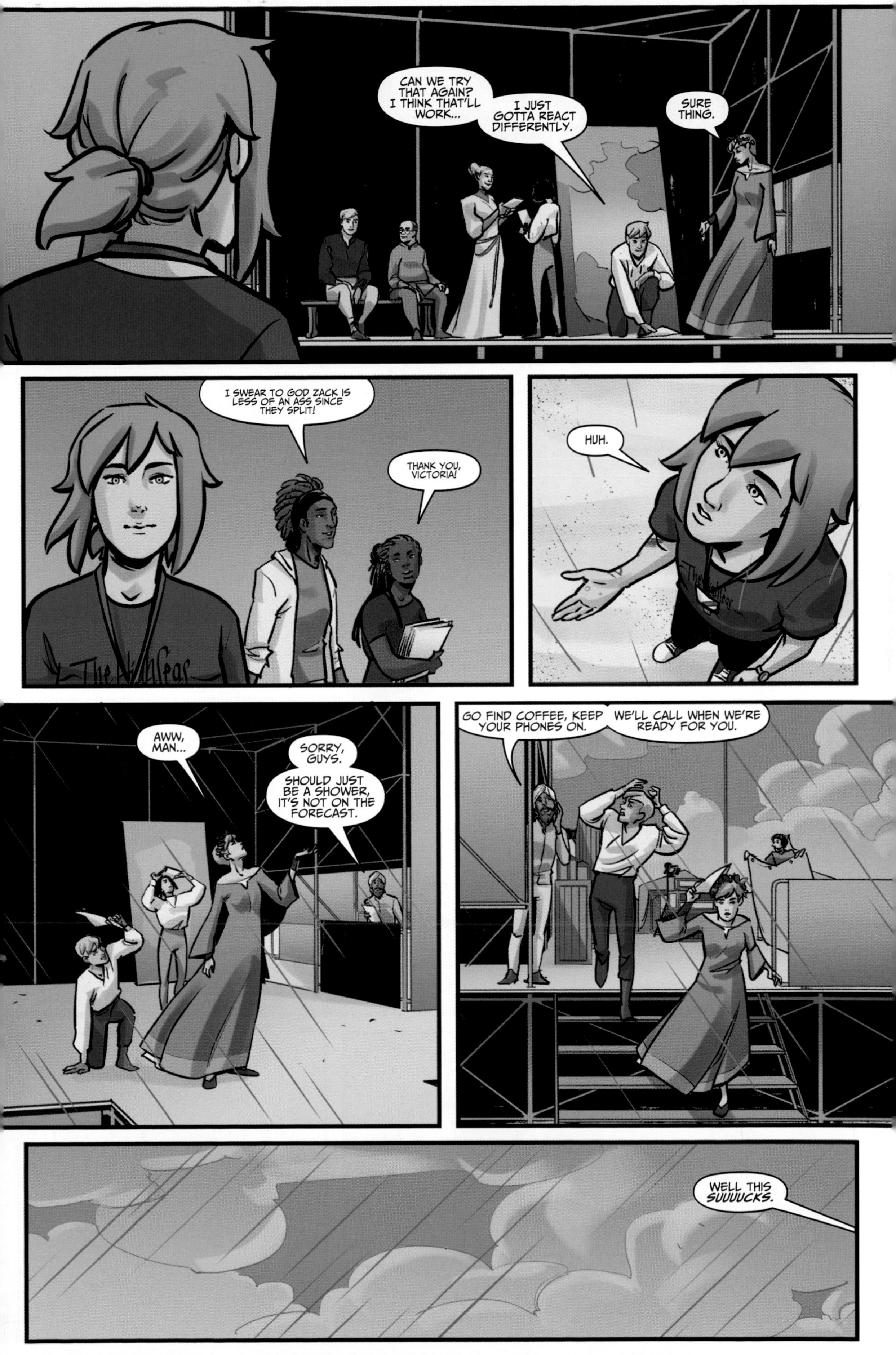
CAN WE TRY THAT AGAIN? I THINK THAT'LL WORK...
I JUST GOTTA REACT DIFFERENTLY.
SURE THING.
I SWEAR TO GOD ZACK IS LESS OF AN ASS SINCE THEY SPLIT!
THANK YOU, VICTORIA!
HUH.
AWW, MAN...
SORRY, GUYS.
SHOULD JUST BE A SHOWER, IT'S NOT ON THE FORECAST.
GO FIND COFFEE, KEEP YOUR PHONES ON.
WE'LL CALL WHEN WE'RE READY FOR YOU.
WELL THIS *SUUUUCKS.*

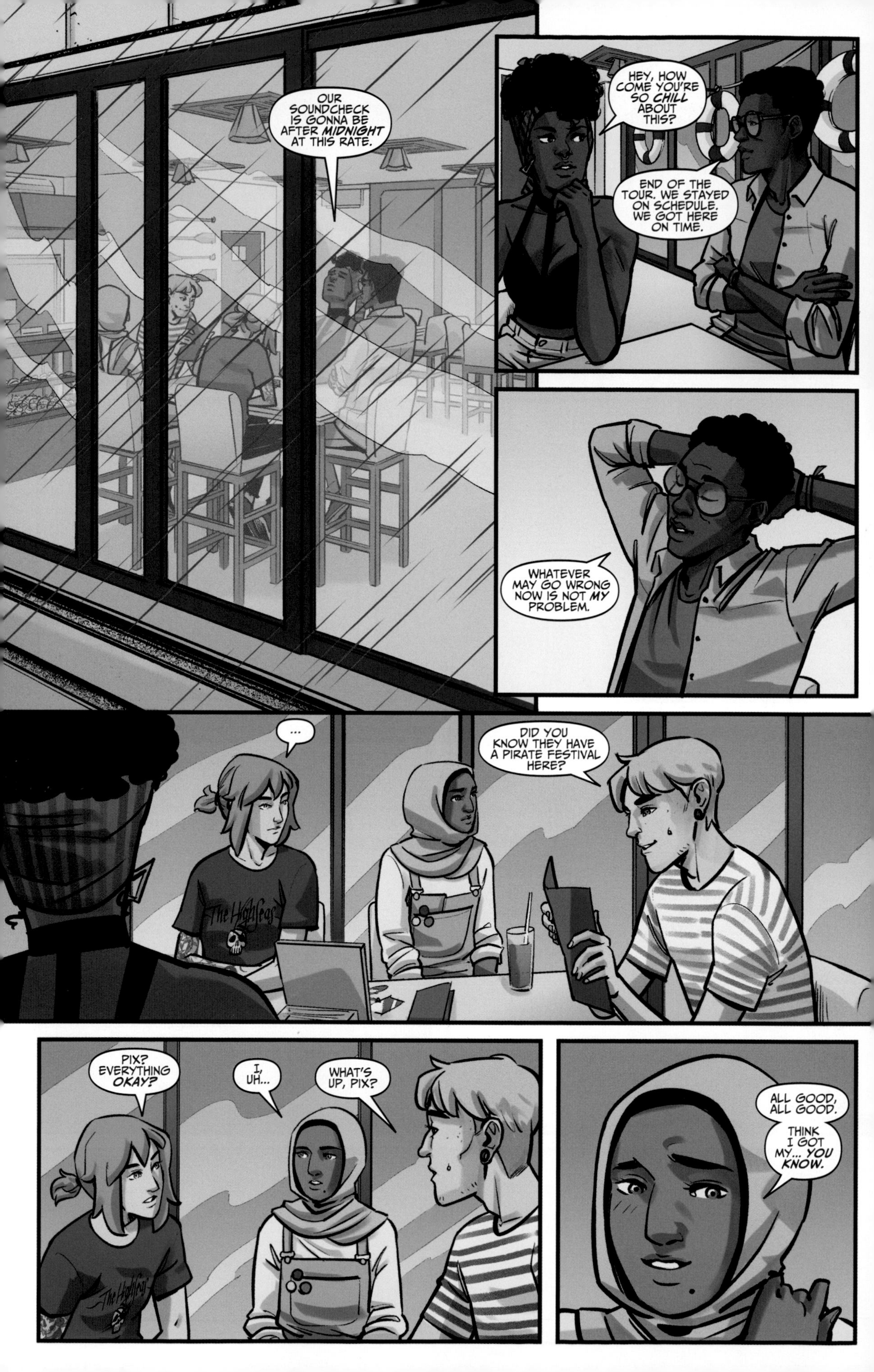
OUR SOUNDCHECK IS GONNA BE AFTER MIDNIGHT AT THIS RATE.
HEY, HOW COME YOU'RE SO CHILL ABOUT THIS?
END OF THE TOUR. WE STAYED ON SCHEDULE. WE GOT HERE ON TIME.
WHATEVER MAY GO WRONG NOW IS NOT MY PROBLEM.
...
DID YOU KNOW THEY HAVE A PIRATE FESTIVAL HERE?
The High Seas
PIX? EVERYTHING OKAY?
I, UH...
WHAT'S UP, PIX?
ALL GOOD, ALL GOOD.
THINK I GOT MY... YOU KNOW.

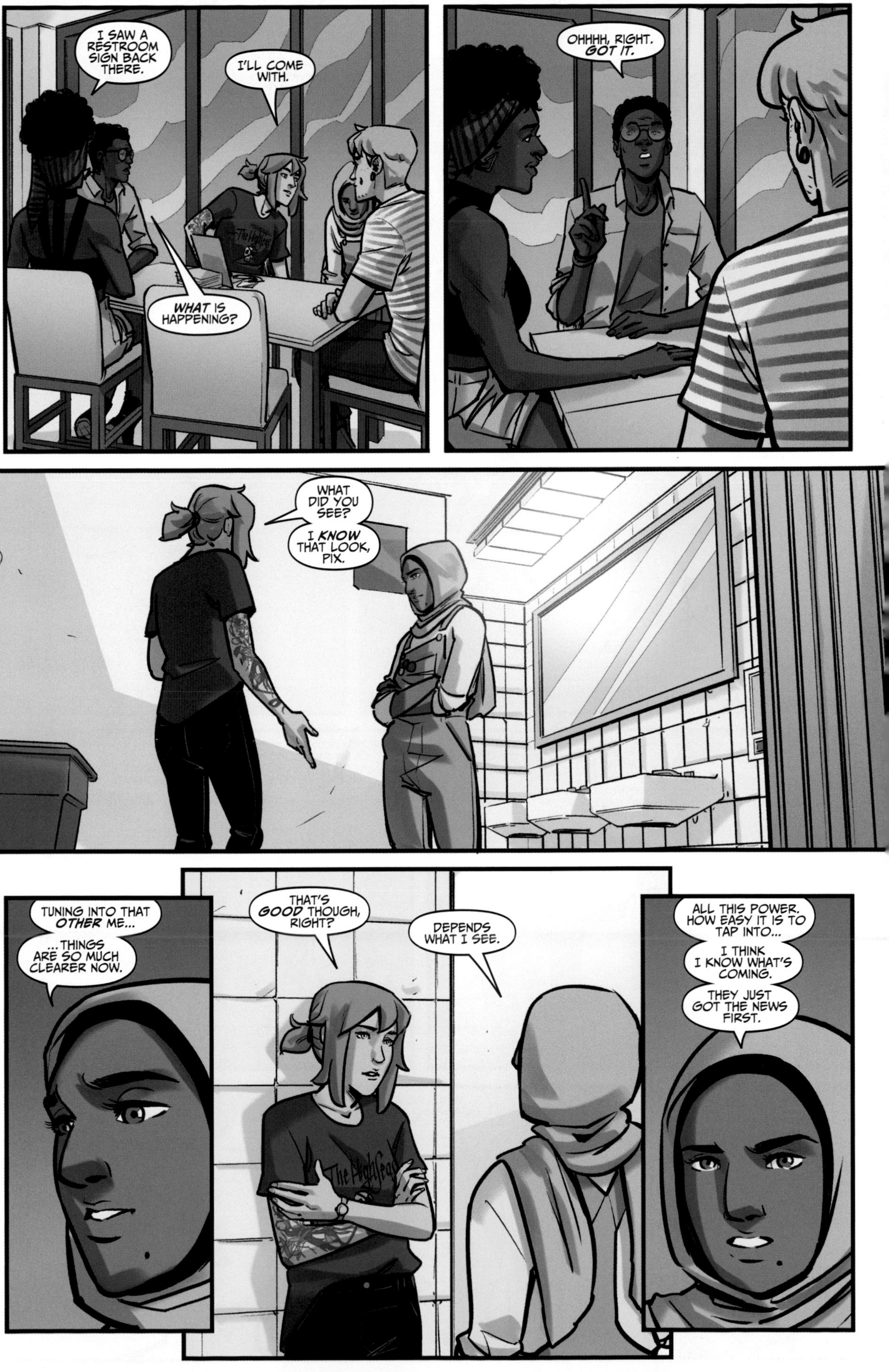
I SAW A RESTROOM SIGN BACK THERE.
I'LL COME WITH.
WHAT IS HAPPENING?
OHHHH, RIGHT. GOT IT.
WHAT DID YOU SEE?
I KNOW THAT LOOK, PIX.
TUNING INTO THAT OTHER ME...
...THINGS ARE SO MUCH CLEARER NOW.
THAT'S GOOD THOUGH, RIGHT?
DEPENDS WHAT I SEE.
ALL THIS POWER. HOW EASY IT IS TO TAP INTO...
I THINK I KNOW WHAT'S COMING.
THEY JUST GOT THE NEWS FIRST.

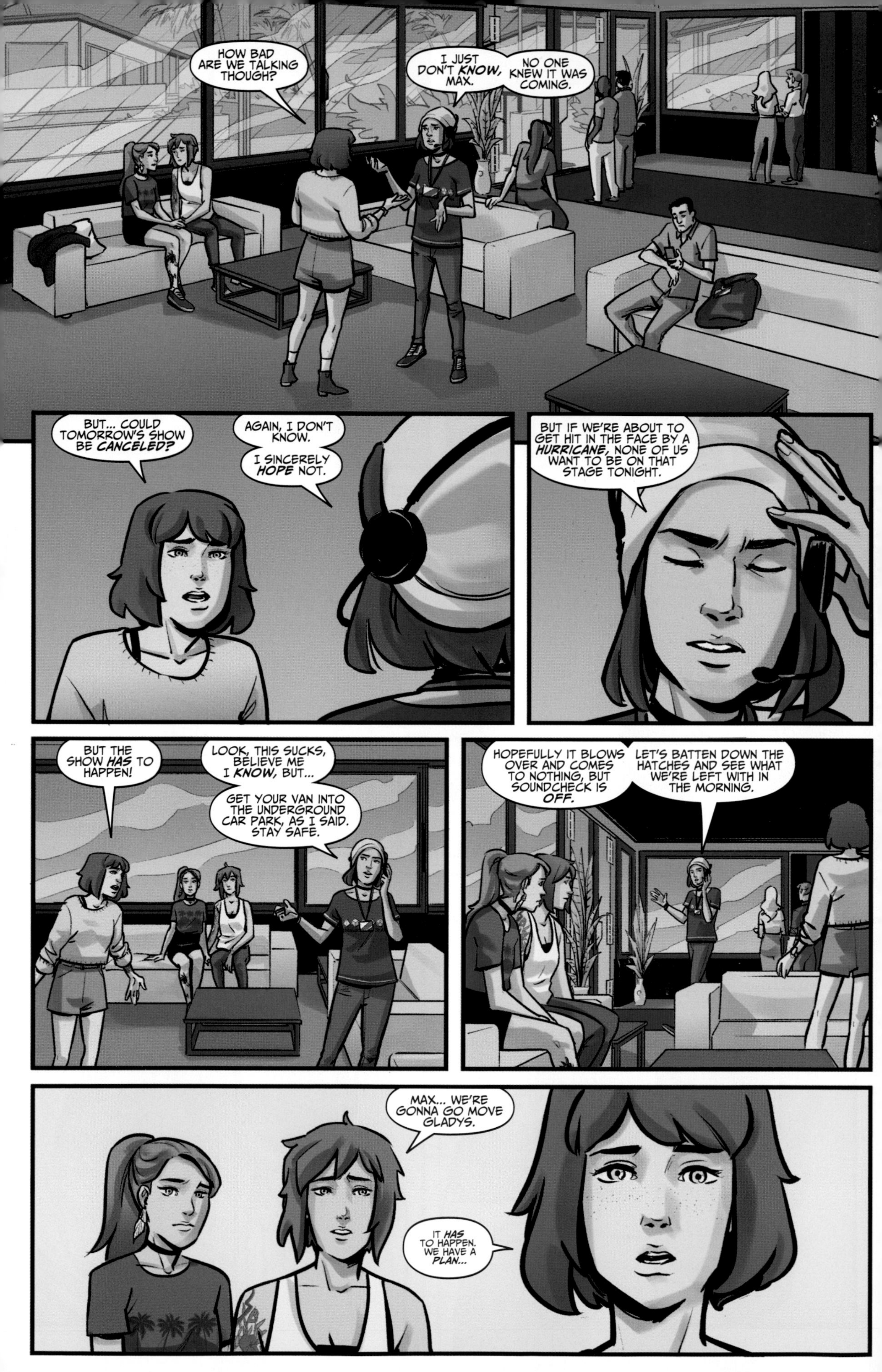
HOW BAD ARE WE TALKING THOUGH?
I JUST DON'T KNOW, MAX.
NO ONE KNEW IT WAS COMING.
BUT... COULD TOMORROW'S SHOW BE CANCELED?
AGAIN, I DON'T KNOW.
I SINCERELY HOPE NOT.
BUT IF WE'RE ABOUT TO GET HIT IN THE FACE BY A HURRICANE, NONE OF US WANT TO BE ON THAT STAGE TONIGHT.
BUT THE SHOW HAS TO HAPPEN!
LOOK, THIS SUCKS, BELIEVE ME I KNOW, BUT...
GET YOUR VAN INTO THE UNDERGROUND CAR PARK, AS I SAID. STAY SAFE.
HOPEFULLY IT BLOWS OVER AND COMES TO NOTHING, BUT SOUNDCHECK IS OFF.
LET'S BATTEN DOWN THE HATCHES AND SEE WHAT WE'RE LEFT WITH IN THE MORNING.
MAX... WE'RE GONNA GO MOVE GLADYS.
IT HAS TO HAPPEN. WE HAVE A PLAN...

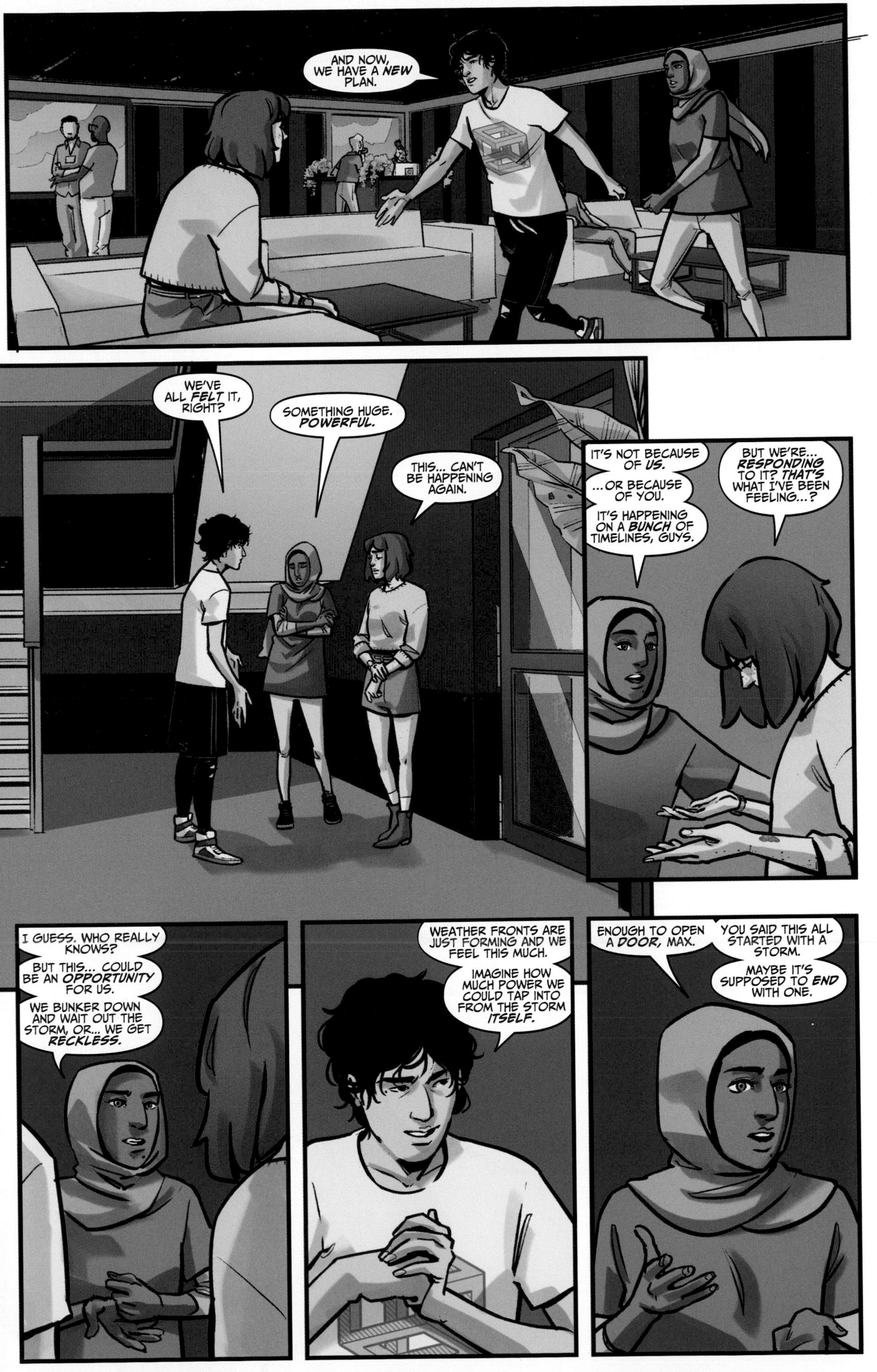
AND NOW, WE HAVE A *NEW* PLAN.
WE'VE ALL *FELT* IT, RIGHT?
SOMETHING HUGE. ***POWERFUL.***
THIS... CAN'T BE HAPPENING AGAIN.
IT'S NOT BECAUSE OF *US.*
...OR BECAUSE OF YOU.
IT'S HAPPENING ON A *BUNCH* OF TIMELINES, GUYS.
BUT WE'RE... ***RESPONDING*** TO IT? ***THAT'S*** WHAT I'VE BEEN FEELING...?
I GUESS. WHO REALLY KNOWS?
BUT THIS... COULD BE AN *OPPORTUNITY* FOR US.
WE BUNKER DOWN AND WAIT OUT THE STORM, OR... WE GET ***RECKLESS.***
WEATHER FRONTS ARE JUST FORMING AND WE FEEL THIS MUCH.
IMAGINE HOW MUCH POWER WE COULD TAP INTO FROM THE STORM *ITSELF.*
ENOUGH TO OPEN A *DOOR,* MAX.
YOU SAID THIS ALL STARTED WITH A STORM.
MAYBE IT'S SUPPOSED TO *END* WITH ONE.

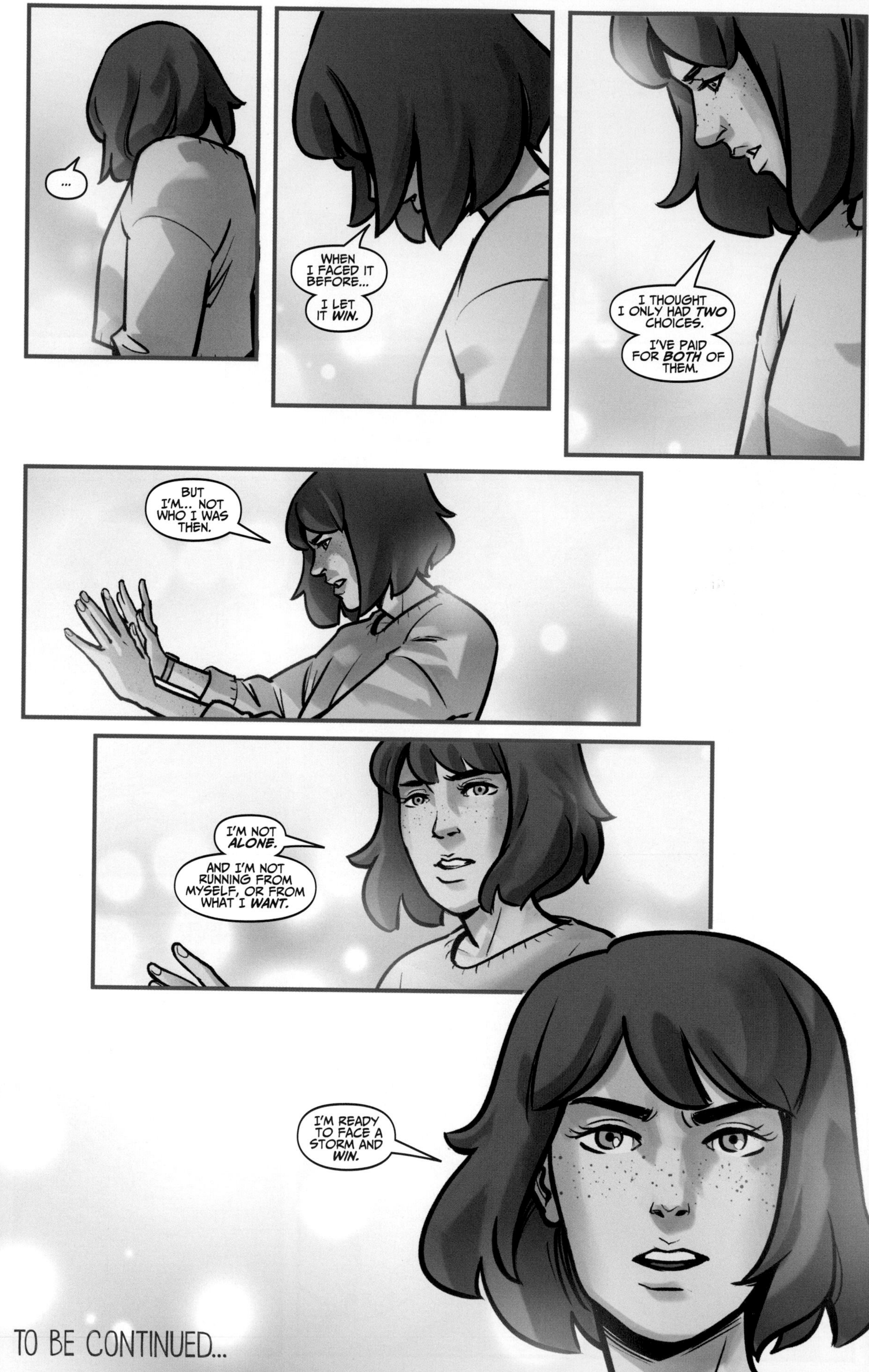
...
WHEN I FACED IT BEFORE...
I LET IT WIN.
I THOUGHT I ONLY HAD TWO CHOICES.
I'VE PAID FOR BOTH OF THEM.
BUT I'M... NOT WHO I WAS THEN.
I'M NOT ALONE.
AND I'M NOT RUNNING FROM MYSELF, OR FROM WHAT I WANT.
I'M READY TO FACE A STORM AND WIN.
TO BE CONTINUED...

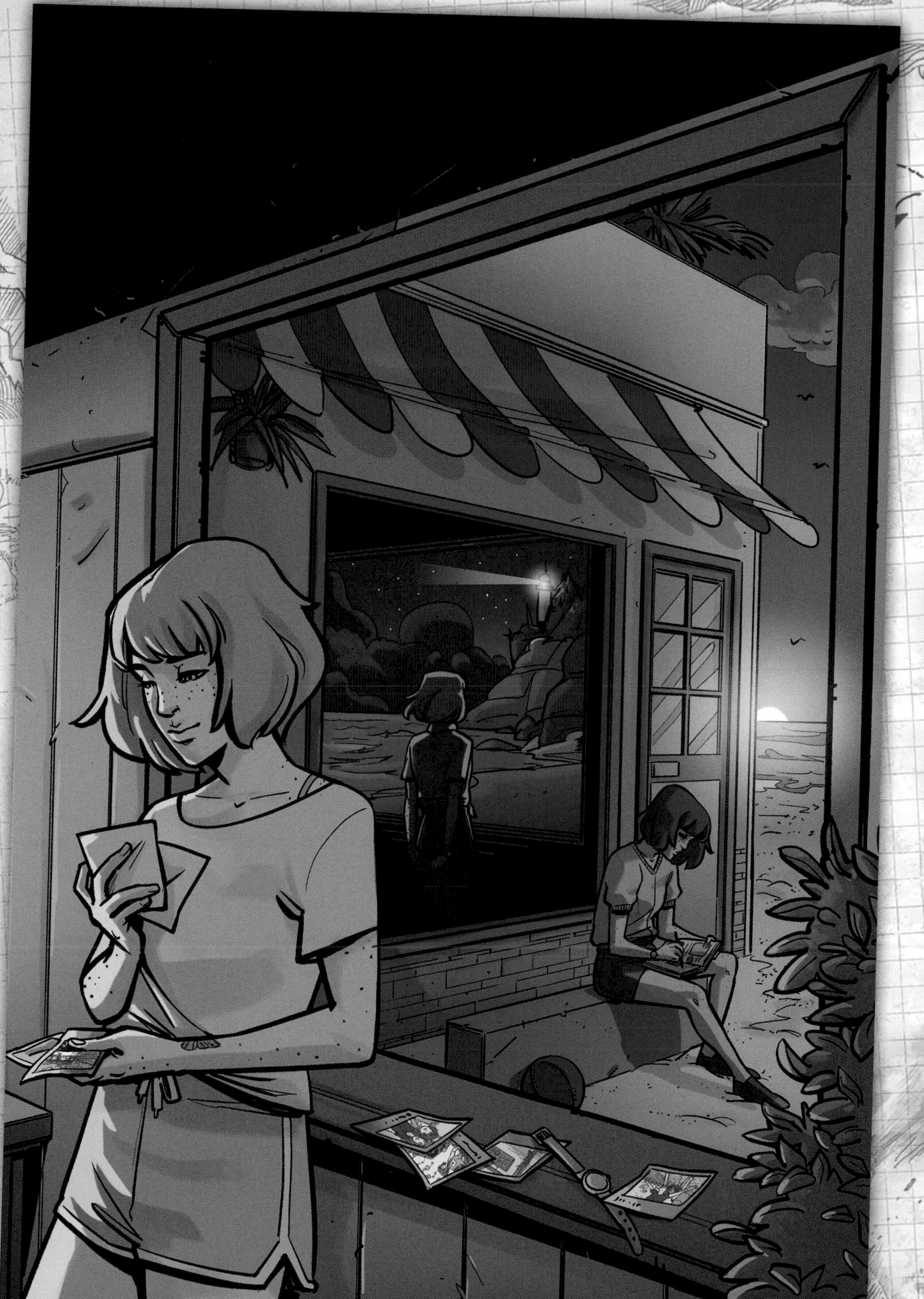

COVER #2B
BY CLAUDIA LEONARDI & ANDREA IZZO

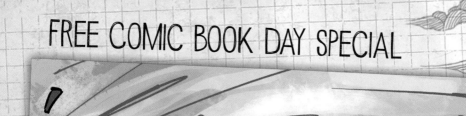

FREE COMIC BOOK DAY SPECIAL

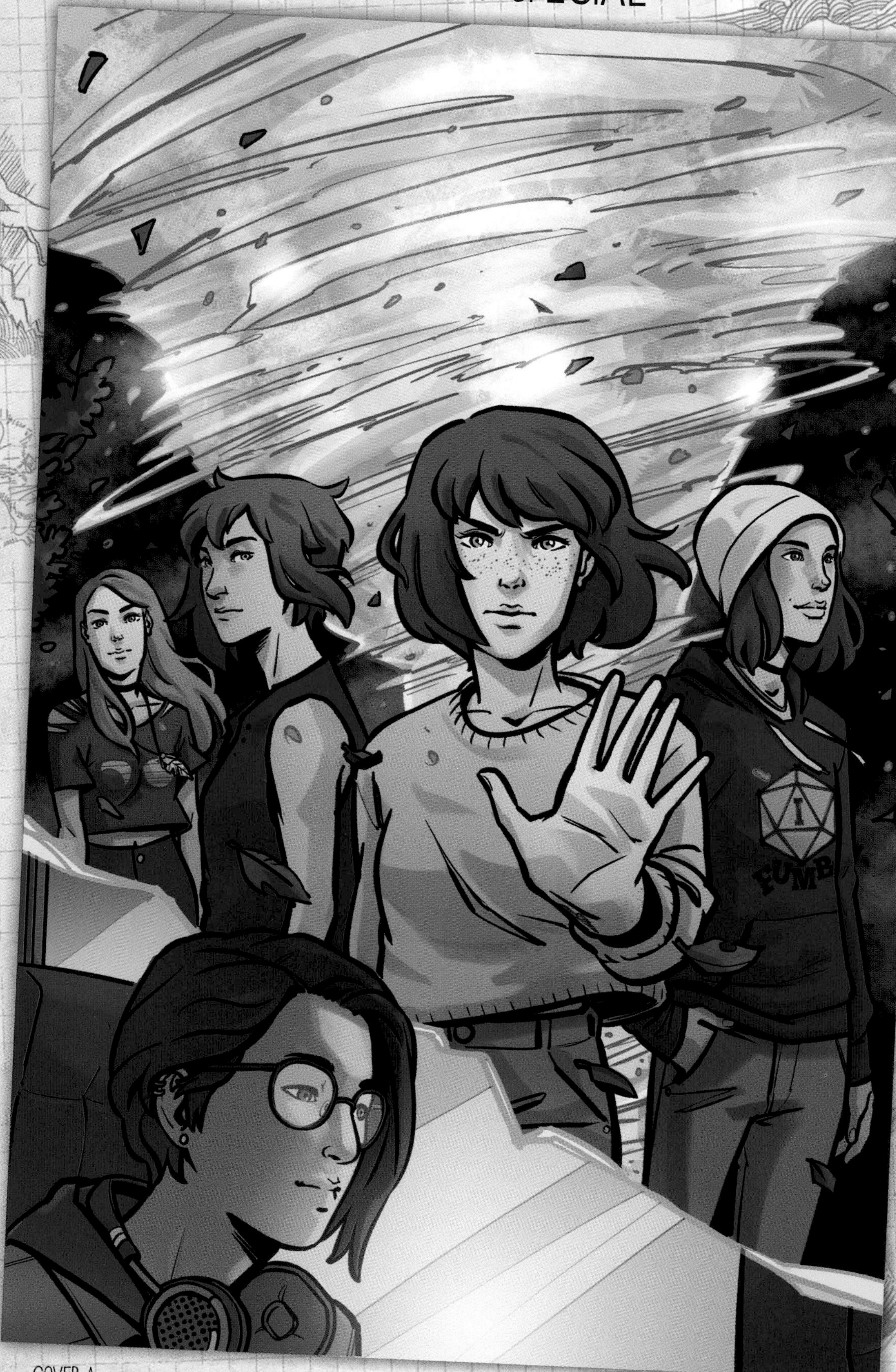

FUMB

COVER A
BY CLAUDIA LEONARDI & ANDREA IZZO

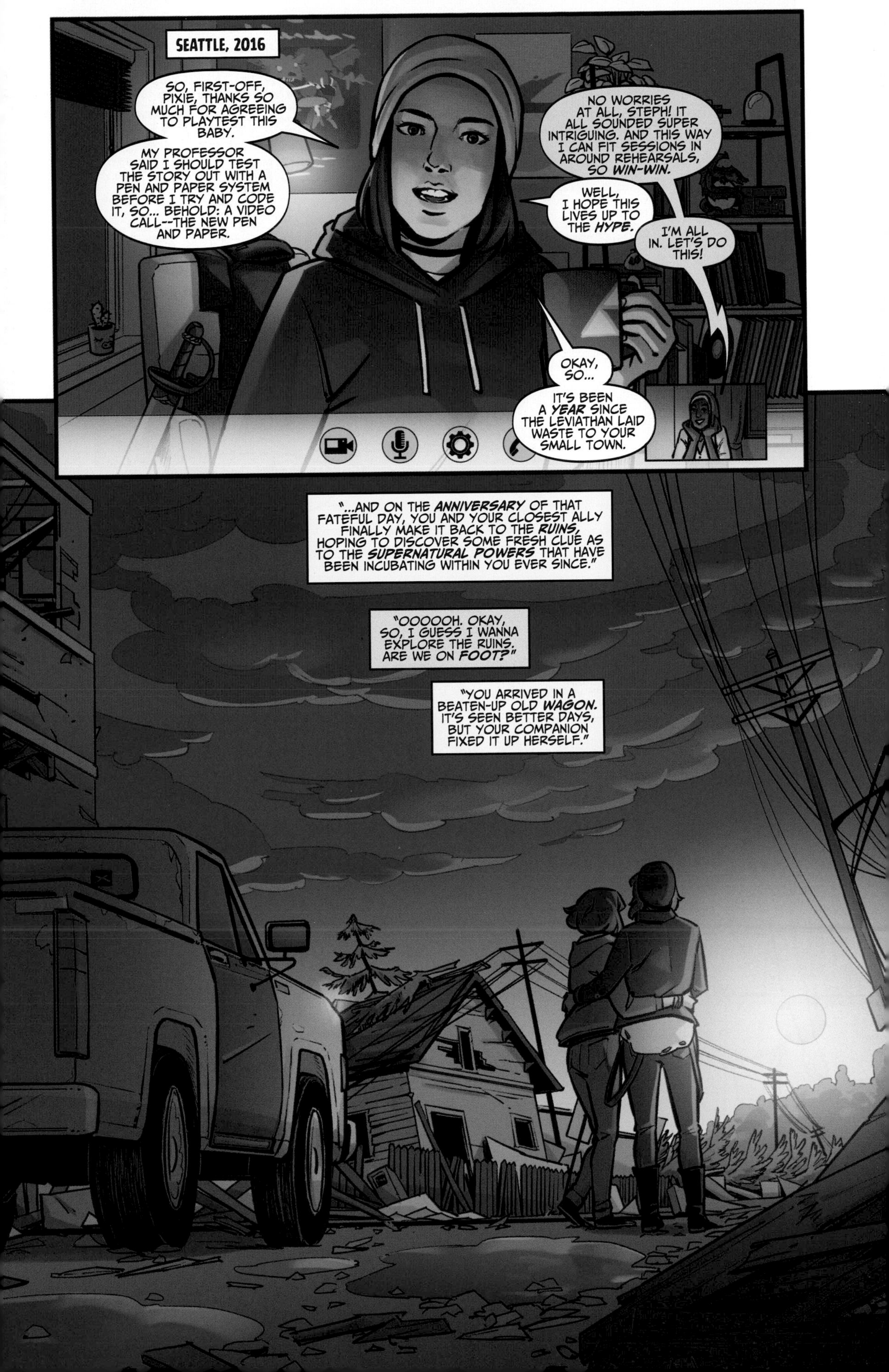
SEATTLE, 2016
SO, FIRST-OFF, PIXIE, THANKS SO MUCH FOR AGREEING TO PLAYTEST THIS BABY.
MY PROFESSOR SAID I SHOULD TEST THE STORY OUT WITH A PEN AND PAPER SYSTEM BEFORE I TRY AND CODE IT, SO... BEHOLD: A VIDEO CALL--THE NEW PEN AND PAPER.
NO WORRIES AT ALL, STEPH! IT ALL SOUNDED SUPER INTRIGUING. AND THIS WAY I CAN FIT SESSIONS IN AROUND REHEARSALS, SO WIN-WIN.
WELL, I HOPE THIS LIVES UP TO THE HYPE.
I'M ALL IN. LET'S DO THIS!
OKAY, SO...
IT'S BEEN A YEAR SINCE THE LEVIATHAN LAID WASTE TO YOUR SMALL TOWN.
"...AND ON THE ANNIVERSARY OF THAT FATEFUL DAY, YOU AND YOUR CLOSEST ALLY FINALLY MAKE IT BACK TO THE RUINS, HOPING TO DISCOVER SOME FRESH CLUE AS TO THE SUPERNATURAL POWERS THAT HAVE BEEN INCUBATING WITHIN YOU EVER SINCE."
"OOOOOH. OKAY, SO, I GUESS I WANNA EXPLORE THE RUINS. ARE WE ON FOOT?"
"YOU ARRIVED IN A BEATEN-UP OLD WAGON. IT'S SEEN BETTER DAYS, BUT YOUR COMPANION FIXED IT UP HERSELF."

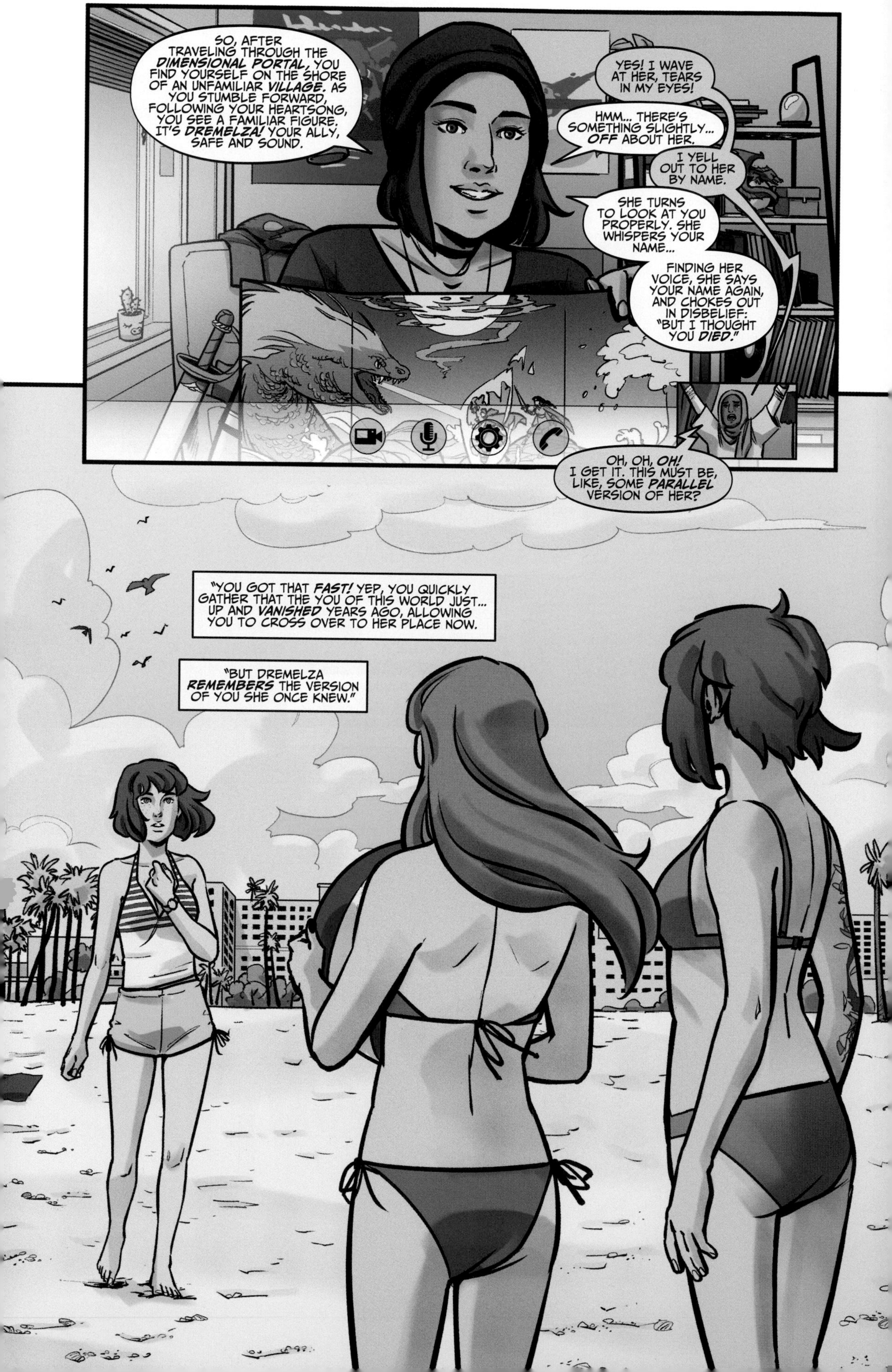
SO, AFTER TRAVELING THROUGH THE DIMENSIONAL PORTAL, YOU FIND YOURSELF ON THE SHORE OF AN UNFAMILIAR VILLAGE. AS YOU STUMBLE FORWARD, FOLLOWING YOUR HEARTSONG, YOU SEE A FAMILIAR FIGURE. IT'S DREMELZA! YOUR ALLY, SAFE AND SOUND.
YES! I WAVE AT HER, TEARS IN MY EYES!
HMM... THERE'S SOMETHING SLIGHTLY... OFF ABOUT HER.
I YELL OUT TO HER BY NAME.
SHE TURNS TO LOOK AT YOU PROPERLY. SHE WHISPERS YOUR NAME...
FINDING HER VOICE, SHE SAYS YOUR NAME AGAIN, AND CHOKES OUT IN DISBELIEF: "BUT I THOUGHT YOU DIED."
OH, OH, OH! I GET IT. THIS MUST BE, LIKE, SOME PARALLEL VERSION OF HER?
"YOU GOT THAT FAST! YEP, YOU QUICKLY GATHER THAT THE YOU OF THIS WORLD JUST... UP AND VANISHED YEARS AGO, ALLOWING YOU TO CROSS OVER TO HER PLACE NOW.
"BUT DREMELZA REMEMBERS THE VERSION OF YOU SHE ONCE KNEW."

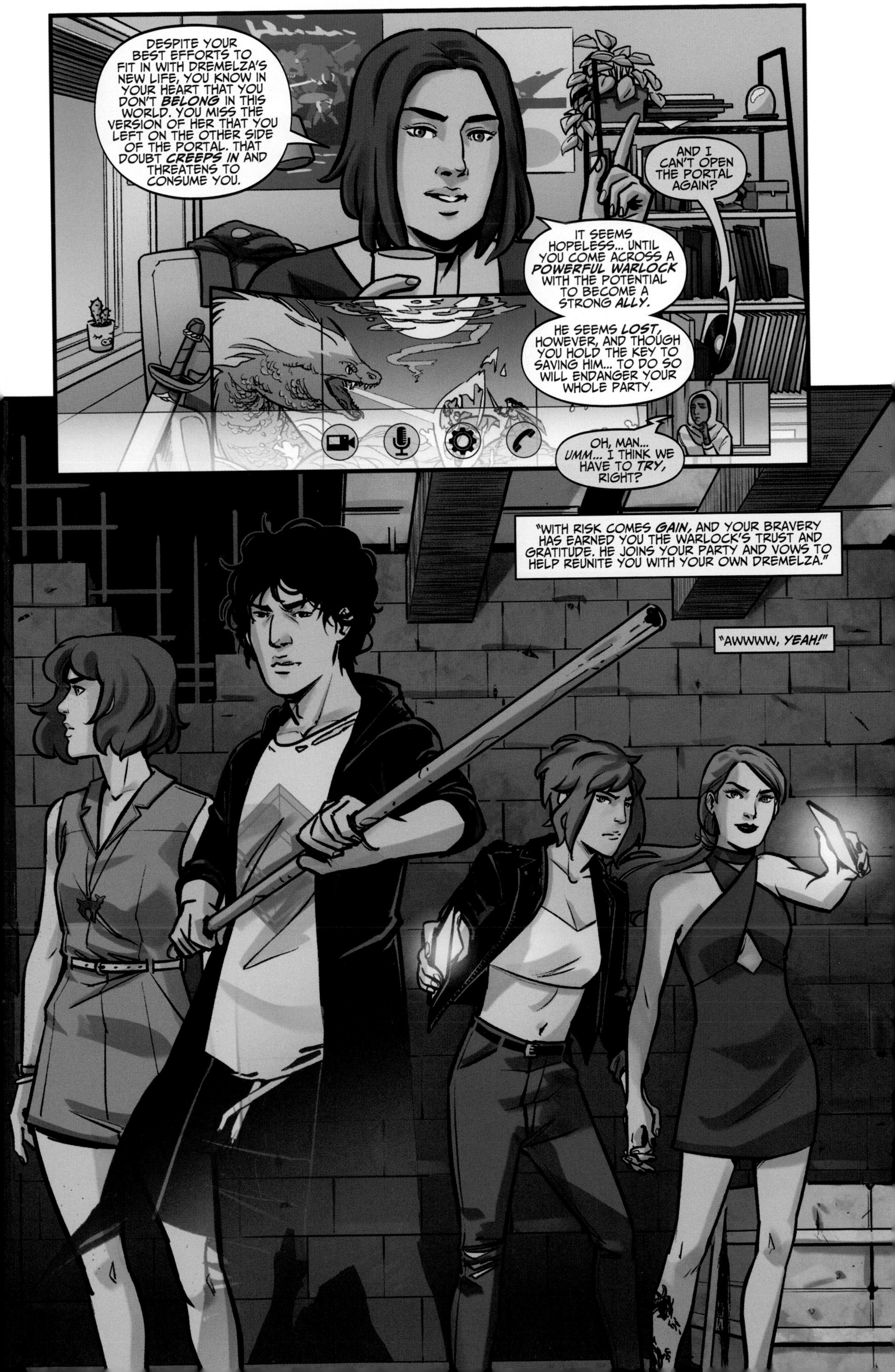
DESPITE YOUR BEST EFFORTS TO FIT IN WITH DREMELZA'S NEW LIFE, YOU KNOW IN YOUR HEART THAT YOU DON'T BELONG IN THIS WORLD. YOU MISS THE VERSION OF HER THAT YOU LEFT ON THE OTHER SIDE OF THE PORTAL. THAT DOUBT CREEPS IN AND THREATENS TO CONSUME YOU.
AND I CAN'T OPEN THE PORTAL AGAIN?
IT SEEMS HOPELESS... UNTIL YOU COME ACROSS A POWERFUL WARLOCK WITH THE POTENTIAL TO BECOME A STRONG ALLY.
HE SEEMS LOST, HOWEVER, AND THOUGH YOU HOLD THE KEY TO SAVING HIM... TO DO SO WILL ENDANGER YOUR WHOLE PARTY.
OH, MAN... UMM... I THINK WE HAVE TO TRY, RIGHT?
"WITH RISK COMES GAIN, AND YOUR BRAVERY HAS EARNED YOU THE WARLOCK'S TRUST AND GRATITUDE. HE JOINS YOUR PARTY AND VOWS TO HELP REUNITE YOU WITH YOUR OWN DREMELZA."
"AWWWW, YEAH!"

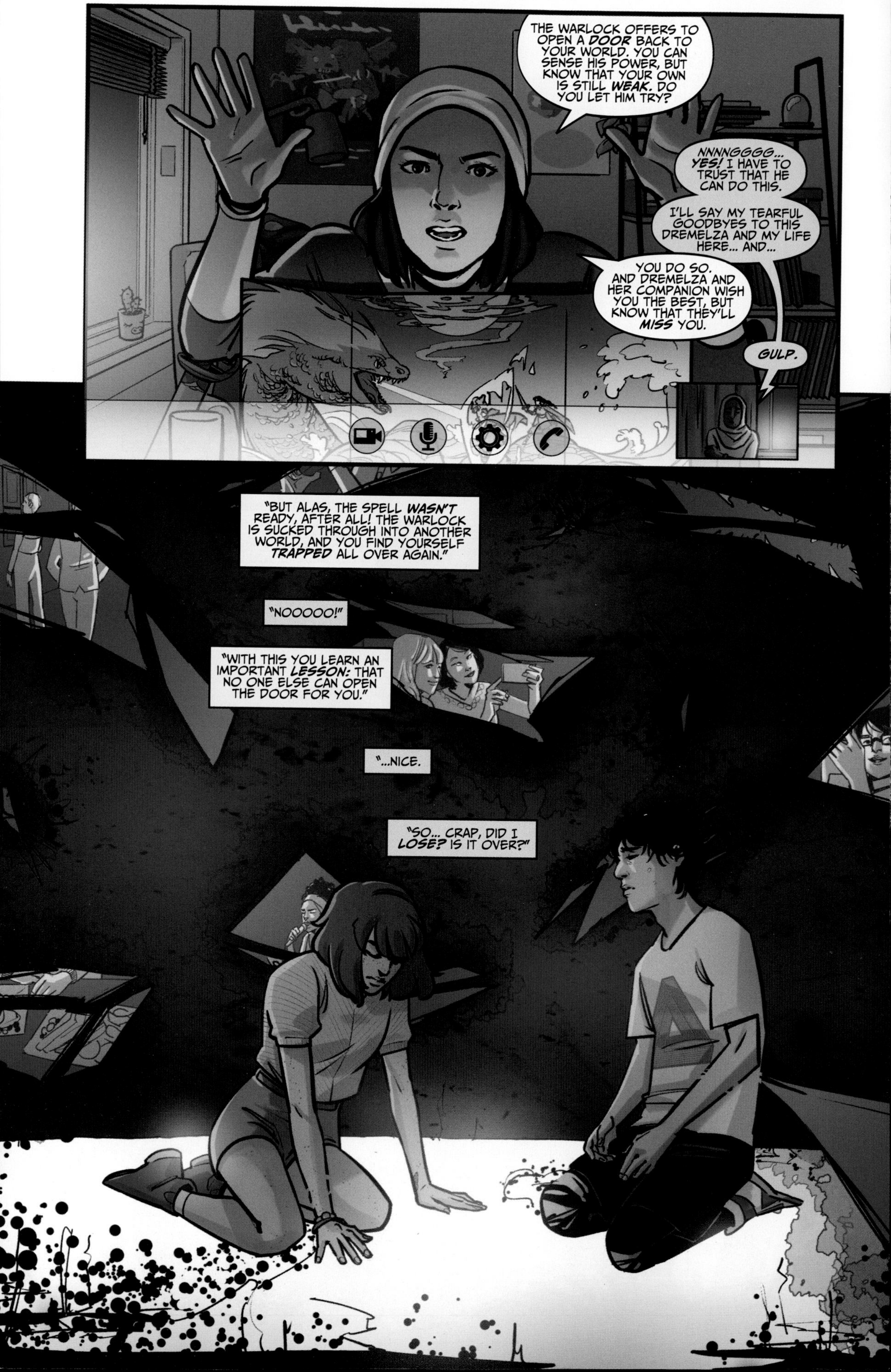
THE WARLOCK OFFERS TO OPEN A DOOR BACK TO YOUR WORLD. YOU CAN SENSE HIS POWER, BUT KNOW THAT YOUR OWN IS STILL WEAK. DO YOU LET HIM TRY?
NNNNGGGG... YES! I HAVE TO TRUST THAT HE CAN DO THIS.
I'LL SAY MY TEARFUL GOODBYES TO THIS DREMELZA AND MY LIFE HERE... AND...
YOU DO SO. AND DREMELZA AND HER COMPANION WISH YOU THE BEST, BUT KNOW THAT THEY'LL MISS YOU.
GULP.
"BUT ALAS, THE SPELL WASN'T READY, AFTER ALL! THE WARLOCK IS SUCKED THROUGH INTO ANOTHER WORLD, AND YOU FIND YOURSELF TRAPPED ALL OVER AGAIN."
"NOOOOO!"
"WITH THIS YOU LEARN AN IMPORTANT LESSON: THAT NO ONE ELSE CAN OPEN THE DOOR FOR YOU."
"...NICE.
"SO... CRAP, DID I LOSE? IS IT OVER?"

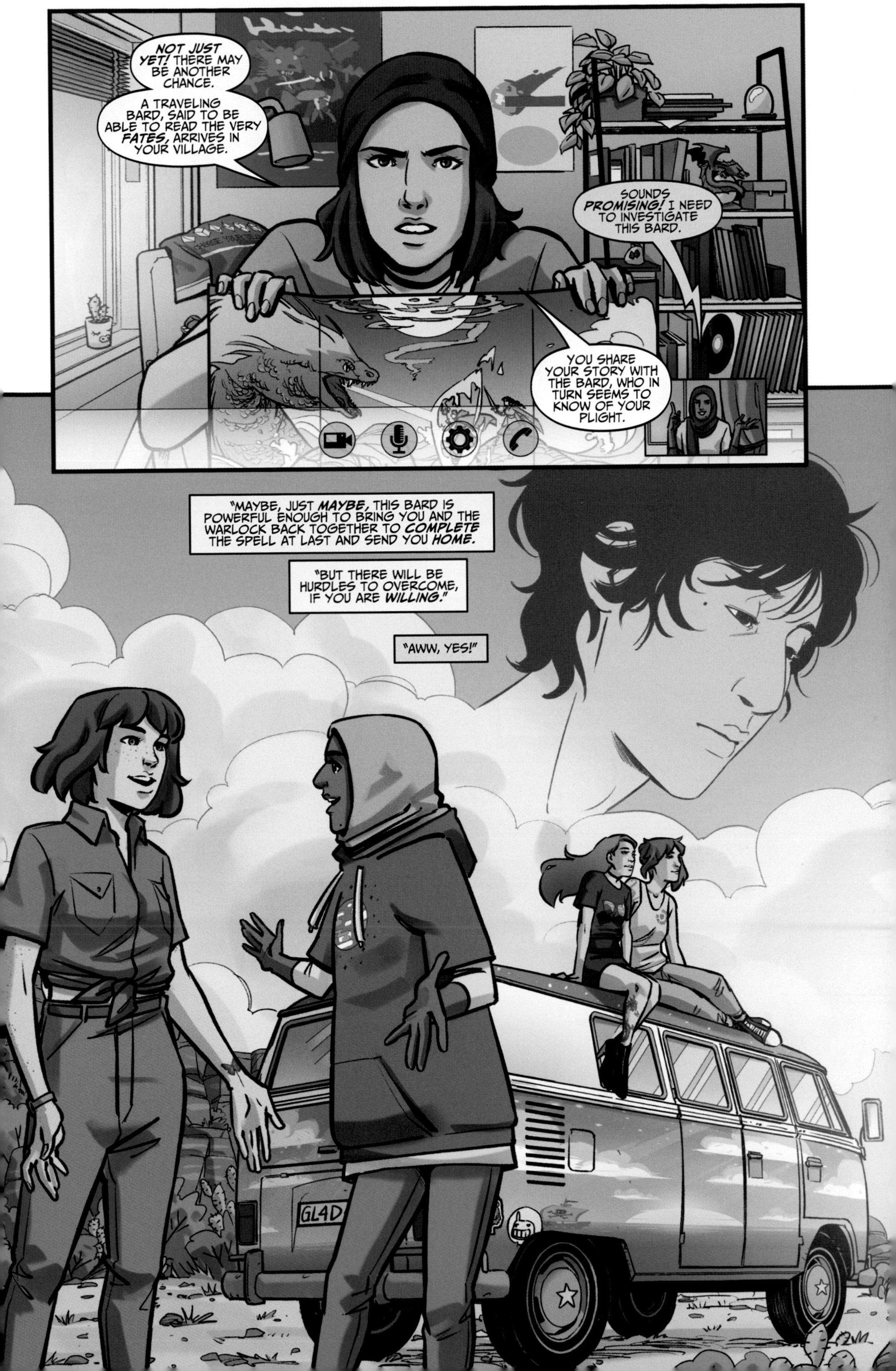
NOT JUST YET! THERE MAY BE ANOTHER CHANCE.
A TRAVELING BARD, SAID TO BE ABLE TO READ THE VERY FATES, ARRIVES IN YOUR VILLAGE.
SOUNDS PROMISING! I NEED TO INVESTIGATE THIS BARD.
YOU SHARE YOUR STORY WITH THE BARD, WHO IN TURN SEEMS TO KNOW OF YOUR PLIGHT.
"MAYBE, JUST MAYBE, THIS BARD IS POWERFUL ENOUGH TO BRING YOU AND THE WARLOCK BACK TOGETHER TO COMPLETE THE SPELL AT LAST AND SEND YOU HOME.
"BUT THERE WILL BE HURDLES TO OVERCOME, IF YOU ARE WILLING."
"AWW, YES!"
GL4D

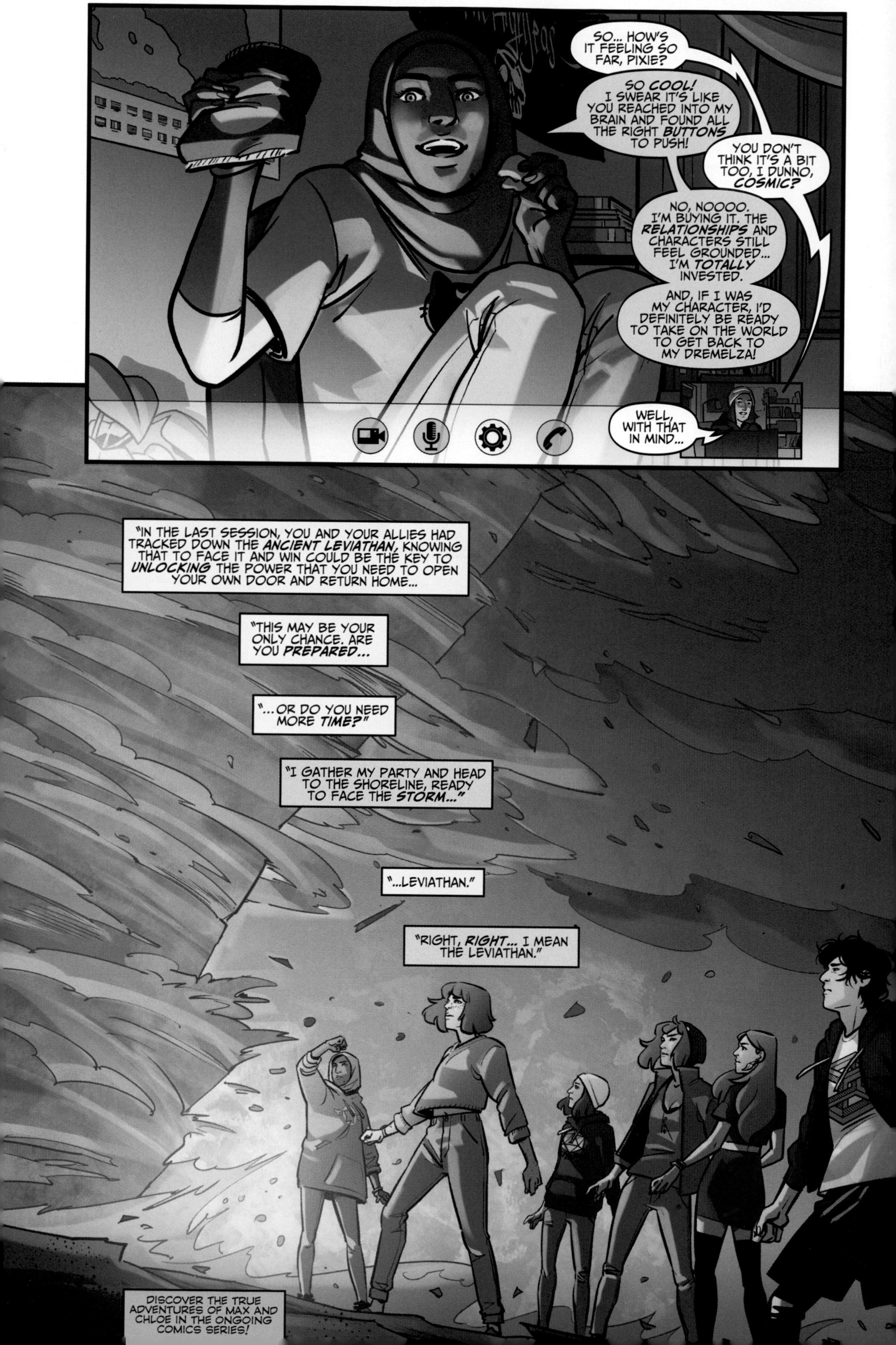
SO... HOW'S IT FEELING SO FAR, PIXIE?
SO COOL! I SWEAR IT'S LIKE YOU REACHED INTO MY BRAIN AND FOUND ALL THE RIGHT BUTTONS TO PUSH!
YOU DON'T THINK IT'S A BIT TOO, I DUNNO, COSMIC?
NO, NOOOO. I'M BUYING IT. THE RELATIONSHIPS AND CHARACTERS STILL FEEL GROUNDED... I'M TOTALLY INVESTED.
AND, IF I WAS MY CHARACTER, I'D DEFINITELY BE READY TO TAKE ON THE WORLD TO GET BACK TO MY DREMELZA!
WELL, WITH THAT IN MIND...
"IN THE LAST SESSION, YOU AND YOUR ALLIES HAD TRACKED DOWN THE ANCIENT LEVIATHAN, KNOWING THAT TO FACE IT AND WIN COULD BE THE KEY TO UNLOCKING THE POWER THAT YOU NEED TO OPEN YOUR OWN DOOR AND RETURN HOME...
"THIS MAY BE YOUR ONLY CHANCE. ARE YOU PREPARED...
"...OR DO YOU NEED MORE TIME?"
"I GATHER MY PARTY AND HEAD TO THE SHORELINE, READY TO FACE THE STORM..."
"...LEVIATHAN."
"RIGHT, RIGHT... I MEAN THE LEVIATHAN."
DISCOVER THE TRUE ADVENTURES OF MAX AND CHLOE IN THE ONGOING COMICS SERIES!

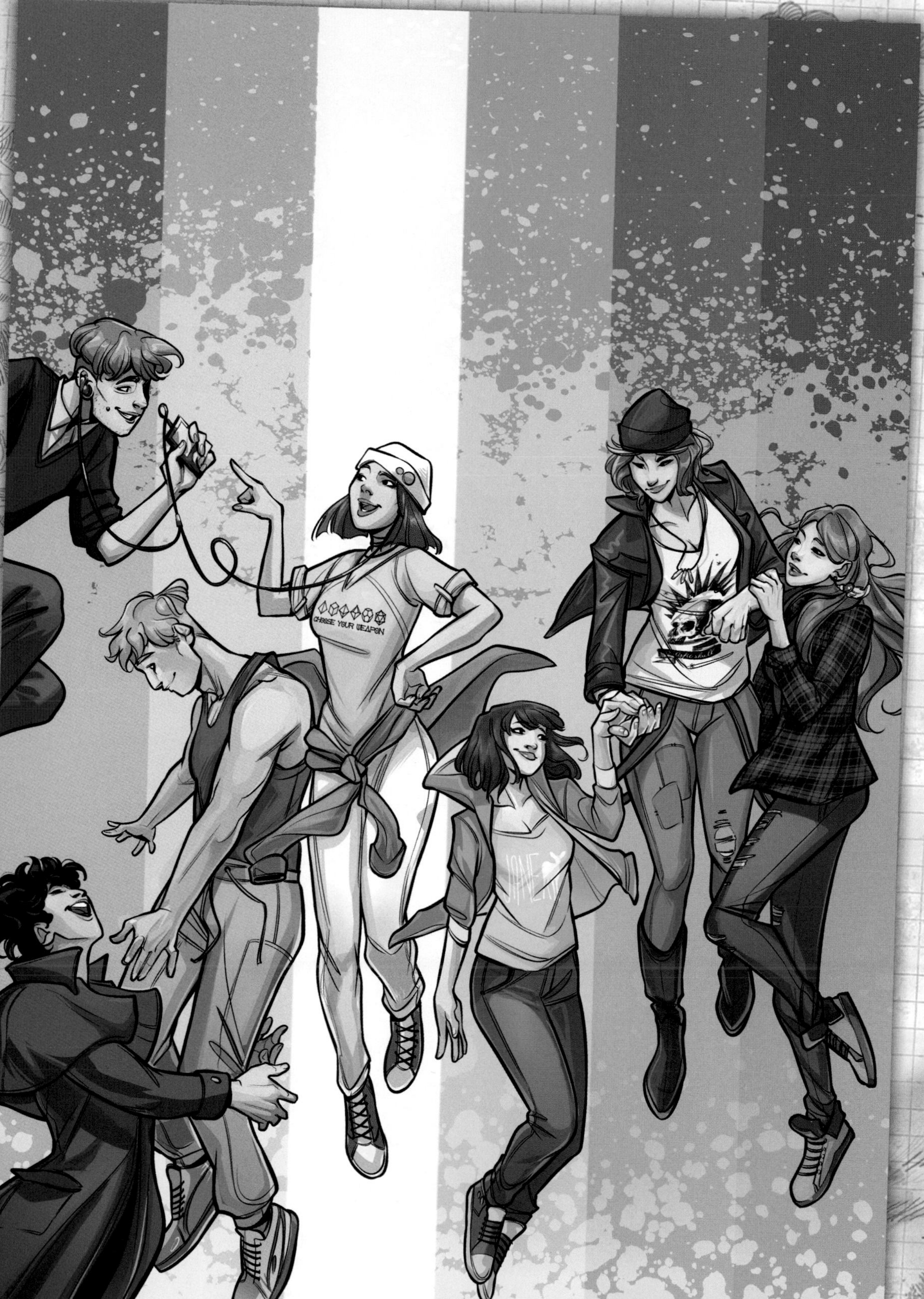
CHOOSE YOUR WEAPON

COVER #2 PRIDE VARIANT
BY IOLANDA ZANFARDINO & ELISA ROMBOLI

Twin Falls Pocatello W Y O M I N G

COVER GALLERY

BY GRETEL LUSKY

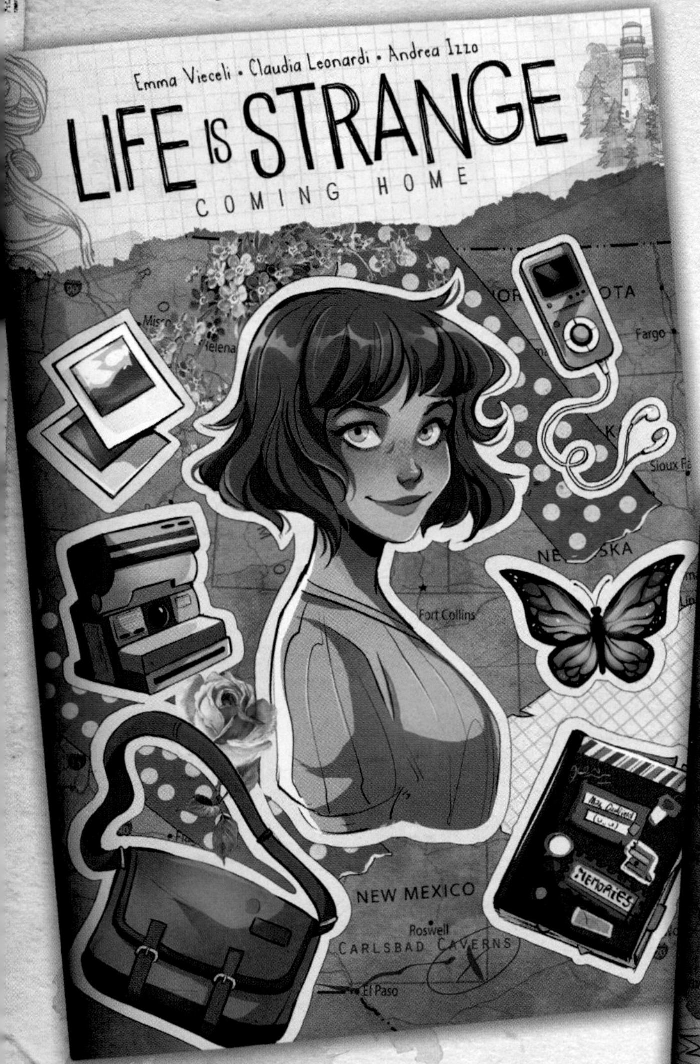
Emma Vieceli • Claudia Leonardi • Andrea Izzo
LIFE IS STRANGE
COMING HOME
NEW MEXICO
Roswell
CARLSBAD CAVERNS
El Paso
Fort Collins
Fargo
MEMORIES

ISSUE #1 COVER C

ISSUE #1 COVER D

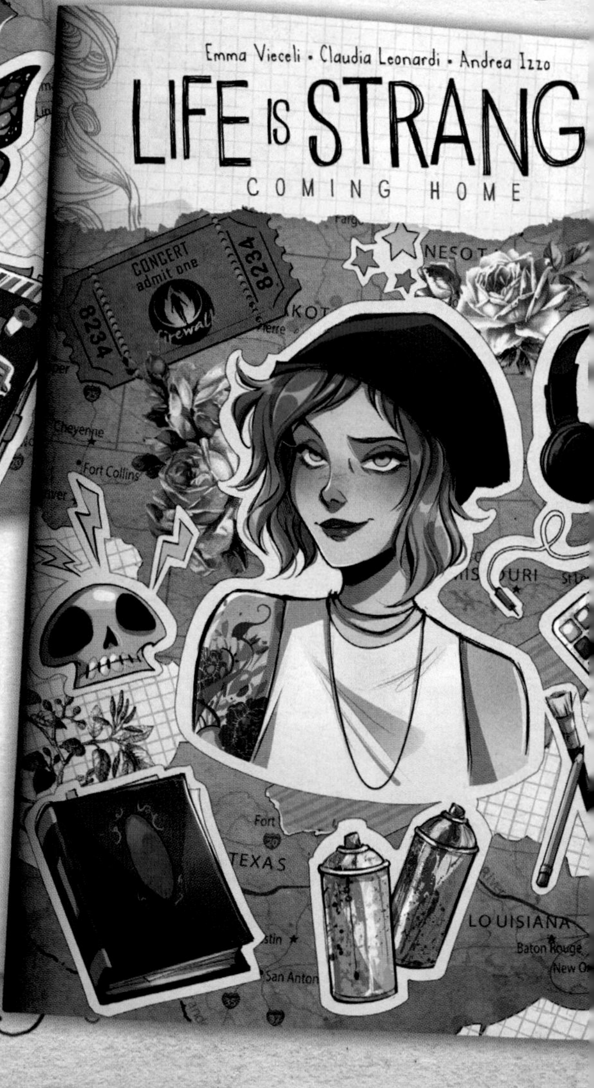
Emma Vieceli • Claudia Leonardi • Andrea Izzo
LIFE IS STRANG
COMING HOME
CONCERT
admit one
8234
8234
Cheyenne
Fort Collins
TEXAS
LOUISIANA
Baton Rouge

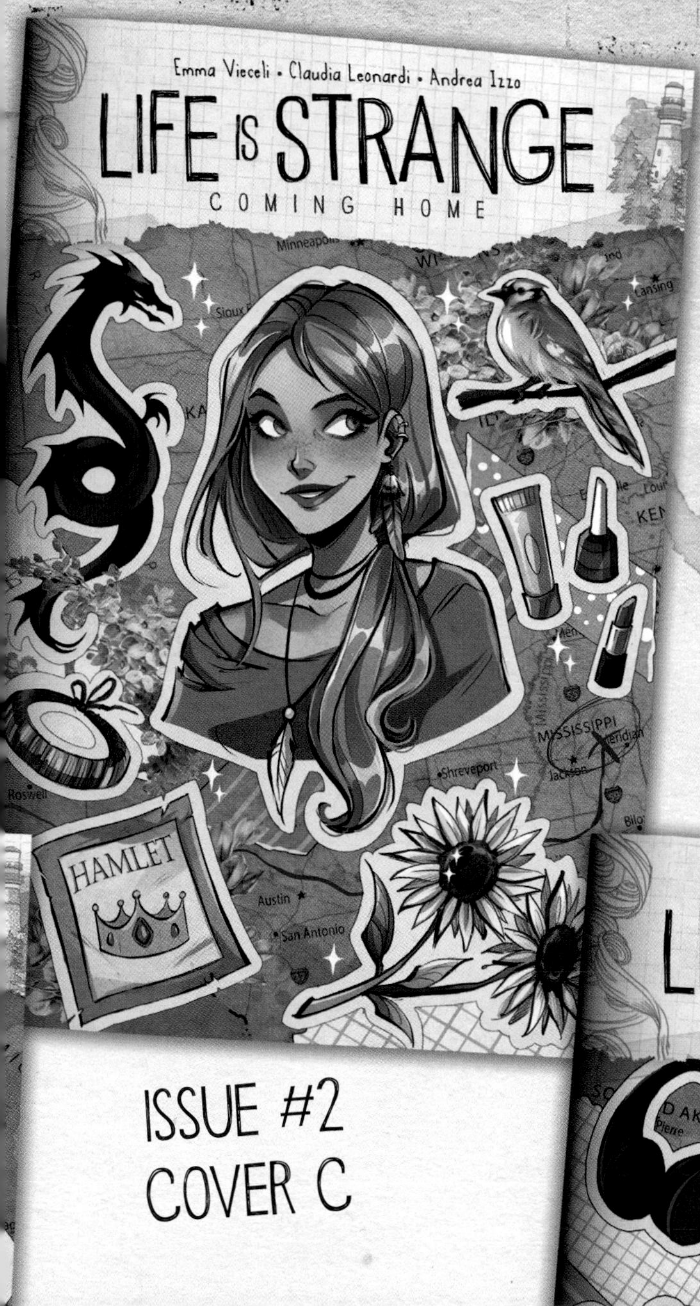
Emma Vieceli • Claudia Leonardi • Andrea Izzo
LIFE IS STRANGE
COMING HOME
HAMLET

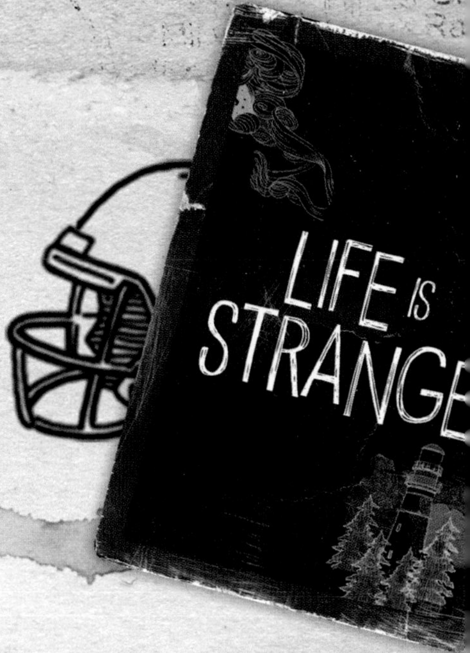
LIFE IS STRANGE

ISSUE #2 COVER D

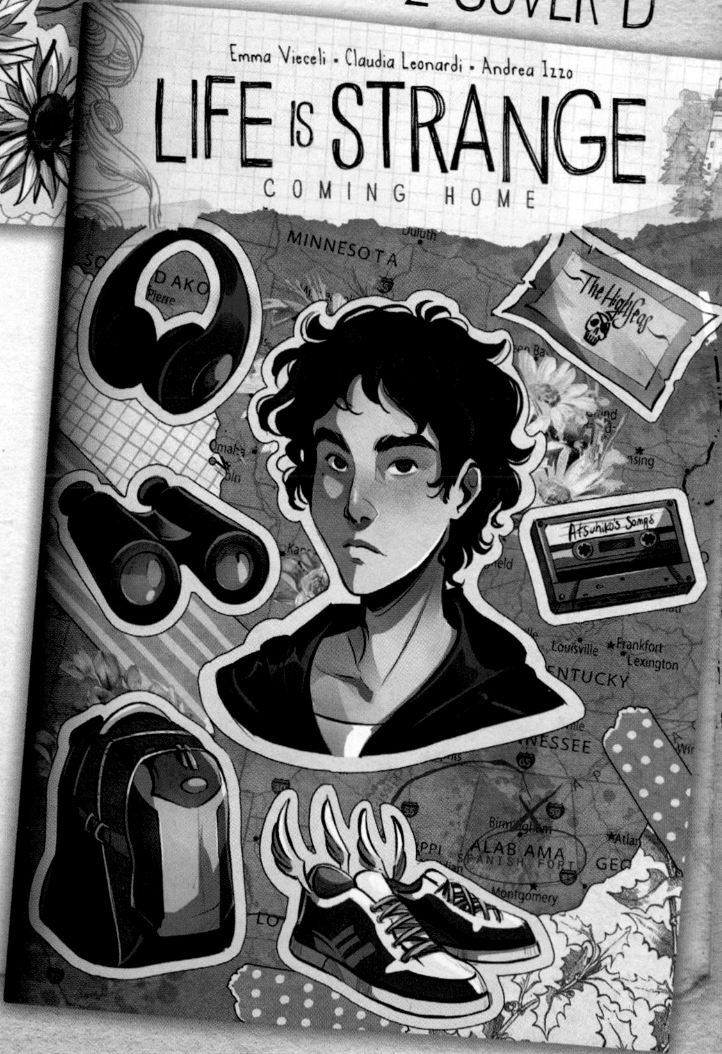
Emma Vieceli • Claudia Leonardi • Andrea Izzo
LIFE IS STRANGE
COMING HOME
MINNESOTA
The High Seas
Atsuhiko's Songs
ALABAMA
SPANISH FORT

ISSUE #2
COVER C

STILL
8-BIT

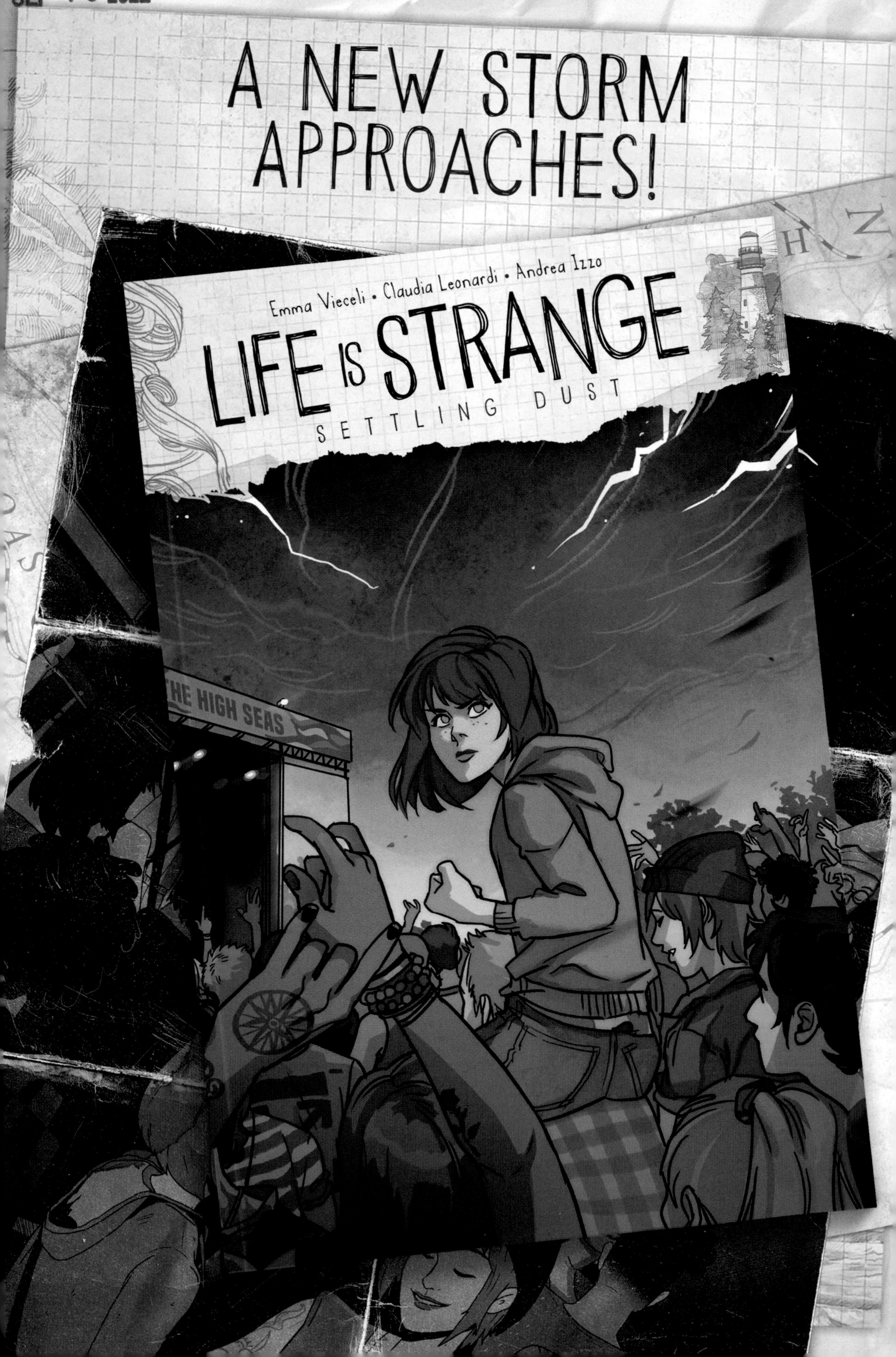
A NEW STORM APPROACHES!
Emma Vieceli • Claudia Leonardi • Andrea Izzo
LIFE IS STRANGE
SETTLING DUST
THE HIGH SEAS